# System,
## Not Circumstance

### Building a Repeatable Core
### Competence for Great Products

**Gregory Scott Youngblood**

ISBN: 1-4392-1672-X
ISBN-13: 9781439216729

Visit www.booksurge.com to order additional copies.

**To Bird**
真実を見せてくれ

# TABLE OF CONTENTS

# PART 2: PRODUCT MARKETING

# PREFACE

When I entered the business world, I believed (as most outsiders do) that successful companies ran like well-oiled machines. I assumed that the people on the inside knew exactly what they were doing. But after ten years working for product companies, I've learned that things are often more chaotic than they seem. I've always been impressed with the intelligence and competence of the individuals involved. But at the organizational level, the techniques and methods used to conduct business were often rather ad hoc. Many organizations left it up to a few key individuals to determine the means for conceptualizing, investing in, designing, and marketing great products. But those means seemed to shift over time as the people or their preferences changed. What I'd hoped to see, but didn't always, was a consistently applied system for creating great products consistently over time.

Throughout my time at Intel and Broadcom this manifested itself in different ways. Both are amazingly well run companies that have thrived over the last two decades because they consistently fielded great products. But each accomplished this in different ways. Much of Intel's success rested on a foundation of very robust product development processes, which were critical for keeping a large and changing workforce on track. These processes were very effective at proscribing what was to be done. But, at times the principles underlying these processes could get lost, leaving only rote compliance. In contrast, Broadcom in its early days tended to rely on a more experienced workforce that had internalized these principles over time. Process wasn't the primary driver of things (of this there was very little), but rather each individual's deep understanding of the art of great products. Unfortunately, this personality-driven environment wasn't optimal for repeatability or scalability as the organization rapidly grew. It also didn't always support the accumulation of institutional learning, as there was no forum for sharing best practices on the business side of the house (it was far outpaced by Broadcom's technical community, which was very good at codifying and sharing best practices). In those early days, everyone just ran on energy, experience, and talent. Broadcom has evolved significantly since, but the situation back then is representative of the state of a lot of young companies that exist today.

Over time, I began to wonder if it would be possible to combine the best of both worlds by creating a playbook of best practices that could serve as a guide to the organization. This system would not simply be a collection of processes, but rather focus on highlighting the fundamental principles related to creating great products. I looked back to my days as an officer in the military, where checklists are used very effectively to transmit years of learnings to a workforce that was constantly being refreshed with inexperienced recruits. That would be the format – a checklist of questions the organization should ask itself at every step of the process of conceiving, launching, and managing great products. Each would prompt the individuals involved to consider some of the key fundamentals necessary to creating great products.

I truly hope this system, as laid out in this work (and the upcoming sequel), can help your product organization sustain its success over the long term. Creating this work has been a passion of mine over the last few years, and the process has clarified my own thoughts about every topic covered. I hope you benefit from it as much as I did.

# CHAPTER 1:

## System, Not Circumstance

Great products make great companies. This is a maxim which cannot be reversed; when the strength of the products wanes, even the giants will fall.

The organizations that thrive over the long term know how to consistently turn out great products. Their formula for success is able to transcend changes in personnel, competitors, market conditions, and technologies. To do so, their methods cannot be ad hoc, but rather codified in a system that is consistently applied over time. This is in fact the central theme of this work: **to sustain success, an organization must move beyond circumstantial factors or ad hoc means and institutionalize a system for creating great products.**

Why is this important? Very simply it is because the circumstances that led to initial success will inevitably change over time. Those first great products are often the result of a fortunate confluence of several factors:

1. Leadership very focused on product
2. A few superstar employees to lead the charge
3. A hyper-motivated rank and file
4. A bit of luck

With these proverbial planets aligned, the product takes off in the market. Confidence and motivation are sky high as the business and organization start to quickly grow. In a few years, it may be large and profitable. At that point, more people, more products, and more customers all need to be managed. Ironically, however, the fruits of your success also may become your biggest problems. This is because a growing business brings it own set of known perils:

- *Current methods don't scale.* The early years are often about a talented core team making all the decisions at 100 miles per hour. But when the organization grows, it is hard to scale these ad hoc techniques to include a larger group of people and products. **How does the organization synchronize all its growing parts and still maintain its ability to execute**?

- *Talented employees leave.* Superstars often leave, sometimes from burnout or a desire to start something new. When they leave, their methods go with them. **How can the organization sustain its ability to create great products while the employee base changes**?

- *Demands of current business distract the team.* As the business grows, it brings with it the grind of managing internal issues and customer problems. This crowds out time spent by Marketing and Engineering on new products, with potentially disastrous effect. **How can an organization balance the needs of its existing business with that of developing great new products**?

- *Luck runs out.* Luck often plays a larger role in early success than anyone cares to admit, but it obviously cannot be counted on in perpetuity. When it runs out, everyone has to work that much harder to develop opportunities, innovation, and differentiation. **How does an organization proactively create new opportunities and reduce reliance on luck in creating them**?

Each of these factors – people, methods, motivation, and luck – all played a central role in the strength of the early products. Unfortunately, these factors are ones that are highly likely to change over the long term. Therein lies the problem: how does an organization maintain its ability to create great products as the circumstances around its success change? Reality shows this to be difficult – consider the number of "one hit wonders" or market leaders who fade quickly. The problem is that the success of many companies is too dependent on circumstance, i.e. that magical combination of people, technology, opportunity, and luck. It exists for a while, but is not necessarily a repeatable event. If an organization is to succeed long term, it must learn to base its competence for great products on something more lasting.

The solution is hard to achieve, but simple to explain: **an organization must base its success on *system, not circumstance*.** This means **developing an organizational core competence for creating great products** by institutionalizing the relevant processes, best practices, philosophies, and organizational expectations. A great product becomes a repeatable outcome rather than the result of happenstance. This is not to say that luck and talent are no longer required. On the contrary, they are still necessary. It is just that there is less reliance on them. As a result, the organization is much more insulated from circumstance. Furthermore, a system provides a playbook of best practices, so the team spends less time figuring out how to analyze and execute, and more time doing it. This increases efficiency and quality of execution, allowing more focus on the product itself. An effective system is not a silver bullet, but it gives the organization the best chance to succeed over the long term, no matter the circumstances.

A system can help us with every one of the perils listed above, starting with the problem of scaling the organization's methods. Small organizations can usually deal with a bit of chaos. The team is small, proximity is close, and communication is high. The superstars will run as fast as they can and do what they do best. There is little need for process to pull everyone into the loop. But when size of the business and team grow, this model can implode on itself. It is the difference between sandlot football, where raw talent and improvisation are enough, and the NFL, where the intensity of competition requires strict adherence to the team's playbook in order to compete effectively.

Relying on a system is equally as important for dealing with personnel changes. Eventually some of the original core of talent will leave, and the organization may find itself heading into battle without the "A" team. Different people will come and go, each with their own way of looking at things. If they know what they are doing, great. If not, the train can quickly come off its tracks. The organization may have come to rely on the General Manager (GM) who asked all the right questions to sniff out bad products, or the talented product manager with a knack for creating differentiation. But his replacement may not be quite as talented. That is why the organization needs to take the methods of the superstars and institutionalize them in a system of best practices. Thus it will matter less if the talent leaves because the core capability and methods for creating great products remains.

A system can also help with the deadly effects of distraction. An ongoing business requires a large amount of tactical work. The grind of maintaining *current* business can crowd out the work on creating great products to win *future* business. Senior Management gets occupied with profit and loss (P&L) analysis and headcount battles instead of asking the tough questions that ferret out substandard products. Product managers and sales people grapple with supply shortages and technical problems rather than finding ways to innovate in the market. And engineers race to meet product development deadlines, crowding out their ability to investigate new technologies. Steven Covey, author of "The Seven Habits of Highly Effective People", would describe this as the "urgent" – the tactical demands of running the business which cannot be ignored – crowding out the "important" – the future-looking product activities that are highly impactful to the business but have longer timelines for completion. Since there is never any shortage of fires to chase, you procrastinate on planning new products right up until it is too late. A system can combat this dynamic in two ways. First, it "automates" some of the basic business processes, compressing the amount of time they take. By freeing team members from some of the burden of these tactical tasks, it frees up time and mental energy for more forward looking product planning. Second, it serves as a forcing function for milestones and deliverables. The system helps forward progress, reducing reliance on overworked, distracted employees. The drive for great new products is no longer a side project that takes a backseat to the day to day business. Rather, it governed by a well-defined set of business processes which are treated with an urgency that matches their importance.

Finally, the institutionalization of our best practices can help mitigate the organization's reliance on luck. It is always good news when luck plays a part in bringing opportunities to the organization. But if the 'possession arrow' is pointed the other direction next time, the organization will have to work a little harder to create the next opportunity or competitive edge in the market. A system offers a playbook for how to go about doing that, presumably lessening the overall reliance on good fortune.

## The System

It may prove helpful to understand what is meant by the term "system". This work will lay out the main elements that comprise a product business, organizing them into four areas (which are discussed later in this chapter). Each element will be explored and boiled down to a few core, underlying principles which govern its dynamic. These are summarized at the end of each chapter in the form of questions. These summaries aggregate into a 45 point checklist which an organization can use to scrutinize every aspect of the business. Application of this checklist to guide how new products are conceived, developed, and brought to market is the essence of the system presented here. Using this system, an organization can quickly identify whether it is doing the right thing to ensure winning products. 'Settling' is not an option because bad products rarely make it through the organization – the system weeds them out. Institutionalizing this system means using it as part of the daily business practice of the organization. Everyone understands it and meets its expectations. These principles, best practices, and processes become part of the organization's DNA. It forms the basis of the organization's ability to create great products, and transcends circumstance because it is so fundamental to how business is done.

We will talk a lot about adding process in order to guide an organization's efforts. But the reader should not confuse adding process with adding bureaucracy, because the two are not equivalent. Bureaucracy is process without knowledge of the underlying principles. In contrast, we approach our subject by first exploring these underlying principles. Once the key people in the organization understand and agree on these, then they can be codified either in explicit process or in action implicitly guided by the principles. The intent is not to create bureaucracy as a way to deal with a growing business.

The proposed system is much more than simply a product planning process. We have a much more holistic view which encompasses the entire business. Our scope includes the four major facets of the product development process: Product Planning, Product Marketing, Product

Management, and Organizational Strategy. The first two are focused on creating the best product possible, and are the subject of this work. The second two, which will be covered in the upcoming sequel to this work, are more focused on how to run the business around the products. The goal is to make these activities as effective and efficient as possible in order to free up more time to focus on the task of creating great products.

We start with *Product Planning*, the phase in which an idea for a product is developed into a full product plan. A concept derived from input from customers and Sales is developed into a set of feature, cost and schedule requirements which Engineering then scopes. Based on what the Engineering and Operations teams believe they can deliver along those three axes, Marketing then creates an financial analysis. With this analysis as context, Management decides whether to invest in this particular project. At the end of the process, the organization is ready to begin executing. We will lay out the fundamentals involved in characterizing a project and creating an effective proposal. Particular attention is paid to ensuring the product has significant competitive advantage, as well as to the importance of driving an organization to converge quickly on a product plan. We also provide significant guidance on how to identify risk areas and vet out bad projects. Individuals in Engineering, Product Management, Sales, Finance, and Senior Management will be interested in this section.

The second major phase is *Product Marketing*. It encompasses the set of activities by which information about the product is communicated to the market. The Marketing team starts with the product's core benefits and amplifies them through creative marketing techniques. This value proposition is then communicated to the market through various channels such as the salesforce, the Internet, product literature, technical documentation, and the press. The goal is to make the target audience believe that the product will solve their problems and is worthy of purchasing at the offered price. The effort culminates with the launch of the product into the market, an effort that requires tight coordination among multiple disciplines. This work will offer a more holistic view of the "product". Rather than just the device itself, it includes the critical elements of ecosystem, positioning, product information, and channel. It examines each path of communication, and how to leverage it to best communicate the value of the product. In short, it provides a set of criteria to ensure that the organization's marketing and sales efforts are effectively presenting the value proposition to the market. Personnel in Senior Management, Sales, Product Management, Marketing Communications, and Applications Engineering will all benefit from this section.

Next is the third facet of our exploration: *Product Management*, the domain of running the business on which the product is based. Even a product line that has great attributes and is marketed well can still fail if the organization can not execute internally to deliver, monetize, and support it properly. Marketing, Sales, and Operations must collaborate to accurately forecast and fulfill customer demand. Marketing and Engineering must execute flawlessly to ensure the products are created, tested, and delivered on time. And Product Managers must be responsive to customer questions and problems that arise during the course of normal business. The aforementioned sequel will offer proven processes for supporting customers and sales teams. It provides the tools to ensure that the right data is being forecast and presented, with the goal being to minimize unexpected changes and the resulting financial and operational impact. It also addresses methods of managing a development program successfully, with insights into the psyche of an Engineering department and a look at the oft-ignored impact of testing. The Marketing, Sales, Finance, Operations, and Engineering teams will all be particularly interested in this section.

The last topic examined will be *Organizational Strategy* – the arena of running the organization and making investment choices across all product lines. Individual projects are considered independently, but also in the context of all other projects that could be undertaken. Organizations must choose the best ones in which to invest, while balancing cost control to maintain profitability now with investment to create greater profit later. Then when these investment decisions are finally made, the execution capabilities of the organization dictate how fast it can get to market. Presiding over all of this activity is the GM – his job is to make sure it all happens. His performance is critical to the success of the product line and organization. We will discuss how a system can optimize each of these elements. A process for managing the P&L and the investment decisions is presented; special techniques for scenario analysis and portfolio management are included. Furthermore, a groundbreaking framework for organizational execution is discussed; the goal is to make flawless execution a core part of the strategy. Next, the role of the GM is examined. A model for excellence in this position is presented, serving as a guide for leaders themselves or the people that work for them. The discussion concludes with guidance on how to hire world-class talent to carry out the organization's plan. Individuals from the Marketing and Engineering teams, as well as the Senior Management team, will benefit from this discussion.

It should be obvious by now that great products are not the sole domain of the Marketing department. Individuals from every part of the organization play a role. The following table highlights some of the tasks that each group carries out:

| | Product Planning | Product Marketing | Product Management | Organizational Strategy |
|---|---|---|---|---|
| **Marketing (or Product Management)** | • Develop product concepts into product plan<br>• Obtain investment commitments from management | • Create product messaging<br>• Guide/approve product literature and technical documentation<br>• Train sales force | • Solve customer issues<br>• Approve final pricing<br>• Manage crises<br>• Forecast demand<br>• Participate in program management teams<br>• Update field on new developments | • Provide project data into Portfolio Planning and P&L planning activities |
| **Sales** | • Facilitate gathering of customer feedback on product concepts/plans<br>• Gather competitive information | • Develop relationships with customers<br>• Create/execute account engagement strategy<br>• Close on business deals | • Obtain customer forecast data<br>• Serves as internal "voice of the customer" | |
| **Operations** | • Provide product cost estimates<br>• Use roadmap and three year plan to assess long term capacity | | • Deliver product on time per the forecast<br>• Ensure high product quality | • Provide long term cost reduction strategies to improve P&L |
| **Marketing Communications (MarCom)** | | • Manage product launch<br>• Manage creation of messaging vehicles such as white papers and product literature<br>• Manage creation of press release | | |
| **Engineering** | • Provide feature, cost, and schedule estimates<br>• Estimate R&D costs for financial analysis | | • Program manage development products to completion | • Provide project level data into Portfolio Planning activities |

| Finance | • Assist in performing financial analyses | | • Monitor changes to near term revenue<br>• Maintain effective pricing controls | • Provide support for P&L analysis |
|---|---|---|---|---|
| Applications Engineering | • Help define technical documentation requirements | • Create technical documentation | • Resolve customer's technical issues | |
| General Manager | • Set team expectations on process and criteria<br>• Ask the hard questions to identify bad assumptions or projects<br>• Approve or reject product proposal | • Push team to create complete product<br>• Drive urgency around winning new business | • Drive business to deliver to quarterly revenue commits | • Deliver healthy long-term P&L through effective investment decisions<br>• Drive team to execute flawlessly<br>• Build a great team through smart hiring |

*Figure 1*

## Conclusion

In the sports world, a team that is able to win consistently year after year is called a "dynasty". This too is our goal: to create a business dynasty that competes and wins in the market, consistently year after year. Despite all the experience and intellect dedicated to the task, only a small percentage of businesses achieve long-term sustainability. Changes, like the ones discussed above, can wreak havoc on the organization's core ability to create great products. As they say, "great products make great companies"; when the product slips so do the company's fortunes. Those companies who have succeeded in building a dynasty may have differed in their path, but all share a common thread. They were able to identify the secret to their success, and then codify it into a way of doing business – a system if you will. The source of their success then became something fundamental to the company, insulated from the effects of circumstance and repeatable over time.

# PART 1:
## PRODUCT PLANNING

# CHAPTER 2:

## The Product Planning Process

*This is where it all begins, with the definition of the product itself. This is the phase in which the great ones are born, but only if handled properly. Delays in this phase are often a major obstacle to getting to market quickly. Many companies struggle to rapidly converge on an approved plan; consensus can be elusive when the issues are complex and the stakes so high. This is why a good Product Planning process is so important – it can serve as a guide and catalyst for assembling and analyzing data to support quick decision making. It also helps focus the talent and creativity of the team members into concrete action. Having an effective process, with a level of rigor appropriate to the size and culture of the organization, is absolutely fundamental to the core competence you are trying to build. Sustained success comes from putting in place a system that helps highlight and resolve critical issues and drives the organization towards convergence on a single plan. Everyone understands the steps and the expectations, and management has made this activity a high priority for everyone. If done right, a good Product Planning process will consistently foster great products and help block weak ones.*

"NOTE: Chapters 2-4 are introductory chapters; experienced readers may want to skim these and then proceed to Chapter 5)."

## Convergence out of Chaos

Product companies are continually evaluating their options for new products to develop. At any given time, an organization will be simultaneously considering early concepts, approving funding for fleshed out proposals, and managing approved products through the design process. These activities involve a large number of variables, imperfect information, and data biased by the individuals involved. Technology and market risks make the picture even more complex. But the lifeblood of the organization is the strength of these products, so the stakes involved in getting it right are extremely high. However, it is not a simple process. It is an exercise in gathering a large amount of data from many individuals and assembling it in a way that leads to a good investment choice. The dangers are real: decisions can be made on unverified data or assumptions, bad decisions can be made on good data, analysis can be incomplete or incorrect, or a critical part of the organization may be left out of the process. The larger the organization, the greater the chance of this occurring. A **well defined Product Planning process can help avoid these situations.**

Most companies will have some form of such a planning process, whether applied informally or rigidly. Generically it is often referred to as a "phase-gate" process, where pre-defined phases of investigation each yield a specific set of data. That data is then taken into a decision making meeting, or the "gate", along with a recommendation. If management feels that the data supports the recommendation, then the project is allowed to proceed into the next phase. If the case is not made, then the team may be asked to re-do the last phase, or the project may be canceled outright. This process exists in order to ensure that good investment choices are made. Resources are too precious to be wasted by ill-advised decisions. The **Product Planning process serves as a forcing function to involve all relevant parties and consider all necessary data and analysis**. It opens up Marketing's assumptions about requirements, value, selling price, and competitiveness to the necessary level of scrutiny. Likewise, it forces Engineering to thoroughly think through what it will take to develop the product. It also ensures that the views and needs of peripheral groups like Operations, Finance, and Customer Support are accounted for. All of this is then merged together into an overall proposal with no internal inconsistencies. Without this process as a forcing function, the immensity of the task would lead to loose ends that could go undiscovered until it was too late. Murphy's Law often conspires to make that one loose end something that craters the entire plan. For instance, Engineering discovers that they didn't plan for an unforeseen resource bottleneck; once discovered, everyone realizes that it will push the schedule out beyond the market window.

The culture of the organization will determine how religiously the process is followed. Larger groups are often more disciplined about following the "letter of the law". With higher numbers of people to coordinate, the process needs to be more comprehensive and thus is more burdensome. But with so many variables spread across so many individuals, it is a necessary evil that helps control the inherent chaos. Yet large companies too often make it untenable by becoming bureaucratic. Each bad decision or misexecution incident over time leads to another process or rule being added. Eventually, the underlying principles of product planning become buried under layers of corporate policy and are eventually forgotten. The intent of the process is lost, leaving only bloated procedures that take too long and don't produce great products. Blind adherence replaces an understanding of the underlying fundamentals. **Keeping the spirit of the process at the forefront is critical for large organizations to maintain an effective product planning capability**.

In contrast, smaller companies are typically better at following the intent of the process moreso than the procedures themselves. This may be because the employees are more experienced and don't necessarily need a process to guide their efforts. Lines of communication are also shorter, so functional groups can quickly converge on a product plan with a minimum of official coordination or approval meetings. Everyone is relied upon to self-regulate, without requiring a process to direct and monitor their efforts. These employees are trusted to have solid assumptions, foresee the critical issues, and coordinate informally with the correct people. Many of the expected deliverables are still required (like a requirements document or engineering specification), but the formality of the analysis and approval meetings may not be necessary. Clearly, such an approach can facilitate speed in getting to market. The danger is that there are fewer checks and balances. Ensuring great products year after year requires a strict adherence to certain principles each time around. **Relying *solely* on the individuals' intuition and experience is risky**. First, humans are subjective, thus their biases will be hidden if not exposed by a process. Second, employees eventually leave the company, taking their techniques with them. This then puts the organization in the position of hoping their replacement is equally as skilled. In both cases, a small organization can benefit by installing a good Product Planning process, even if it is not rigidly followed.

## The Process Steps

Every company will have its own terminology, but all Product Planning processes essentially boil down to a basic phase-gate format. Each organization will be differentiated by the level of control management exerts, detail required, and number of phases or gates. Figure 2.1 below is a generic template for the basic steps of the planning process. This is a high level summary; later chapters will explore each phase in greater depth.

| Phase | Gate |
|---|---|
| **Concept Phase**<br><br>• *Activity:* Use knowledge of customer problems and requirements to generate a concept for a product. Flesh out the concept, test feasibility and potential for further exploration. Process led by Marketing.<br><br>• *Outcome:* High level analysis on attractiveness and feasibility of a product concept.<br><br>• *Participation:*<br><br>  o MKT: Discover market problems/ requirements and create product concept to satisfy. Characterize target markets, functionality, financials, competitiveness<br><br>  o ARCH: Assess technical feasibility and scope of work<br><br>  o ENG: Create gross estimate on schedule and resources (±25%)<br><br>  o OPS: Create gross estimate on product cost (±25%)<br><br>  o FIN: Perform sanity check on basic ROI | **Concept Approval**<br><br>• *Characterization:* "This is my idea for a product, and it makes enough sense to explore it further"<br><br>• *Approval implies:*<br><br>  o Concept is sound and can proceed to Product Approval<br><br>  o A larger number of resources in Architecture and Engineering can be enlisted to support analysis |
| **Product Definition Phase**<br><br>• *Activity:* Turn concept into a complete product definition which Engineering will scope and commit.<br><br>• *Outcome:* Official Market Requirements Document (MRD). Early architecture spec.<br><br>• *Participation:*<br><br>  o MKT: Characterize segmentation and market problem; create detailed feature definition, pricing strategy, competitive analysis, and financial analysis<br><br>  o ARCH: Perform deeper feasibility analysis, create architecture spec<br><br>  o ENG: Create gross estimate on schedule and resources (+/-15%)<br><br>  o OPS: Estimate product cost (+/-15%)<br><br>  o FIN: Approve financial analysis | **Product Approval**<br><br>• *Characterization:* "This is what Marketing wants Engineering to build."<br><br>• *Approval implies:*<br><br>  o Product is competitive and meets markets need. Financial return is attractive.<br><br>  o Project can proceed to Implementation Approval<br><br>  o Engineering must now dedicate more resources to analyze and scope project |

| Phase | Gate |
|---|---|
| **Implementation Phase\*** <br>• *Activity:* Analyze product requirements and create an engineering plan for satisfying them. <br>• *Outcome:* Full engineering plan for how to deliver product <br>• *Participation:* <br>  o MKT: Clarify requirements and tradeoff decisions where necessary <br>  o ARCH: Translate between market requirements and implementation specification <br>  o ENG: Provide commits on features, cost, schedule, and necessary resources (±5%) <br>  o OPS: Estimate product cost (±5%) <br>  o FIN: Help estimate development expense | **Implementation Approval** <br>• *Characterization:* "This is what Engineering can commit to." <br>• *Approval implies* <br>  o The product plan is sound and meets the market need Engineers can be staffed and design can start |
| **Mid-Course Review** <br>• *Activity:* Assess committed product definition and current project status against market requirements. <br>• *Outcome:* Clear statement on whether current project meets current market requirements. If not, recommendation on how to close the gap. <br>• *Participation:* <br>  o MKT: Re-assess market requirements <br>  o ENG: Present latest engineering status <br>  o OPS: Present any cost or manufacturing issues that deviate from prior assumptions <br>  o FIN: Re-assess financial situation | **Mid-Course Review Approval** <br>• *Characterization:* "We have re-assessed the current project against market requirements, and these are the recommended changes (if any)" <br>• *Approval implies* <br>  o Project can proceed as-is or with any change recommendation |
| **Product Launch** | |

*Figure 2.1*

*\*In subsequent chapters, this phase will be combined with the Product Definition Phase*

*Key: ARCH = Architecture; ENG = Engineering; FIN = Finance; MKT = Marketing; OPS = Operations.*

It should be clear that the amount of detail and analysis increases as the process progresses. Therefore, each successive phase represents an escalation in the number of required resources. It begins with a marketer analyzing the market; it ends with a large number of engineers working on the implementation proposal. This is why the phase-gate process is needed – it allows the organization to wade into the analysis phase slowly, periodically making sure the direction is right before progressively adding more heads to study the project. Also, before a large resource commitment is made to the development effort, the process helps ensure all the relevant criteria have been met. Few businesses can absorb the wasted resources caused by needless false starts, not to mention the accompanying negative impact on morale. A good phase-gate process will help avoid both of these situations. And it need not do so in a way that adds bureaucracy. This process could take months or less than a week. The interval does not matter; each organization can proceed as quickly as it is able.

## Keeping the Process on Track

The Product Planning process is designed to bring order to chaos born of complexity. Without structure, most approval meetings can descend into "thrash", which means participants are arguing about data and analysis rather than making decisions. A common reason for this is a **lack of consensus on the criteria for passing each gate**. There are four areas in which this often manifests itself:

- *Required financial metrics.* There are a number of commonly used metrics (Net Present Value, Gross Margin Turns, Expense) – which does the company choose to use? What are the numerical targets? Are those targets firm or does the company qualitatively factor in other aspects, such as strategic value?
- *Level of detail of analysis.* There is a high probability a particular participant will cause a stir because they want to see more depth in the analysis than is actually required for that phase. There is always someone who is expecting a Product Approval (PA) level analysis during the Concept Approval (CA) phase.
- *Types of analysis performed.* Analyzing project proposals is a complex task with a lot of subjectivity on how to characterize and analyze the situation. It is hard to ensure you are covering every base – both presenter and audience bring their own biases and ways of looking at the project. Leaving out a critical type of analysis can leave certain audience members with important unaddressed questions or doubts.
- *Method in which data is presented.* This is the most superficial of the four, but no less significant to achieving consensus. Even if a general agreement exists on the analysis, poor presentation of the facts can cause confusion. People often think about data in a certain way. A slide that presents it in an unfamiliar format may be distracting enough that they miss the message.

Any of these four has the power to cause enough thrash to prevent convergence in the meeting, even for a product that is clearly good. This can cause significant delays to a program. Failing to achieve approval because of these factors means the presenter must regroup, modify the analysis or presentation, and schedule another meeting. With busy calendars being the norm, this can mean weeks of delay. While some delays can be absorbed, they may eventually delay the launch date of the product. This can be a real problem when you have a market window that does not move to compensate for the organization's bickering. As the pressure builds to start, the organization may be tempted to compromise on the product definition or approval criteria simply in an effort to "get started on something."

**The solution to these problems lies in having a template for the approval meeting presentations**. By setting joint expectations for metrics, detail, analysis types, and methods of presentation, they are removed as factors of debate. The attention can then stay on the content itself. To do this, it can be effective to assign a small team of individuals representing Marketing, Engineering, Finance, and Operations (Sales could possibly be included) to help design the Product Planning process. Once ratified, it should be sent out to the rest of the organization. At the beginning of each approval meeting, a slide should be shown that reiterates the agreed upon expectations for data and analysis for the particular gate at hand. This properly calibrates expectations before the meeting begins.

Another impediment to good execution of the Product Planning process is a **lack of a sense of urgency in moving through the phases.** At the end of a development program, there is always intense pressure on Engineering to deliver. Often programs start too late to allow adequate time for development, so they are constantly digging out of a schedule hole. More often than not, these situations are created because Marketing did not solidify requirements early enough, or the organization did not crisply execute on the whole process. Every slip on the front end of the planning process usually translates into an equal slip on the backend of the product schedule. **Yet somehow the pressure to deliver on the backend is not typically felt on the front end.** To ensure motivation to execute is equally high in all phases of the program, a simple concept called *Endpoint Management can* be used. Typically an organization will schedule its approval meetings, or gates, when the team is ready with the proper level of data and analysis. Instead, it is recommended that the timing of the Product Planning process phases and gates be dictated by the project end dates. This can be accomplished this by mapping out the program milestones onto a timeline, as shown in Figure 2.2. Start to the far right with the market window milestones, including "Volume Shipments", and other interim deliverables such as "Product Samples". In collaboration with Engineering and Program Management, work backwards on the timeline to establish intervals between each preceding milestone in the development process leading up to the market window. Next, fill in the architectural deliverables upon which Engineering relies, such as the Product Requirements Document (PRD). Do the same for deliverables (like the MRD) upon which Architecture would rely. Finally, work backwards all the way to CA, using what Marketing says are the timeframes they need to move the product through the planning process.

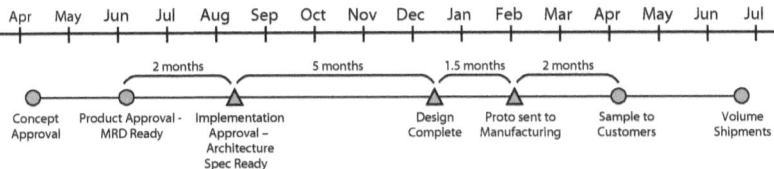

*Figure 2.2: Endpoint Management Template*

With this in hand, you now have a target for when CA and PA must happen. The **product planning dates are driven by the market window, rather than by the readiness of Marketing**. The organization would then frequently review this tool in order to bring visibility and a sense of urgency to the early phases of the planning process. The eventual impact of poor front end execution will be immediately apparent to all. It may be helpful to assign an owner to the overall Product Planning process who can ensure the proper organizational focus and drive the appropriate cadence.

One final comment deserves mentioning. There is not a General Manager (GM) on the planet who will tell you that product planning is not important to him. But don't believe his words. Rather, judge him by how well he staffs this activity with marketers and architects. Many organizations chronically understaff here, with predictable results. It is not so much a conscious decision as a failure to recognize how the *urgent* will always push out the *important*. An organization that tasks its product managers on both existing business and new products will find that this happens, with product planning always getting the short end of the stick. And architects are always in short supply because they have to spend significant time with both Marketing and Engineering. **A successful organization will overinvest resources in their Product Planning process** in order to ensure a steady pipeline of innovative, differentiated projects.

## Conclusion

Getting the Product Planning process right is one of the cornerstones of building a repeatable core competence for great products. Occasional winners may emerge from ad hoc means, but consistent success requires a robust process. This is because of a very simple fact: product planning is hard! There are a lot of variables to deal with. Marketing must determine what customers will value (even though the customer may not know) while also predicting competitors' moves. Trends in technology, regulation, and standards bodies must also be foreseen. Engineering contends with the challenges of development and scheduling in the face of unknown risks and issues. You are making high-stakes, semi-irreversible decisions with imperfect information. Once the organization starts to move in a certain direction, inertia is often high and so recovering from the wrong path is difficult. The Product Planning process helps an organization deal with these uncertainties and variables in a predictable way.

# Checklist:

### Has the GM set up a robust Product Planning process?

A lack of clarity around the expected analysis and deliverables will inevitably lead to mis-execution and delays in the Product Planning process.

## What to Look For:

- The process steps and deliverables are documented and available
- The specific process has been followed for the last two products

### Is the process actively managed for great execution?

Because it is such a long term activity, product planning requires a forcing function to keep it on track.

## What to Look For:

- The planning calendar is reviewed each week in the GM's staff meeting
- An assigned owner drives the process using Endpoint Management

### Has the GM made product planning a high priority?

Tactical fires will always pull the organization's attention away from product planning. It is the GM's responsibility to ensure it gets the focus it needs.

## What to Look For:

- The GM holds the team accountable for product planning milestones
- The GM staffs the product planning activity for success

*(Further discussion on this checklist available at www.systemnotcircumstance.com)*

# CHAPTER 3:

## Concept Phase

In the first years of life, children are for the most part helpless and highly dependent on their parents. They need a nurturing environment to gain the strength and capability to stand on their own. This is much like the Concept Phase, where emerging ideas for a product are guided into a more robust state. A corporate environment can be brutal to new ideas, where the intense need for details and financial justification can kill them before they have a chance to bloom. It is simply too early to be able to answer all of the inevitable questions. But a consistent string of great products is going to require a healthy supply of potential concepts, much like a professional baseball team relies on its farm system for prospects. A great organization will provide a safe haven for new ideas and an effective process for incubating them without setting the bar too high. Rather than requiring irrefutable proof of financial return or feasibility, effort is focused on recognizing fertile target markets, identifying inherent competitive advantage, and highlighting issues for deeper analysis or validation.

## The Content

All products start out as a simple idea about how to uniquely solve a perceived problem in the market. During the Concept Phase, that idea will be developed into a full concept proposal. This will require enough data gathering and analysis in order to do a first pass judgment of its merit. It is primarily a Marketing driven exercise, with a small amount of support from other groups such as Engineering, Architecture, and Finance. The end result is a Concept Approval (CA) meeting in which Marketing presents the concept and seeks approval to proceed with deeper analysis. As it is early in the product planning process, a considerable degree of freedom is granted – it is not necessary to have all the answers or details. Assumptions are fine as long as they are identified and reasonable.

The Concept Phase is an exercise in bringing concrete form to a fuzzy idea. There are a standard set of analyses that need to be performed in order to enter into the CA gate:

- *Target Markets:* The "market" is not simply a monolithic group of individual customers. It is, in fact, comprised of smaller groupings, each characterized by a common set of needs. Each is slightly different, and rarely will a single product competitively address them all. **The organization needs to pick its battles by identifying which segments will be targets and which won't** (discussed in Chapter 6 "Market Segmentation") A critical component of being competitive is knowing exactly who your market is and creating products specifically for them. Lacking this knowledge, the organization defines a product that is presumably designed for all segments but ends up being competitive in none of them.

- *Problem and Solution:* **The best products are always those that solve real and significant customer problems.** Forget about features, price, performance, or anything else. Before proceeding any further in the exploration of the concept, identify the actual problem the product would solve (discussed in Chapter 7 "Market Problem"). If the problem is vexing enough, presumably customers will pay well for the solution that solves it best. Discovering the *Market Problem* starts with spending significant time with customers, prompting them to share their challenges. Once identified, the Concept Phase is used for developing a solution to these problems.

- *Market Window*: For every product, there is an ideal time for it to become available to the market. It may be driven by customer needs or the competition's schedule. Missing the market window will result in product failure or a significantly reduced financial opportunity. Engineers will commonly tell you that given enough time, they can build anything. But a specific schedule requirement for interim milestones and end dates will dictate what they can actually deliver (discussed in Chapter 10 "Schedule"). **Schedule requirements at this stage need not be exact** or definite, but close enough to serve as a reasonable planning factor.

- *Financial Analysis*: A basic analysis is performed to prove to the company that it can make an attractive return from investing in the project (discussed in Chapter 13 "Financial Analysis"). A common set of analysis tools are employed (Net Present Value, Revenue Turns, Gross Margin Turns, Time to Payback, etc). These tools require the Marketing team to estimate what the customer will pay and how many they will buy. Engineering will estimate product cost and the overall development expense. As it is early in the process, the accuracy is expected to be low. This is fine – the main purpose of this cursory analysis is to **highlight obvious problems or inconsistencies early in the process**.

- *Competitive Analysis*: It is not enough to solve a customer's problems – **you must be able to do it better than the competition can.** An understanding of what they have planned is essential (discussed in Chapter 11 "Competitive Analysis"). Of course they are doing their best to hide their plans from you. Nonetheless, assemble the best data that can be found, and make the necessary extrapolations and predictions as to their intentions. With this data in hand, you can then make a clear statement of the product's inherent competitive advantage – an absolute prerequisite for exiting the Concept Phase. If the product is truly great, it should be easy to succinctly characterize exactly how it wins in the market.

- *Plan to Get to Next Stage*: The goal of the Concept Phase is to **get more resources assigned to do deeper analysis** in the Product Definition Phase. So a key deliverable here is to show a plan for utilizing those individuals to get to the next gate. Some key points to be addressed are:

- Which specific individuals, and how much of their time, will be needed for the next phase of analysis? Identifying them now ensures their manager will allocate their time appropriately.
- What are the key areas of investigation to be explored? Important assumptions must be identified clearly in a *Validation Plan* that is executed in the next phase.

## The Process

Less experienced marketers often have a hard time getting started with this process. They have the idea, but now what? Kicking off the program should be easy. Assuming you have a reasonable concept in mind, get started by following the standard set of steps summarized below.

- *Assign a code name*: Code names are used to refer to the project internally before the market name gets assigned. It obscures the nature of the project in the event of competitive leaks. It also gives the concept an internal identity, something that can be helpful at an early stage when Marketing is peppering Engineering with inane questions about 'some new idea'. The familiarity that a code name provides is a subtle aid in getting mindshare from those who have the expertise you need to explore the concept. It is common for Marketing to establish some type of consistent theme for the code names of a particular product line – similar geographic locations, historical names, sports teams, and so on.
- *Develop the concept*: Here you are verifying your understanding of the Market Problem and developing the solution to solve it. It will involve spending a significant amount of time with customers to determine their problems, as well as with Engineering to brainstorm a solution. Subsequent work goes into assessing the value such a solution would provide to the market. It is expected that many assumptions will need to be made in that process, but this is acceptable as long as each is documented for later validation.
- *Validate the concept*: Concepts and assumptions are then validated in the market by circling back with a few trusted individuals within the customer base. They'll confirm if you correctly understand the Market Problem, as well as the solution's value proposition. Keep the

group limited in order to control competitive leaks, but recognize that this type of feedback is valuable enough to take the risk. What sounds good within the walls of the ivory tower sometimes does not hold water in the real world, so this step is absolutely critical.

- *Set date for CA presentation*: Long term activities like product planning often get de-prioritized against more urgent tactical tasks. Human nature and the dynamics of a fast moving business make this unavoidable. Use an *Endpoint Management* template (see Chapter 2 "The Product Planning Process") to set a date for the approval meeting. This will serve as a forcing function for the team to prioritize their time appropriately.

- *Document the concept*: Getting the concept onto paper (discussed in Chapter 8 "Requirements") is critical to getting Engineering and Architecture to take it seriously and spend enough time on it. It also makes it easier for them to help scope the concept, as well as spot inconsistencies. A short document will suffice; it should contain an early version of the basic information described above. Marketing should try to have this document ready before seriously engaging the technical team.

- *Scope the concept*: Now it is time to assess both the technical feasibility of the concept as well as the magnitude of development effort necessary to create it. The Architecture team usually takes the lead in translating the concept into a high-level specification. Marketing and Engineering will assist. The result is a coarse estimate of features, cost, and schedule of such a product. This may be followed by an iterative tradeoff process to balance the three to best meet the market's needs (discussed in Chapter 10 "Schedule").

- *Analyze the financials*: Analysis from Engineering and Architecture should have yielded the approximate product cost and development expense. Marketing should then create a *Strategic Pricing Plan* (discussed in Chapter 12 "Pricing Strategy") that reflects the market's willingness to pay given the value that the product offers. They also need to generate sales volume estimates. All of this goes into the financial models that indicate the product's potential return.

- *Prepare the presentation*: It is now time to prepare your presentation (discussed in Chapters 14 "Presentation Fundamentals" and

15 "Product Concept Template"). The preparation process can be invaluable in helping bring the plan together. Thinking through your analysis is one thing; preparing to present it to others tends to invoke a higher level of clear thinking. Problems or inconsistencies are likely to stand out more. Trust your instincts – don't ignore them when they tell you the plan has a problem. Be sure to document all assumptions and create a plan to validate them in the Product Definition Phase.

- *Deliver the CA presentation:* The goal of the presentation is to get management's explicit approval to proceed further in developing the concept into a full product plan. By definition, this requires a larger number of resources, and the approval is an implicit commitment to make these available.

## Conclusion

A successfully concluded Concept Phase is a very good thing. It provides a mandate for spending further time to develop the concept into a product plan. This is extremely helpful for marketers trying to get busy engineers and architects to do analysis for them in support of this effort. Also, passing CA allows Marketing to confidently engage Sales and customers with more information about the roadmap. Since changes to the roadmap cause too much confusion and loss of confidence, it is better to wait until the CA is passed before positioning it as part of your future plans. Finally, getting through the CA helps quell any dissent within the organization. There will always be a multitude of opinions on what the next product should be. Even those individuals that "don't get a vote" often feel the need to vocally express their opinion. An approved concept has the power of the GM behind it; dissenters can now be told, "You had your chance, now it's too late". Taken as a whole, being post-CA is a much better state in which to exist. It is in the best interest of the Marketing and Architecture teams to apply the necessary time and discipline to reach it as soon as possible.

A running example of a product effort will be presented, spanning across all chapter of this book. It reflects the experience with a real product from the author's career, although the names and some details have been changed to mask the specific companies involved. Chapters 3 and 4 give an overview of the entire process for Mason; later chapters will dig into a deeper level of detail.

# The Concept Phase: Real World Example

*TechCorp is a very successful semiconductor maker with sales of approximately $1 billion per year. Several years ago they began a new business around network communications chips which allow computers to talk with one another over a network. The first product was moderately successful, and they were able to capture one significant customer out of a concentrated market of about ten personal computer (PC) original equipment manufacturers (OEMs). They achieved this in the face of fierce resistance from a dominant incumbent who previously claimed eight of the ten OEMs as customers. It was now time to follow up with the next product, which needed to be highly competitive in order gain the necessary market share to support a profit and loss (P&L) picture that was sustainable over the long-term.*

*The Product Planning process was initiated. The first step was to decide which market segments would be targeted with the new product. A candidate list was drawn up, mostly specialized segments within the overall PC market. The team knew that the best products solved customers' really ugly problems. It was quite simple: make the customer's life easier in a meaningful way, and they will willingly pay well for the product. So the Marketing team knew that it was imperative for them to figure out what those problems were. Like all good marketers, they went out and spent time talking to their customers face to face. The subjects of improving battery life and data security for laptop PC users came up a lot. With this knowledge in hand, they then turned their attention to brainstorming ways to solve some of these problems through their product. They quickly produced some good ideas, including special power modes (which they initially called "cable sensing mode") and the integration of a security technology called TPM ("Trusted Platform Module"). Potential looked good, so they chose the code name Mason, and kicked off the project. Within three weeks of working with the Architecture team and a few engineers, they had a strawman concept in hand. The team was excited, but initially unsure of how well it would be received by customers. Did this concept really solve their problems in a way that would get them excited? To find out, they made a list of a few customers whom they knew well and trusted to give good, discreet feedback. Reviews of the concept with this group went well – all seemed to like it at a high level. This step was critically important, as it gave the marketers the confidence in Mason to take it forward. Setting a date for the CA of six weeks hence, they proceeded with a formal analysis of the project. Markets were segmented and sized, and the problems of each*

documented. The solution concept was formalized, and the schedule requirements were fleshed out. Then, the most important part of the analysis was
performed – a clear characterization of how the product would win in the
market. Not quite a full competitive analysis, it still needed to clearly explain
why customers in the target segments would certainly choose this product
over the alternatives. The marketing team knew that if this section wasn't
convincing, their proposal would never gain approval, so they spent significant time developing it.

With this completed, the financial analysis was up next. Although based
on estimates, it tended to vet out the truth in any project. If the numbers didn't
work, the organization would surely never fund the project. And even though
all the assumptions are guesses at this early stage, the audience was still
expected to scrutinize the analysis for the qualitative underlying logic.

With all the analysis complete, a plan for getting to the next stage needed
to be created. The team requested that three architects, a software manager,
and two hardware designers be made available for six weeks at 25% of their
time. With this support from Architecture and Engineering, the Marketing
team felt comfortable committing to a PA date three months from the date of
the CA.

# Checklist

## Is the market opportunity evident?

At this stage, the details need not be fully ironed out. Rather, the goal is to ensure that, at a high level, there is a potentially profitable market opportunity.

## What to Look For:

- Analysis shows sizable segments with real Market Problems to solve
- Marketing can state exactly what it will take to win in these segments
- The envisioned solution is both feasible and clearly defensible

## Is the analysis sound?

The analysis in the Concept Approval need not be bulletproof. But it should be comprehensive and pass a basic reasonableness test.

## What to Look For:

- All assumptions are documented in an actionable Validation Plan
- Sales and Engineering certify that assumptions are reasonably correct
- Financial analysis is consistent with overall plan, shows acceptable return

*(Further discussion on this checklist available at www.systemnotcircumstance.com)*

# CHAPTER 4:

## Product Definition Phase

*Obtaining approval for the concept is a significant step, but there is still a long way to go. Until now, a lot of latitude was given to make assumptions in order to keep the focus on the big picture. But the level of scrutiny on require-ments, implementation, and financial analysis will now increase significantly. Great companies employ a repeatable template to make this transition from conceptual to specific. It guides the entire team in quickly converging on a feature set and schedule which meet the market need, sustaining a significant and demonstrable competitive advantage, and offering an attractive return even in the face of uncertainty. With a shared expectation on what is required, products move more quickly to the design phase and into the market. The system helps the team deal with complexity and imperfect information while satisfying the corporate need for clarity, risk mitigation, and decisiveness.*

## The Content

The type of content for the Product Approval (PA) is not wholly different from that of the Concept Approval (CA). It contains the same basic analyses, but with more detail. Let us look at some instances where the bar is raised:

- *Target Markets*: What started as a basic characterization of customer groupings must now evolve into a detailed description of the four main characteristics of a segment (this is discussed in detail in Chapter 6 "Market Segmentation"):
  - o Unique problems and functional needs
  - o Willingness to pay for a solution to their problems
  - o Requirements for making the product easy to use
  - o Method of learning about and buying the product

  A full characterization of the financial opportunity represented by each segment is necessary (a TAM/SAM analysis).

- *Problem and Solution:* The **Market Problem should be fully validated** as being real and significant at this point. Likewise, the results of the Validation Plan should have given the team a fair amount of confidence in the product's value proposition. Here the analysis should include a detailed picture of the customer's usage environment and how the specific problems arise. This will then need to be translated into a very concrete set of product feature and cost requirements. When entering the approval meeting, the definition should be 95% locked so that Engineering knows exactly what they are expected to scope and design.

- *Market Window*: A fully validated set of required deliverables and dates should be defined, including interim development dates, customer product sample or demonstration dates, and technical documentation. A push back from Engineering is inevitable, so Marketing should be ready to confidently defend them. The consequences of missing the market window for a particular segment should be noted, as this could be relevant in later scenario analysis.

- *Financial Analysis*: A recommendation to invest needs to be justified with hard numbers. So **previous gross assumptions are now replaced with credible and validated data**. Pricing is supported by a full Strategic Pricing Plan. Cost estimates are based on documented analysis from Engineering and Operations. Also volume assumptions need to be supported by either a good top down or bottom up model, consistent with segment sizes, market share, and pricing. More sophisticated tools, such as a sensitivity analysis (discussed further in Chapter 17 "Financial Analysis"), should be employed in order to help crisply answer the inevitable "what-if" questions about the input variables.

- *Competitive Analysis*: The simple overview of possible competitive alternatives must evolve into a detailed analysis (discussed in depth in Chapter 11 "Competitive Analysis") of company-, product-, and strategy-level comparisons based on confirmed sources. From this, specific action plans should be laid out on how to mitigate weaknesses and exploit advantages. Mostly importantly, a very clear answer should be given to the most important question: How do we win? If the product's advantage can't be verbalized in simple layman's terms, it probably isn't compelling. Astute management will not let a project pass unless it can show a strong and sustainable competitive advantage based on features, cost, quality, brand name, or distribution.

- *Productization Plan*: **A real product is more than just the "device" designed by Engineering.** It is the device plus all of the surrounding pieces necessary to easily learn about and use the product (discussed further in Chapter 17 "Creating Complete Products"). This must be clearly laid out in the PA presentation. It includes the intended positioning in the market, the ecosystem of necessary products and partners, the required marketing collateral and technical documentation, as well as a channel plan for effectively accessing customers. Early planning for these elements demonstrates to management that the team recognizes everything it takes to make the product successful. It also helps account for the necessary effort and cost to take the product to market so that an adequate headcount and budget are reserved.

- *Engineering Response*: The earlier feature/cost/schedule estimates from Engineering are replaced by an official commit. It includes the headcount level required to deliver the product. Here the stakes are high because the product cost, project expense, and features (specifically their effect on pricing) all have a big impact on the project's financial return. The **organization is basing it P&L on these commits, so they need to be solid**.

- *Engineering Plan*: Engineering will need to show their plan for executing on the development program to which it just committed. Much of this is concerned with *who* is doing *what*. The number of engineers and their skills mix should be described, as well as what they are working on and for how long. A plan needs to be shown for how engineers roll off their current project onto this new one, or for any necessary hiring. Finally, any required outsourcing or technology acquisitions should be accounted for.

## The Process

As soon as the CA is achieved, preparation for the PA should begin. Presumably the date for this is already set and time is of the essence. As before, there is a relatively straightforward process that can be followed:

- *Execute on the Validation Plan (Market)*: Start by seeking to validate the market assumptions highlighted in the Concept Phase. For the market questions, there is only one way forward – face to face time with customers. Employ the sales team to get meetings with the right people. As it is so early in the process, you'll need to balance the risk of competitive leaks (via these customers) with the benefit of their feedback. But realize that the validation of plans and assumptions is absolutely critical for marketing to confidently and effectively set the product direction for the organization.

- *Execute the Validation Plan (Technical)*: A number of technical issues were identified which need further exploration. The Engineering team should be spending their time doing so. Because of the mandate gained by passing CA, a larger number of resources should be available for this.

- *Finalize the market analysis*: The Validation Plan should yield better cost, price, features, and volume estimates. It is time to feed this back into the market and financial analysis. Look for any problems or inconsistencies that may have arisen. Do the features, cost and schedule still allow you to capture all of the target market segments? Does the feature set still support the pricing structure? Is the product still competitive? New information can sometimes change a good project into a bad one, and it usually shows up in the financial model

- *Finalize the requirements*: Based on feedback from the market and the validation of the technical assumptions, Marketing and Engineering will presumably iterate on the plan to bring features, product cost, and schedule in line with the market's needs. Once completed, a critical step is for Marketing to finalize the product definition in the Market Requirements Document (MRD). This is a highly symbolic step. Much of the product discussion and planning is done verbally. In the end, everyone may believe they understand the plan, but having the decisions and results documented in an MRD gives Engineering an official basis for finishing off their own planning and making a commit to the organization.

- *Create the Engineering plan*: At this point, Engineering will perform their analysis of how to deliver to their commitment. This is mostly a process of engineering managers working with their teams to create detailed schedules and assign specific individuals to tasks.

- *Deliver PA presentation*: In this presentation you are seeking to get management to agree to fund the project – in other words to dedicate real engineers to begin developing it. This will require Marketing to present a credible product proposal, and Engineering to provide a credible plan to develop it.

## Conclusion

Successful passage of the Product Approval stage is an exciting event. The uncertainty of not knowing what the next product will be is stressful to everyone in the organization. **Without an approved "next" product, there is always the possibility that there is *no* next product**. Team members may begin to wonder if they will have a job going forward. Sometimes this is justified, other times it is just pure paranoia. But it will exist, particularly within Engineering as they are more isolated from this process until the product is approved. Management and Finance will also be nervous about the financial viability of the product line until Marketing can find a product that will justify continued investment. Rallying the organization around a strategy and a plan helps dissipate the tremendous pent-up energy. Passage is exciting and good for organizational morale.

But it is not without some personal risk for those driving the process. Marketing must definitively declare that if the proposed product is built, then it will provide the promised financial return. Engineering is committing that if given the requested resources, they can deliver the product on the promised schedule. Reputations are on the line, as well as a large amount of money. Everyone had better be right.

# Product Definition Phase: Real World Example

*The Mason Concept Approval was a success, and the team was given the green light to proceed towards Product Approval. The stakes just got a lot higher. Instead of enjoying the freedom of a concept, the team now had to deal in hard facts and a real product plan. The first step was to execute the Validation Plan. In the prior phase, many assumptions had been made about the special power modes and Trusted Platform Module (TPM) being good solutions to the market problems related to laptop PC battery life and data security. The organization would demand that they get direct customer feedback on this, as the value proposition they represented was the product's foundation. There was no more room for assumptions about what customers would value, and so Marketing hit the road to get face to face with them.*

*In parallel to this, Engineering began their own analysis of what it would take to deliver these features. In the last phase, they had also based their analysis on assumptions and gross estimates. This needed to be turned into a solid commit, so more work was clearly required. By pulling in a few more engineers for this analysis, a bottoms-up schedule was created. Program Management helped put it into Gantt chart format so it could be understood. As with most projects, the analysis initially showed that, with current resources, it would not be possible to hit the feature-cost-schedule combination that Marketing was requesting. Some tradeoffs were going to be necessary. It turned out that one of Mason's target markets, the desktop personal computer (PC) market, was driving a significant schedule hit while only contributing a small amount of the product's projected overall profit. It was a painful choice, but Marketing reluctantly agreed to drop this segment as a target. This made Engineering's job a lot easier, and they were able to better align their commitment with Marketing's requested schedule.*

*Next the Competitive Analysis was done, populated with higher confidence data than before. Members of the Marketing team had to spend a fair amount of time extracting data from customers and the market, with an emphasis on cross-checking facts with more than one source. And instead of simply a feature comparison checklist, this analysis covered product attributes and strategy, as well as the competitor's company level strengths and weaknesses. Capping this analysis off was the "How We Win" statement. It succinctly and clearly declared why the product would win in each individual target segment. Mason had a clear advantage in the laptop PC space* with its cable sensing mode (now dubbed "Intelligent Power") and integrated TPM, and so the team felt a strong case could be made that it would win in the market.

The Pricing Strategy was then created. Rather than simply a projection of what the price would be, it was broken down by the value contributed by each individual feature. Also, all contextual elements, such as macroeconomic conditions and price elasticity, were factored in. This was in turn fed into the Finance Analysis. While in the Concept Phase this was mostly used as an indicator of the product's attractiveness, the stakes were now much higher. It would be used as one building block of the organization's P&L, and would dictate the financial make up and staffing level. As such, it was considered a commitment, and was expected to receive commensurate scrutiny of all the embedded assumptions. Sales volume assumptions would be questioned and needed to be defended using customer information and the Competitive Analysis. Pricing assumptions would also receive a lot of skepticism, and so a clear understanding of the value of Intelligent Power and TPM were necessary. Detailed sensitivity analysis was also done to show that the financial case for Mason was robust even if some of the assumptions changed within reasonable bounds.

Lastly came something that was not within the scope of the CA – a productization plan. This meant Marketing would need to show how the battery life and security benefits of Mason would be positioned in the market. This was mostly centered around a core theme – "True Mobility through long battery life, secure data, and stable technology". Ecosystem partners were identified, including the need to pre-integrate with at least one TPM software stack provider so that customers would not have to do so themselves. A staffing plan was also created. Mason would require 13 more engineers to be hired to deliver on time, including some with the specialized TPM knowledge that the organization currently lacked. This hiring requirement was clearly identified and accounted for in the projected expenses. Engineering also mapped out the specific individuals that were to work on each part of the project, accounting for when they became available after rolling off existing projects. Finally, they laid out exactly how they would assemble the necessary testing and design tools and infrastructure that were needed. In all, they presented a complete plan to get Mason into the production phase.

# Checklist

### Are all assumptions validated?
The Product Approval should yield a commit by the organization to move ahead. The stakes are too high to have uncertainty in the major assumptions.

## What to Look For:
- Pricing assumptions are supported by a full Strategic Pricing Plan
- Cost and schedule are based on detailed engineering analysis
- >3 key customer have given positive feedback on the entire plan

### Is it clear the product will win profitably in the market?
To commit a large amount of resources to the project, it needs to be very clear to the organization that the product will win and return strong profit.

## What to Look For:
- Competitive advantage is clear and has been validated with >3 customers
- The ROI is strong and robust to a reasonable level of uncertainty

### Is there a full product plan?
More than just a product definition and committed schedule is required. All elements necessary to get to product launch must be planned for.

## What to Look For:
- Marketing has identified ecosystem, channel, documentation requirements
- Engineering has identified staffing assignments, project risks, and needs

*(Further discussion on this checklist available at www.systemnotcircumstance.com)*

# CHAPTER 5:

## Changing the Plan

At this stage a large of amount of time, effort, and pride has gone into the product plan. The project is somewhere between the Product Approval and completion. Then a worst case scenario happens: new information comes in from the market or internal sources and suddenly the product is no longer viable as defined. Without a change to the plan, whether minor or major, there will be significant negative consequences for the organization. But making a change is not always easy, especially if the remedy is project cancellation. Like an investor that has lost serious money on a stock, it is hard to cut one's losses and move on. A big part of a core competence around great products is being able to detect and react to a project that is unexpectedly misaligned with market realities. This requires a system that encourages constant review of a program's alignment with the market, facilitates agile change, and rolls out the new plan smartly and decisively. If done well, it can minimize thrash within the organization and optimize the chances of releasing the right product.

## The Need for Change

Getting past the Concept and Product Approval gates is a comforting accomplishment. A direction is set, Engineers are busily designing the product, Marketing is pitching the product to customers, and Management now has some insight into expenses and profits going forward. The rigor of a sound Product Planning process should give the organization confidence that the product is solid given the best information at the time. Unfortunately, the world is not static. Unforeseen events may arise, causing some fundamental assumptions to change. A new competitor may enter the market with disruptive technology or a price bombing strategy. The needs of the customer base may change. Macroeconomic conditions may affect buying behavior. Or Engineering might suddenly find that it needs to de-commit on a critical aspect of schedule, cost, or features. Whatever the cause, these **new circumstances may dictate a mid-stream change to the product plan**. If the organization is lucky, the situation is addressable by minor modifications to the product definition or resourcing plan. However, some gaps can't be solved quite so easily. Sometimes, only a dramatic change to the plan of record (POR) will re-align the project with the realities of the market. Anything less will only lead to inevitable failure and the waste of significant resources and opportunity in the process.

**The responsibility to recognize and act on such a situation rests primarily with Marketing**. They are the voice of the customer; if the current plan does not meet the market's needs, they need to make sure it does. Whether due to the customer changing his mind, Marketing changing their view, competitors making unexpected moves, or an Engineering de-commit, it is always Marketing's job to address the gap. This is because they are the only ones with visibility into the market. Engineering is proverbially locked in their cubes doing their job with little exposure to customers. They are not in a position to notice a problem. It is Marketing that needs to remain vigilant after the PA gate is passed, continuing to stay in touch with customers regarding their problems and needs. Product definition is not a 'fire and forget' exercise, as the world is always in flux. The capabilities and plans of competitors should also be continually monitored and assessed. Remember that your competition is an intelligent opponent who will be executing their own plans but also reacting to yours. Never take a static view of what they may be doing. At any given time, all available market data needs to be compared to the current POR to ensure that the product is still compelling and competitive.

**Realization of a problem always emerges slowly**, rarely in an instantaneous epiphany. It often begins with initially fuzzy and unconfirmed information trickling in from customers and the salesforce. As this progresses, concerns about a potential gap will begin to tickle at the edge of your consciousness. If you feel it, dig more. With effort you may begin to realize the specific problem and its magnitude. It is at this point that you might realize that a change needs to be made.

## Obstacles to Change

In theory, Marketing should then simply stand up and tell the organization that the plan should be changed. But real life does not work this way because human nature works against you. There are several common factors that hinder such a direct course:

- *Momentum*: Unifying the organization around a single plan is great. The problem is that once set, changing the plan is like changing the direction of an aircraft carrier. Momentum works against you. And while smaller organizations are often more nimble, they are not immune to this effect. Humans, by nature, would rather execute a plan than search for one. Early in the product planning phase one of the dangers is the temptation to "just pick a direction" rather than persevering to find the right one. That danger still exists, but now even more strongly because the project has already started. Engineering and Marketing have both invested a considerable amount of time and energy on the current plan. This is especially true for the engineers, who are energized by working on technical challenges but find their morale wrecked when their efforts are wasted on a plan that changes.

- *Ego*: The creators of the product strategy will naturally have pride in it. But they can often have blind spots when it comes to accepting that the plan may no longer be the best course of action. There is a risk that doing so would reflect poorly on them, as some could perceive the situation to be a result of their inability to understand the market. So, the fragile human ego often does whatever it can to avoid this. It is this dynamic that keeps some marketers from driving a change.

- *Confidence*: Advocating a change to the plan can cause significant impact to the organization because of the potential for significant waste of resources and the resultant ill will. Wrenched from the comfort of an agreed upon plan, the organization must now seek out a new, likely riskier path. This is a lot to ask for. And so a marketer who is not 100% confident of the need for change may have a hard time raising the issue. Certainty in these matters is rare – product decisions are often made with imperfect information. Inexperienced individuals might never be able to clear this hurdle.

- *Technology*: New, disruptive technologies are sometimes the source of unforeseen change in the market. By their nature, such technologies are more likely to not be fully understood by the Marketing team. This makes the threat harder to assess. Human nature is such that we are more likely to discount or ignore those things we do not immediately comprehend. And when we do finally grasp the threat of a new technology, it may still be unclear as to how to react.

- *Time*: Recognition of a problem often comes late in the game, only after the competitive and market dynamics have had time to play out. So, rarely is there much runway to react. This often scares off many marketers from pushing for change. They may be subconsciously driven by a belief that it is better to have *some* product that is on time (even if not quite the right product for the market) rather than no product at all or an extremely late one.

- *Bandwidth*: Most marketers are extremely busy. The nature of their job pulls them in a hundred directions at any given time. Getting to the point of having an official product plan often takes a herculean effort. Once done, it allows the Marketing team time to get back to catching up on the rest of their job. They know that going back to revisit the product plan will require an immense amount of further effort. There is a fatigue factor that can often hinder one from diving back into the Product Planning process.

- *Self Preservation*: An ongoing project offers both a chance to shine as well as job security for the Marketing team member that owns it. These are desirable facets of a job situation, even more so if the company or industry may be going through tough times. Canceling that product represents the loss of both factors. While it would be nice if professionalism led everyone to make the right decision for the company, the reality is that self-interest can play a role and at times cloud one's judgment regarding the viability of a product.

While your gut may be telling you that something is wrong with the plan, the forces described above can become an obstacle to action. It can be tempting to ignore the problem rather than address it. But the Marketing team needs to understand and accept their weighty responsibility here. They are the scouts in the arena of product development: where they lead, the organization follows – even if right over the proverbial cliff. **It is Marketing's job, and theirs alone, to raise a red flag when the current plan will not profitably meet the market requirements**. No one in Engineering or Management has the market knowledge to fill this role. So, if any of these forces are holding you back, push through it. While the issues raised about momentum and time are a concern, ultimately the *wrong* product on time is never better than the *right* product late. If you truly cannot meet the market window, it may be better to simply skip a cycle and focus on the next market window. It is better to retreat now and come back strong enough to regain competitiveness and market share. If a lack of confidence or knowledge is holding you back, seek help from more experienced individuals in the organization. Quietly express your concerns and ask for their assistance in understanding the new market circumstances and exploration of the right course of action. You'll find that most will be flattered that you've approached them for help; on the flip side, you can leverage their knowledge to avoid mistakes, making yourself look better. If bandwidth is a problem, you will simply have to temporarily put aside other concerns. This is a personal choice, and you will surely take heat from those expecting other urgent deliverables from you. Of all of these issues, overcoming the ego may be the hardest. But the business of creating great products is a complex one, and far too difficult to do if you can't admit you are wrong once in a while. Suggesting a change to the plan means you have to admit you may have made a mistake in the original plan. That is tough. All you can do is try to avoid the situation by doing better due diligence the next time around. Then you can rest easy in the knowledge that you've made the best plan possible with the best knowledge available at the time. If circumstances change in a way that was unforeseeable, it need not threaten your ego to have to modify the plan. Marketing must never be afraid to stand before the organization and say "My view has changed" if this is what is truly best for the business, as long as they are doing good due diligence up front and not making frequent or capricious changes.

## Proceeding Smartly

**Once you do decide to make a change to the plan, don't prematurely publicize your view.** It can be deadly to team productivity. Engineers are easily demotivated by the notion that the product on which they are working could be cancelled. They know that a strong project means interesting work and job security. A natural human reaction to a project in danger is to immediately look around for a new project or job – no one wants to be the last one off a sinking ship and vulnerable to layoffs. The senior guys who have been around the block may be able to handle it, but junior engineers are particularly susceptible. So it is important to keep your concerns to yourself until the appropriate time. If you broadcast your concerns and they turn out to be unwarranted, then you have lost precious development time and unnecessarily hurt the product – possibly creating an unintended self-fulfilling prophecy.

Start by working quietly behind the scenes with some of the management staff to build your case. Eventually you may be telling the organization that they must change direction; you'd better have a clear and convincing analysis which shows why it is necessary. While your skills of persuasion will come in handy, you should rely mostly on the bare truth – the current plan will not lead to success. If you can give a clear picture of that outcome, and clearly demonstrate how the current path leads to it, a rational organization cannot argue. If you've done a good job of identifying your assumptions in the original Product Planning process, you can simply show which of your assumptions has changed. If the particular assumption in question was not explicitly stated, don't worry. Identify it as implicit, and show the chain of logic that necessitates the change to the plan (of course, it goes without saying that your new assumption needs to be strongly validated – you wouldn't want to be perceived as capriciously changing the plan). It is most effective if you can quantify the effects of the new assumption on the financial analysis. The effects of most circumstances can be quantified in either one of two variables in the financial analysis. The first is a lower selling price; some common causes may include:

- Less perceived value because the product lacks a feature which turns out to be a market requirement.
- Less perceived differentiation because a competitor unexpectedly matches a key feature in the product, requiring you to fight on price.
- A negative macroeconomic environment which leads to tighter spending by customers, requiring lower prices to drive a sale.
- A competitor unexpectedly decides to utilize a price bombing strategy.
- A late schedule relative to competition, requiring you to lower the price to entice customers to wait for your product.

You may also experience a change in circumstances which manifests itself in lower overall volumes. Some common causes include:

- A lack of a specific required feature may eliminate your ability to capture any business in a certain market segment
- Your schedule is late relative to the market window or competition, meaning you lose market share or miss specific opportunities

You would then calculate the effect of the change to these input variables upon the output metrics. If the metrics change significantly in the wrong direction – particularly if they fall below the corporate target – then it is a strong indicator that a program modification may be necessary.

Now that you have characterized the effects of the problem, it is time to consider a solution. It is said that mediocre employees are oblivious to strategic problems and good employees can spot such problems, but it is the great employees who offer a proposed solution. So before raising the issue to management, you should seek to find an alternate path. There are many forms this could take. You may ask for a significant addition to the feature set in order to meet a new market requirement or your competition. Of course, doing so will add to the schedule or resources required since Engineering won't have planned for it. Alternatively, you could choose to give up another feature. This means a bit of soul-searching is required; reducing features may impact competitiveness in certain markets. You may have to make the hard decision to drop any requirements that are not absolutely must-have, even if it means losing certain peripheral opportunities.

To accommodate some of these changes, it may be that a significant addition of resources is required. On paper it sounds simple; if management will agree to approve a few new heads, the program could be put back on track. Of course, nothing is that simple. First, nearly every company in the universe is short on resources. Existing heads are likely already committed, and there is always resistance to creating an imbalance in the P&L by overhiring. Second, rapid hiring is nearly impossible in most cases. It is too hard to find, recruit, and train engineers in the middle of a program in time for them to contribute meaningfully. So while having extra people on the program may seem like an ideal solution, one has to consider the impact to the financial picture as well as the feasibility of getting those resources in place in time.

Unfortunately, there are also those situations where recovery is not an option. The gap is simply too large and time too short to redirect the program to success. In cases such as these, cancellation may be the only viable option. As painful as it is to everyone involved, no organization can responsibly go forward with a program knowing that it will likely not be successful. And any marketer that hides or ignores the now-recognized gap is committing a grave breach of business ethics, not to mention common sense. Every marketer will be faced with such a dilemma at some time in his career. In such cases, this advice is offered: **it is *always* better to avoid a losing battle than to fight it and lose**. Better to regroup and fight in the time and place where you can win. While cancellation means giving up on the current market opportunity, at least those precious resources could be deployed onto other more promising projects.

However, this brings up an interesting risk. **Cancellation of the program may raise fears within the corporation that this particular line of business does not have a long-term future.** The resources saved may be better deployed to another business unit (with their own P&L) that has convinced management that they have the potential for strong financial returns. These types of turf battles are common in mid to large size companies that have begun to mature (and thus are managing their finances in a disciplined fashion). Everyone is fiercely fighting for resources because the corporate finance community is doing everything they can to keep a cap on headcount. Therefore, it is wise to have another promising project queued up before other greedy GMs begin to hungrily eye your idle resources.

So to avoid a negative impact to morale and poaching from other business units, **it is wise to quietly vet another project concept to a reasonable level of detail before going public.** Initially work with a trusted circle, likely other members of the Marketing and Architecture teams. Once you have confidence in your position, begin to approach selected engineering managers in order to gain their support. Doing so on an individual basis is very effective; it allows them to provide feedback in advance that you can fold into the new plan. It also allows them to vent – having them express frustration privately makes you look better and allows them to enter a meeting on the topic in a more constructive frame of mind. Take the arrows in private rather than in a meeting in front of senior management. The first task is to convince them that there is a problem. Until they believe that, any suggested change you make may only anger them, as they will see you as indecisive and causing thrash in their organization. Also, marketers have an annoying habit of essentially saying to Engineering "this is the new requirement…just go do it." Engineers tend to find this condescending, and may resist it. An alternate method is to say "here is the problem as I see it…can you help me find a way to meet these new market requirements?" Once you convince them there is a problem, they will be much more receptive to (and will be asking for) your proposed solution. When you believe you have enough support among key managers, it is time to take the problem and proposed solution to senior management. At this point, you will presumably re-enter the official Product Planning process.

## Conclusion

No one in the organization likes the prospect of changing a plan midstream. The revenue, morale, and stress impact to the organization can be significant. Nonetheless, it is an occasional fact of life in the product business. Marketing bears the responsibility of recognizing and reacting to circumstances that merit a change. **The most egregious organizational sin is for a project that is unaligned with market realities to be allowed to go forward.** Marketing needs to avoid any self-delusion and take a critical eye to all projects. Management needs to play their part and ask the hard questions to vet bad projects out. Once one is discovered, it must be dealt with decisively but skillfully. Changing a product plan is tricky. Fumbling this process will inject unwanted thrash into the organization, and also hurt the credibility of the Marketing team and the organization's senior leaders in the eyes of the rank and file.

# Changing the Plan: Real World Example

*We fast forward to three months after the PA. Engineering had completed about 30% of the design. Everything was on track per the original schedule and morale was high. Sales and Marketing had begun to sell the product broadly across the customer base. As this progressed, some new information began to emerge about the interface by which the communications chip connected internally to the personal computer (PC). Today's technology was a low performance interface called PCI. But the industry was rapidly transitioning to a higher performance technology called PCI-Express. This was in fact the interface implemented in Mason. But as the selling process progressed, customers were saying they were nervous about the stability of the new interface technology. They would feel more comfortable with a product that had both the new and the legacy interfaces so that they would have a fall back plan in case the new technology had problems. The first few times this came up, the Marketing and Sales teams did not really react. But as they heard it more and more, one of the Marketing team members began to get worried because Mason only implemented the new interface. Back when the product was initially defined, the industry seemed squarely pointed towards using PCI-Express, and so removing the legacy PCI interface to reduce product cost was a logical choice. Now that the new interface technology was progressing slower than expected, it cast doubt on those assumptions. What if the notion of a dual interface product suddenly became a firm requirement from customers? In retrospect, it was a big oversight not to have a better plan to bridge between an old and a new technology. This was clearly going to be a problem that needed to be addressed. But how? The design was almost half done. Marketing would have to upset the entire program to add in a legacy interface, not to mention the fact that they would have to own up to their own mistake in not anticipating this problem when the product was first defined. Of course, there was no choice – they just needed to face facts and go get it done.*

*The first step was to assemble what was known and discuss it among Marketing, field applications engineers, and Sales. All were in unanimous agreement that given what they now knew, adding the legacy interface was the right thing to do. Next, the product manager asked the architect on the project to discreetly help scope the effort in terms of product cost impact and design complexity. This allowed Marketing to understand how significant* this change might be without alarming any of the engineers actually doing the design work. The answer came back that the cost impact would be small, but the work was moderately complex and could add six weeks or so to the schedule. With this in hand, the Director of Marketing approached his boss, the GM. He wanted to alert him about the new information, and that Marketing would be approaching Engineering to analyze what it would take to make a change. The two teams would report back to the GM in a week or two to make a recommendation. The GM appreciated the heads up and approved the course of action.

In the subsequent meeting between Marketing and Engineering, there were some heated emotions. The schedule was already tight, and engineers were working long days in order to keep things on track. The Marketing team did their best to lay out the situation and the impact to the product if not addressed. Probably more from emotion than anything, some of the first line engineering managers stated that they could never add this feature and still meet the schedule. But the meeting ended with promises to go off and analyze the problem. Luckily, the Director of Marketing had spent a lot of time prepping the Director of Engineering and had his support. In the end, the analysis came back that, with some reshuffling of resources, and a two week delay in another project (which Marketing determined they could accept), the legacy interface could be added with a three week hit to the schedule. This would still be within the time frame that met the customer's needs, although with little cushion (meaning there would be greater program risk if something else caused the schedule to slip). With the analysis done, the new feature was made part of the POR, and added to the marketing presentations and technical documentation.

# Checklist

## Can the organization detect a POR-market gap?

Product planning is not a 'fire and forget' exercise. The organization must stay vigilant to continually ensure that the plan is still the right one.

## What to Look For:

- A mid-course review has been scheduled to review POR vs. market need
- The GM holds Marketing accountable for identifying any gaps

## Does the organization react rapidly to a gap?

To overcome an organization's natural inertia, the GM must install a mindset of rapid, decisive reaction to any gap between the market and POR.

## What to Look For:

- Marketing quickly validates the data and presents alternatives to the GM
- If a project is cancelled, Engineers are quickly moved to a new project

*(Further discussion on this checklist available at www.systemnotcircumstance.com)*

# CHAPTER 6:

## Market Segmentation

*Walk in to a dark room, and all you'll likely see is a monolithic black. But stand still for a few moments and shades of gray will emerge as faint edges of objects become apparent. As your vision adjusts it becomes possible to navigate the room. The process of identifying segments within a large market is much like this. Initially our untrained eyes only see a monolithic mass of customers with homogeneous needs. But over time our knowledge of the market grows and we begin to discern distinct groupings within the mass. This awareness can be applied to help create better products for unique parts of the market. And if your vision is a bit better than your competitor's, you can spot these groups just a little bit sooner. In skilled hands this can quickly be turned into a competitive advantage. This is what is possible for companies that systematically and proactively employ Market Segmentation. Although one of the most powerful weapons in the Marketing arsenal, it is surprisingly underutilized because it not always well understood.*

## The Myth of Big Markets

The antithesis of market segmentation is the notion of "selling a toothpick to 1% of everyone in China"; if you could simply get 1% of the population of China to buy your product (only 1%! Should be easy...), then you would have a huge market success. So, you define a product that addresses this entire market, and then sell with gusto hoping to capture that mere 1%. Yet along the way you notice the product getting beaten in certain competitive situations. In each case you investigate, you are losing for something specific that you are lacking. At times you seem to be missing a minor feature that a small group of customers desire; you label them as outliers. In other cases, the customer expects some ridiculously low price; again, you write them off as cheapskates looking for a bargain, not a real product. As time goes by, you realize the losses aren't exceptions – they appear to be the rule. Suddenly, the dream of capturing that 1% begins to look like a long shot. Before too long, it is clear that your product is a failure.

What happened? The explanation is simple: **you tried to make a product that was all things to all customers, and ended up with a product that wasn't competitive in any situation**. You fell into this trap because you so badly wanted to go after a market of 1 billion buyers. So you called them all "a" market, and attacked it with a single product. Yet you soon realized that it is very hard to have one product address the needs of an entire market. You failed to harness the power of Market Segmentation.

## The Evolution of a Market

Let's begin by examining the way in which a market is created and grows over time. We will make the case that the need for segmentation is the result of a predictable pattern. A "market" can loosely be defined as a group of customers that share a common need; a product that meets this need would presumably be uniquely attractive to them. So, the "birth" of a new market is often coincident with the discovery of the common need.

Early in its life cycle, a new market is monolithic. It hasn't taken enough form to be sub-divided. Suppliers are still trying to figure out its unique characteristics, problems, and dynamic. Likewise, the market itself is still trying to fully understand the value of the new products targeted at it. Therefore, such products are aimed at all customers within the fuzzy boundary of this new, monolithic market. Suppliers are running as fast as they can to rush product to market to establish first mover advantage. Revenue growth comes from a land grab for early market share. As things progress, further growth comes from market expansion, as the rising tide raises all boats. Furthermore, early competitive pressures tend to be manageable, and so price pressure is minimal.

Of course, all good things come to an end. New competitors begin to notice the developing market, and hungrily eye the profits being taken by existing suppliers. With the benefit of being able to copy existing product offerings, they enter the market hoping to take a piece of the pie. Although behind at first, they begin to catch up and can soon provide reasonable alternatives to those of the incumbents. As the market is maturing and growth slows, these new competitors are directly stealing market share and revenue from the incumbents.

With only a few suppliers, making a product decision was relatively easy for customers. But now, with so many choices, they have a harder time choosing which particular product is best suited to their needs. They very much want one of the products to stand out so as to make their buying decision easier. A product that appears to cater specifically to their own unique needs probably would. Customers may even be more willing to ignore a lack of incumbency or brand name. But in the absence of one product standing out, these customers will revert to choosing on price, at which point commoditization sets in.

Clearly no supplier wants to be in this situation. So as a market saturates, products must continue to become more specialized to the unique needs of each customer. A customized product for each individual customer may not be feasible, but it is possible to find sub-groupings of similar customers that share a "unique commonality" – a set of needs that is common within the grouping, but unique from the larger market. If the unique commonality is significant enough, and the size of the group large enough, then it can be designated as a market segment. **A product specifically designed for this group's unique needs would likely experience greater success within this set of customers than products which are geared toward the larger market**. Within the context of a saturating market, identifying and serving unique groups is a way to maintain or grow market share. This is often easiest for incumbents – the market knowledge and intimacy they built during the growth phase should help them discern that the market is not monolithic, but in fact contains unique groupings of customers that have common problems. Furthermore, profits reaped during the growth phase can fund a broadening of the product line across multiple segments.

## Defining a Market Segment

Determining the boundaries of a market segment is not always easy. Let's say you are Oracle selling databases. Your customer base encompasses multiple industries; one such customer type might be hospitals. Does this mean you can define a hospital segment, given that the boundaries of this group are rather well-defined? Not necessarily, because a segment is not defined by identity but rather the unique commonality of needs. What unique challenges and needs do database users within a hospital setting share? **This is the key to segmentation – discerning and defining the unique needs of a particular group of customers**. To do so properly, you need a comprehensive framework for describing the characteristics of a segment.

There are four main components of such a framework. The first is the most familiar: the *functional needs* of the customer. Given the unique information that database users are trying to organize and the unique way they access it, what do they need the product to *do*? For instance, the health care industry may be having a problem maintaining the security of certain information in their patient database. The scientific research community may be grappling with the need to quickly execute large scale simulations. Each of these examples represents the respective segment's Market Problem (discussed further in the Chapter 7 "Market Problem"). The Market Problem is the fundamental difficulty that the customer is experiencing. **Discovering a functional problem that is common to a group of customers is the first step in defining a segment**. Presumably, a feature that addresses a segment's unique needs would make the product more valuable and competitive. To clarify, you are identifying the functional needs and problems of the segments, but not yet the features that would address them. Leading with features is a mistake. You inadvertently limit your engineering team's creativity when you tell them what to build rather than giving them a problem to solve (more on this in Chapter 8 "Features"). Furthermore, it will be very apparent to an experienced audience (during your product planning presentation) that you do not understand your target segments if you do not fully describe the functional Market Problem first.

The next characteristic that defines a segment is its "willingness to pay" for the product, reflected in a *price point*. This willingness to pay is a result of the value the product offers them. The magnitude of the Market Problem being solved and the lack of otherwise available solutions dictate this willingness. If the need is not critical, or if most of the products on the market meet it, then there will be little willingness to pay more. Therein lies the power of segmentation. If the rest of the market doesn't recognize a segment, it is because they aren't discerning the unique needs of a particular subgroup. So in establishing and addressing a new segment, you can be the first to provide a unique solution to its unique problem. This is good, because solved problems drive a perception of value and thus a higher price point (discussed further in Chapter 12 "Pricing Strategy"). A grouping of customers with a relatively homogeneous set of problems should have a similar willingness to pay for the solution, and thus each segment will have its own natural price point.

Now, that was the easy part. Most marketers understand what has been discussed so far. Unfortunately, too many companies go no further in characterizing their target markets. But experienced marketers know that **customers don't always choose just on features and price**. There are other decision criteria they use which may not always be obvious. Some customers may choose a product which is simply the *easiest for them to use*. Since customers within a segment are likely to use the product in a similar way, attributes that make it easier to use are often an identifying characteristic of a segment. Consider two examples:

- Some products require a fair amount of effort and technical prowess to implement. Each segment using the product may have its own unique challenges with implementation in their specific usage environment. Therefore technical documentation customized for a specific customer's application of the product would be highly desirable. This would relieve these customers from having to maintain the technical skills and expend the effort to figure out the implementation details themselves or extract it piecemeal from your Applications Engineers.
- Some products are used in conjunction with others, and interoperability is a requirement. This can be a challenge to users, as they

are required to both take a leap of faith that it will all work to-gether. If it doesn't, they have to go through the painful process of doing the integration themselves. Users would highly value this uncertainty being removed and the integration work being done for them. You can make this happen by doing the integration and testing of the product with the complementary products upfront. This removes a potential buying obstacle – i.e. "I wonder if it will work with what I have now?"

In each case, the segment had unique needs which were wholly sepa-rate from function or price. This illustrates that the characterization of a segment's needs for ease of use must be included in the segmentation exercise (discussed further in Chapter 17 "Creating Complete Products").

The final component used to characterize a segment is the *channel* by which customers learn about and buy the product. Typically this refers to a salesforce or distributor, which is the conduit for marketing a certain category of product to a certain group of customers. In the Internet age, it is based on building a brand name (through creative use of popular media and viral marketing) or some mechanism to drive web traffic to the appro-priate website (such as Google advertising). Or, it could be alliances with partner companies (who presumably have complementary products) that already have access to the right customers. All of these take time to build, as personal relationships, market segment knowledge, staffing, and infra-structure are slowly put into place. If the organization is selling to its tradi-tional markets with its traditional products, a channel is probably already in place. But what if the product resides in a new category, or is being sold to an entirely new and different market? **Without a channel providing access to the target markets, the product will have no chance to suc-ceed**. Yet marketers conveniently forget this. They believe that the right product at the right price will sell itself. Implicit in this is an assumption that customers will become aware of the product, understand the value proposition enough to investigate further, and trust the company enough to buy it. Yet this is precisely the situation you may find yourself in if any of your target segments are outside of your traditional targets. The Internet is littered with tens of thousands of incredibly useful software tools, but no one knows about most of them! There is simply no way for the user to pick these proverbial needles out of the haystack, and the providers of these tools don't have an effective way make users aware of them. So, any study of a segment must include a characterization of how the customer becomes aware of, learns about, and buys products.

This discussion should illustrate that segments are characterized by much more than simply functional needs and price. Each is a complex combination of all four vectors which Marketing should include in their segmentation exercise. Each represents an opportunity to better discern and address the unique needs of the target segments. Of course, customers will tell you that they want a product that optimizes on all four vectors simultaneously – "full features, low cost, effortless to use in my unique application, and readily available to me". But the truth is that each segment has its own "ratio" of value that it places on these characteristics. For any particular segment, one of the four criteria will likely be dominant. The product decision will ultimately boil down to choosing the product that best optimizes on that criterion, with enough consideration given to the others. The marketer needs to ask himself "On what criteria will a particular segment make a buying decision?" Optimize a version of the product with that in mind.

Let us consider the example of a company which is planning to sell an industrial chemical product and therefore is analyzing various market segments. The product offers a combination of extremely low emissions and very high viscosity. Let us examine a few of its potential target markets and the value each places on the four vectors:

- Segment #1 uses the chemical in a manufacturing process governed by strict Environmental Protection Agency (EPA) emissions guidelines. The cost of penalties far exceeds the cost of the chemical itself. Few products meet the emissions threshold, so the customer is willing to pay more for those that do. Most customers have a skilled staff, and thus know how to safely handle the chemical. Customers in this segment acquire the chemical from one of the larger manufacturing distributors that supplies much of their other equipment. It is clear that this particular segment cares most about *function*. A product for this segment would emphasize its emissions characteristics, and a premium could likely be charged.
- Segment #2 uses the chemical in a recycling process. There are few emissions in this process, so little value is placed on the product's

low-emissions characteristics. In fact, most functional needs are served just fine by most of the available products. The recycling process is basic, so there are no critical requirements for usability. Finally, the recyclers also use the same chemical distributors to buy the product. It is clear that this particular segment would likely care most about the *price point*. Here, a product would have to be priced to meet an aggressive price point.

- Segment #3 is comprised of small photographic shops that use the chemical to arrest a chemical reaction inside the automatic developer machines. The segment's functional needs for the chemical itself are not extreme; most available products adequately meet them. But it does need to be mixed with two others chemicals, and placed in the machine by a trained individual. Frequently a mixed batch has to be discarded because the mix ratio was incorrect. In fact, such mistakes were leading to an average 30% chemical waste rate and 40 minutes wasted worker time. A customer in this segment may not place high value on any particular functional characteristic of the product, but would be extremely interested in having it easier to use to eliminate the waste. One possibility would be to package the primary chemical with pre-measured amounts of the complementary chemicals, eliminating waste as well as the need to train the employee. A need to optimize the *usability* of the product likely dominates the buying decision criteria for this segment.

- Segment #4 is comprised of laboratories that perform pathology tests on tissue samples. The chemical is used to prepare certain tissues for a particular test. They also value the low emissions properties of the chemical process. EPA limits are not the issue (amounts used are very small), but because it is used by individuals in close quarters, it is safer for the users to have low amounts of noxious fumes. So this segment places moderate value on the emissions characteristics, and so has a mid-level price point. But Segment #4 is unique in one respect – its users do not buy from the large chemical distributors. They typically purchase their other lab supplies from the distributors of medical equipment. They are not willing or able to change this buying pattern. So they place a lot of value on having a product available through these medical equipment distributors. In fact, they will likely only buy a product available in this channel; they would simply never get exposed to any other channel. All functional, price, and usability benefits are trumped by the need of this segment to have the product available in the right channel.

This simple example illustrates how every segment has its own unique combination of needs. These shape the perception of your product and drive the buying decision. You need to clearly understand the target segments at this level, including all four factors and the weight placed on each. This is the level of knowledge necessary to truly understand what makes a customer buy. And **that is the basis of any good product plan – knowing exactly why a customer would or would not buy your product**. As mentioned before, strive to move beyond the superficial characterizations of segments; operate at this very fundamental level and your products will be more in tune with customers' needs.

## Spanning Multiple Segments

The point of segmentation is to pick a specific segment and customize your product and marketing efforts around it. Doing so will likely increase your chances of success within that segment; of course the flip side is that you have limited your available market. The ideal situation is to have a unique product for every segment of the market. You could dominate with the right product for each grouping of customers. Unfortunately your resources will always be too limited to allow this. You will be forced to choose your target segments and attack them with a few products. But a little creativity can allow you to maximize your Total Available Market (TAM).

One option would be to create a product that had the superset of attributes required by all target segments. But a problem arises in that each of the target segments likely has its own unique price point. Those with greater needs for functionality and ease of use will accept a premium, while others may only be willing to pay mainstream or commodity pricing. So with this single product, if you price high to capture profit in the premium segments, you won't be able to sell into those with lower price points. But if you price aggressively to capture the mainstream, you leave money on the table within higher end segments. The **challenge**

**is to somehow charge different price points in different segments for the same product**. If each segment would only kindly pay as much as they are able, then the problem would be solved. This would be akin to a progressive tax (such as income tax), where each individual pays an amount of tax relative to their income. Too bad it doesn't work that way. There are laws against discriminatory pricing, and there is inevitable channel conflict that arises with disparate pricing across customers. So instead of an attractive but infeasible progressive tax system, you'll have to fool the market into it.

This can be done with a technique called Spanning, whereby multiple segment-specific products are created from a single base product. The base product boasts all the attributes necessary to address the entire set of target market segments. For each particular segment, a unique product version (called a "SKU", or Stock-Keeping Unit) is created which only contains those attributes relevant to the specific segment. The perception is created that it is a product designed specifically for that segment. This is further enhanced with positioning, ecosystem, and channel considerations that are appropriate for the segment. This process is repeated for each of the target segments. Because they appear to be different products, the organization is then free to price each independently in a manner appropriate to each segment. The result is that a single development effort (which conserves precious resources) that can yield a lineup of products customized to a broad set of segment's needs and willingness to pay. **Maintaining the perception of each being a unique product is critical**. Buying habits are like water – they migrate to the lowest point (in this case, price point). If the illusion is broken, it will be hard to stop customers from migrating to lower priced versions of the product. Organizations can take a few basic steps to reinforce the differences between SKUs. Each product SKU should have its own unique:

- *Market Message:* Target the message specifically to the needs and language of the segment. Done well, it will resonate more with the market and also better differentiate from other versions.
- *Marketing Collateral:* The mere existence of segment-specific collateral will strongly reinforce the market messaging and the illusion of a unique product.
- *Product Name:* Rather than simply adding a suffix to a base name, use an entirely different numbering or naming scheme.

- *Channel*: If possible, only expose a particular channel to the products it will sell. Ignorance is a powerful tool in maintaining multiple versions of a base product.
- *Technical Documentation*: Don't let the Applications Engineers get lazy and try to create one document for all versions. Create unique documents for each segment and customer usage environment.
- *Sales Training*: As with the channel, only expose the sales team to the products they will be selling. Train them rigorously on differences between versions they may be selling so they can help maintain the illusion of the differences between SKUs.

While the Spanning technique can do a great job of maximizing TAM while minimizing development expenses, it can create some problems. A common one is the angst Operations will feel from having to manage multiple product versions. It creates more overhead to track them all, and tends to lead to higher levels of inventory. It may require some incremental qualification effort. And, sometimes, it can increase product cost, as the total volume is now spread over several products which may not qualify for the same volume price breaks from the manufacturing partner. Some Operations groups will take a hard line, implementing a blanket policy. This is in their nature. But they are not exposed to the market and its variety of needs; they only know to pursue the goals of cost reduction given to them by the corporation. They've seen the effects of version proliferation from marketers run wild, and so feel the need to push back.

Another group that is often impacted by SKU proliferation is Engineering. Spanning may have helped minimize their *development* resources, but it can increase their *testing* resources. Each version may have to be treated to some degree as a unique product in the testing process. Unless the market availability of these unique product versions can be serialized, they all must be tested at once. This can create peaks in staffing requirements that are hard to accommodate. So, be aware of the schedule and resource impact of your segmentation strategy.

Your customer support resources, whether Applications Engineers or the support call center, will also be taxed by multiple product versions. You are creating an illusion, so any group that is customer-facing must also maintain the illusion. Applications Engineers must create unique documentation for each version of the product. Customer service personnel must be trained to track and respond to each unique SKU appropriately. Overall, their workload will increase.

Expect the managers of each of these teams to provide some resistance to offering multiple SKUs from a single product. The best way to deal with this is to prepare a quantitative analysis that clearly shows how the costs of the strategy are far exceeded by the incremental profit that can be obtained. Meet proactively with these managers to gain their support well before the product planning presentation. Find ways to address their concerns and fold them into your plan. With this approach you can usually diffuse some of the inevitable points of resistance.

## Segmentation as an Offensive Weapon

Too many marketers take a passive approach to segmentation. They simply accept the segment boundaries that are generally recognized in the market at that time, assuming this represents the "natural" groupings of customers. But experienced marketers understand that the definition of any segment is not fundamental to the universe – it is in fact "man-made". Your understanding of the boundaries of a particular segment only exists because another market player has shaped your perceptions through their own marketing efforts. They have identified a grouping of customers with a unique problem and then created products for it.

In doing so, these companies were able to attack the new segment first and establish incumbency. They are in a position of strength. In military terms, this is the equivalent of allowing your enemy to choose the place of battle and establish defensive positions before you arrive. Using the generally accepted segmentation of the market only leads you into the strength of the incumbents. This is why segmentation should be used proactively, as an offensive weapon. **Instead of using someone else's definition of the market, seek to define new segments**. To do this, go back to basics; look to identify unique problems or usage models that could form the basis for the definition of a new segment. You only accomplish this by spending significant time with your customer base, seeking to understand their world. Find that "unique commonality" that your competitors haven't, and then create the product offering that addresses it. Instead of accepting the rules, you are changing the game on your competitors. Before they realize it, you are marketing products that cater more closely to the needs of a group of customers. Before they can react, you are stealing those customers away and establishing a leadership position within the sub-segment. You change the rules to suit your strengths.

**Offensive segmentation can be used by newcomers to enter a market with a very entrenched incumbent.** As leaders in a market develop, they will naturally cater to that market in a way that captures the most customers. In fact they probably do recognize small pockets of sub-segments within their larger market. But many find themselves in a situation where addressing the needs of these sub-segments would defocus the effort and resources applied to addressing the mainstream market. This phenomenon was well-described by Clayton Christensen in *The Innovator's Dilemma*, where incumbents, by necessity, must focus solely on their mainstream customers who have mainstream needs. Luckily for these incumbents, the sub-segments settle for the mainstream product because there are no alternatives. This is the window of opportunity that incumbents often leave open for a new player to identify and address the needs of an ignored sub-segment. Such a new player may lack the brand name, resources, economies of scale, and relationships that the incumbent possesses. But customers with specialized needs may be willing to overlook these shortcomings for a product that they perceive as better meeting their unique needs. With this opening, a new competitor can establish a beachhead in the market from which to expand. Because sub-segments tend to be small, you can possibly operate under the radar and not provoke a competitive reaction from the incumbent. As you succeed you will begin to draw more attention, but now you are armed with a revenue stream, greater market knowledge, and more credibility. By using this beachhead strategy, many newcomers have taken a complacent incumbent by surprise and proceeded to steal significant market share.

Of course, **incumbents can use segmentation to defend their market share.** They continually sub-divide the market into new segments, then extend unique versions of their product line into them. Upstarts have no openings with which to enter the market. By definition, incumbents should be in a much better position to do this than the new guys. Their position in the market should afford them a high level of customer intimacy and knowledge that can be leveraged in defining new segments. Their current products should provide an easy jumping point for segment specific offerings. And their current product line should provide the profits to fund custom development for a particular segment. These are all strengths that an incumbent should be using to defend its market share and lock out new competitors.

## Segment Analysis in Product Planning

We now turn our attention from the art of segmenting a market, to that of integrating the analysis into the Product Planning process. Beginning with the Concept Phase you will be required to identify, characterize, and size your target market segments. This analysis will provide important context for every product choice you make. The four vectors previously discussed should enable you to provide a very comprehensive analysis. Your audience will be evaluating how well you understand the market. As you conclude your presentation proposal, they will look back to your target segment analysis for consistency. Does the product fill the segments' needs, including both functional and usability requirements? Are the price points being met, and supported by the underlying cost structure of the product? Do you have ready access to the channel from which the target segment typically buys? All of this will be scrutinized; it is easy to see the importance of clearly identifying and characterizing your segments upfront.

They will also expect that you understand the financial opportunity each segment represents. So the target segments need to be sized. The marketing profession uses three common terms to describe market size, the first of which is *TAM,* or Total Available Market. This represents the sales potential of the group of potential customers whose problems can be addressed by a particular category of product. Such products include those that your company or competitors currently offer, or could conceivably develop with a reasonable amount of engineering effort. TAM numbers are intended to convey the attractiveness (i.e. potential returns) of a particular market in the context of the investment necessary to gain and maintain market share within it. TAM can be applied to an overall market or to a market segment, as long as the characterization is made clear to the audience.

The next term is *SAM,* or Serviceable Available Market. Many marketers have a hard time distinguishing between SAM and TAM ("Aren't *Serviceable Available* and *Total Available* the same thing?"). The most effective definition is that **SAM represents the sales potential of markets that your company can address with existing products**, up to and including the proposed product. **TAM, on the other hand, represents the market size that could be addressed with today's products and reasonable future extensions** to the product line. SAM is by definition equal to or (more likely) a subset of TAM.

With both SAM and TAM, many marketers struggle to quantify them. The numbers can be built bottom-up or top-down. Forecasts can be built from bottom-up when the customer base is finite and you have intimate knowledge of the sales potential of each. But in more diffuse markets, this is impossible and the market size must be constructed top-down. The best case scenario is that market analyst reports exist from 3rd parties. Typically these are only available for mature markets. So, what do you do when the market is emerging or entirely new? As each situation is unique, little concrete guidance can be provided. But the best advice is find concrete reference points from which to infer your market size. As long as you are able to show a reasonable chain of logic for your assumptions, your audience is likely to play along. Of course, **the most credible market size assumptions come when you can show both a bottom-up and top-down analysis, with the two numbers roughly in agreement.**

Finally, we look at *SOM,* or Share of Market. This represents the share of the market which the proposed product could reasonably expect to capture. Essentially, this is your volume estimates divided by the SAM. It provides a nice check on your volume estimates. Many marketers make the mistake that their sales volume predictions require capturing a clearly unrealistic share of the market. By showing the SOM on a chart, you give an easily understandable indication of what type of success against competition you are assuming. The audience will be evaluating your share assumptions in the context of current market share, number of viable competitors, your company's market power, and the strength of the product. They are looking for consistency of your share assumptions with these market realities.

**The growth (or decay) rate of target market segments is as important as the current size itself**. A significant investment in a small market may be justified if that segment is growing rapidly, as you can be the first to establish an incumbency position that will pay returns later when the segment is large. Likewise, significant investments in innovation for a large but shrinking market may not be warranted; instead this may suggest a cost reduction path, or a milking strategy that reduces investment and harvests the profits.

## Conclusion

Clearly, Market Segmentation can be quite a powerful tool for redrawing the boundaries of the playing field to suit your strengths. But it requires you to give up on the larger battle and focus where you have the best chance to win. It has the potential to reduce P&L expenses through Spanning, where one product development allows you to attack multiple market segments. You can also use the power of segmentation to enter a market against an entrenched competitor, or help defend your own incumbency, by creating customized products for each market niche. Yet, surprisingly, many marketers fail to exploit the full power of this technique. A common cause is a lack of appreciation for what this tool can do. Inexperience is usually the culprit – many new product managers simply haven't seen a truly successful segmentation strategy up close. In other cases, the marketer succumbs to temptations of high revenue potential for a product that tries to attack the entire market, trying to be "all things to all customers". Just as likely is that the product manager has lost intimate contact with the market. From the distant viewpoint of the ivory tower, he can no longer discern the patterns and groupings of customers who share similar problems and needs. Finally, it is possible that internal reasons are the cause, whether from limited development resources or pushback from Operations and Engineering on SKU proliferation. But all of these can be overcome. **Segmentation is a powerful tool that can be used to successfully change the rules of the game**. It can be a key element of a core competence in great products.

# Market Segmentation: Real World Example

*The main market for Mason was an established one: the PC market. The incumbent had treated this as if it were monolithic, selling one network communications chip for all computers. But there were a few different types of computers which used the product. The Marketing team decided to explore whether they could create some new sub-segments, each of which could be addressed uniquely. The trick was to determine if each segment had its own unique characteristics (function, price, ease of use, or channel).*

*The first segment was business users (as opposed to home users) of desktop computers. They were made by companies (called PC OEMs) such as HP, Dell, and Lenovo; TechCorp already had a direct salesforce calling on these accounts. Although packed with features, the required functionality was already commoditized and innovation opportunities were scarce. Thus, these products were under enormous price pressure. The product category was also relatively well understood from an implementation standpoint, so only the standard datasheet and design guide were required by this segment. This was a very large segment, exceeding 100 million units per year, but was relatively flat, and predicted to begin shrinking within a few years. The sheer size made it potentially attractive, but the lack of growth or innovation and the intense price competition was potentially problematic for any organization to make a big investment in this segment.*

*A second class of desktop computers called "White Box PCs" also existed. They were made by Tier 2 manufacturers who usually lacked a strong brand name or global presence. The fact that most manufacturers of these PCs were located in the Asia-Pacific region made this segment unique. Unfortunately, the salesforce was primarily U.S.-based. A new salesforce would need to be built in the local region, with people that had relationships there and spoke the local languages. Regarding the product, the demand for quality was lower. These were also purchased by businesses, but ones that cared less about support and technology. Price was nearly the only buying criteria; advanced features were not, as there were few perceived problem left to solve in this segment. This market was somewhat smaller, running at about 40 million units per year. But it was beginning to grow rapidly as more computers were purchased in developing countries where cost was valued much more than features. The growth made this segment attractive, but the emphasis on cost made the Marketing team question whether there was any room for innovation that would provide adequate pricing power.*

Another type of computer was a laptop PC, made by companies like HP, Dell, Lenovo, and Toshiba. These customers were well covered by the existing salesforce. Cost was less important – the focus was on small size and long battery life. This was an exciting segment because it was already large and growing rapidly, taking share from desktop PCs. At 50 million units per year and a 24% growth rate, it represented a fertile opportunity for the product. There was also significant potential for innovation around size, security, and battery life. Thus, the price point could naturally be higher for products that could elegantly solve problems related to these areas.

Finally, the team became aware of an emerging category of computers: blade desktop computers. Instead of a discrete box that each user owned individually, the computer was a small module housed in a chassis (that held up to a hundred of such modules) in the information technology (IT) department. Keyboard, video, and mouse were then extended out to the user over a cable. To the user it appeared to be a local computer, but the brains were centralized for easier maintenance and repair. While a very small segment – only 1 million per year currently – the fact that the architecture was very new and different suggested the potential to innovate and gain an early technology lead.

With this information, a summary of the segments could be created around the four vectors as shown in the following table:

| Segment | Function | Price | Ease of Use | Channel |
|---------|----------|-------|-------------|---------|
| **Desktop** | Mostly commoditized | Low | TBD | Covered by existing salesforce |
| **White Box** | Highly commoditized | Very low | TBD | Need to create Asia-Pacific salesforce |
| **Laptop** | Strong need for small size, low power, security. Explore further. | Moderate premium | TBD | Covered by existing salesforce |
| **Blade** | Extreme small size and low power. Explore further. | Premium | TBD | Existing salesforce would need to expand coverage to new groups and companies |

*Figure 6*

The "Function" and "Ease of Use" information would be filled in further as the team moves on to considering the Market Problem for each segment.

# Checklist

## Does Marketing really understand the market?

Products designed to appeal to everyone end up winning no one. The organization must understand the unique groupings within the larger market.

## What to Look For:

- Segments are characterized by function, price point, channel, ease of use
- Marketing declares specific targets and non-targets, with explicit rationale
- Segments are sized bottom-up or top-down using objective 3$^{rd}$ party data

## Is segmentation being used offensively?

Segmentation can be an extremely effective way to create differentiation, especially if the organization uses it proactively to attack the market.

## What to Look For:

- Marketing has defined previously unrecognized sub-segments
- Custom functionality/messaging is used to uniquely appeal to each segment

*(Further discussion on this checklist available at www.systemnotcircumstance.com)*

# CHAPTER 7:

## The Market Problem

*Problems are something most of us try to avoid. In the case of a particularly vexing problem, one might be willing to pay handsomely to make it go away. Your customers are no different. They have their own problems related to their daily operating environment. Whether it is high costs, low productivity, long engineering cycles, a particular inefficiency, or complexity of use, there is always some type of problem to solve. Any product that provides the solution in a way that is clearly superior to alternatives is sure to be desired by the market. This manifests itself in the form of strong sales volume or pricing power. So the ultimate question to ask is, "Do I really know my customer's problem?" Be careful with the quick "of course!" response. Countless customers have found themselves sitting through a marketing pitch from a vendor who simply talked about features and technologies without once seeking to understand what the customer was grappling with. "A technology looking for a problem" is a cliché within the realm of product marketing. Sustained success comes only when the question "What is the market problem we are trying to solve?" is deeply embedded in the organization's DNA.*

## The Reference Point

A product concept always begins with some "reference point" – some attribute upon which the product improves. It might be a characteristic of your current product (cost, performance, etc) which will be improved in the next. For example, you might decide that dramatically increasing the processing speed of your current product will be the main thrust of the new product. This "same as before but a little better" method is certainly easy to explain to customers, but it puts blinders on you and limits your ability to innovate. Cost reduction projects – "same as before but cheaper" – are also in this same category of one-dimensional thinking. And then there is the most egregious reference point you can use – your competitor. In other words, you copy what they are doing but try to make it just a little bit better. This reference point nearly always leads to commoditization and price compression. In all three cases the focus is inward; the first two examples are "ivory tower thinking" at its finest, while the third represents a reactive mode of product development. None tries to evaluate the true needs of the market.

Instead of using internal reference points, one of the most fundamental principles in this profession should be considered: **great products solve _real and significant_ customer problems**. Clearly the customer's problems need to be truly understood in order to address them. Turning your eyes inward tends to close off the mind from taking a fresh look at the customer's situation. Using internal reference points to evaluate competitiveness or value proposition is fine, but only after Marketing has asked and answered a very fundamental question: _What are the customer's most vexing problems?_ **Understand problems first before any consideration of the solution.** You will find that it opens up a fertile world of opportunities for innovation. If you can't clearly articulate the set of problems the customer is grappling with before entering Concept Approval, it is a sure sign you should head back to square one and spend more time with your customer. If you look back at products that don't do well in the market, chances are it is because they were designed around internal reference points and not around solving real market problems.

Let's look at an example. Consider a consumer electronics company building a new DSL router (the box that sits in a user's house). One of the vendors to this company provides the device's main processor, and is considering the definition for a next generation product. The vendor's product manager embarks on the definition process, and is deciding on the reference point. Part of the success of the last processor product was that it contained enough processing power to handle a large number of applications that would run on the DSL device. Speed is always easy to sell, so if "fast" won this time, surely "faster" would also win going forward? This was clearly an example of internally focused thinking, with the current product's speed and processing power as the reference points. This product manager was also hearing some competitive information from Sales that the main competitor was promising a 50% cost reduction over the next two years. The immediate impulse was to begin to consider a cost reduction path in order to survive in the brutal pricing environment the competitor would create. Again, this approach is not particularly market-focused. In neither case was any time spent with customers discussing their problems. So he smartly tabled those ideas and began a dialogue with his customers. He was surprised to find that, while power and cost were important, most customers were drastically trying to reduce the heat within the DSL box. It turns out that end users were demanding smaller, quieter boxes. More heat meant a large and noisy fan was required to cool the box. But heat generation typically increases proportionally with processing power. So, in fact the initial concept of improving processing power would have *hurt* the product's value. So, excessive heat generated in the box turned out to be the *real, significant problem* with which customers were struggling. And the product manager only knew this by spending time talking to his customers without any pre-conceptions.

The resulting product concept was a processor with similar performance and price to that of today's product, but with reduced power consumption (and therefore heat generation). In fact, the product manager asked his customers to define the level of power reduction that would be valuable to them. It turns out that a box with a power budget of 25 total watts (vs. the 38 watts of today's DSL routers) would allow a significantly smaller and quieter fan to be used. This meant that the power budget for the processor would be around 10 watts, representing a 25% reduction from today's product. With this data from the customer in hand, this became the product concept: a processor that provides today's performance at 10 watts of power consumption in order to allow customers to use the next smaller size fan. From this concept emerged a powerful but unexpected benefit: the smaller fan was also cheaper by around $8. So without changing the price of the product at all, the product could save the customer $8 in solution cost. It is interesting to note that the 50% cost reduction (on today's price point of approximately $10) promised by a competitor would have only saved the customer $5. This path allows the product manager to have created a more attractive product (because it enabled the use of a smaller, quieter fan) that offers a lower overall solution cost than that of a price bombing competitor. This is a perfect example of creating more competitive and profitable products by listening to one's customers.

Of course, the example is purposely constructed to illustrate our point that great products are always based on:

1. Real problems (that are relevant to your product) that have been directly validated across a representative set of customers.
2. The customer's *most vexing* problems. Solving a minor problem may not create significant enough differentiation and pricing power.
3. A solution that is cheaper or simpler than that from the competition. Always remember the LCW principle: "Low Cost Wins".

You will find that this problem-first mentality makes the marketing and selling process much easier. You will be fighting to get mindshare from customers who are very busy and not easily inclined to make time for their vendors. But there is a reason they are busy: they are heads-down trying to solve their problems (i.e. the Market Problem!) Every day they invest effort and pride in pursuit of a solution, and likely sacrifice a significant amount of personal time. Their compensation and professional advancement are based on their success. If you are able to discover, understand, and solve their problems for them (via your product), rest assured you will get their attention and time. **Understanding and solving their real problem transforms all the energy and anxiety of their job into enthusiasm for your product**. Skeptics are turned into internal advocates. They become willing to accept some of the product's other shortcomings (e.g. schedule) because it solves their main problem. And their willingness to pay goes up dramatically, giving you significant pricing power. Finally, the credibility and goodwill you generate from being so customer-focused translates into an advantage in the next selling cycle. Clearly, having a product definition based on a deep understanding of customers' problems pays dividends many times over. Contrast this with a product based on internal reference points, which is a clear sign that you don't understand (or appear to care about) what the customer is really grappling with. Customers pick up on this quickly, and Marketing and Sales will feel like they are flying into a significant headwind as a result.

## The Real Source of Differentiation

Clearly, a customer focus is a requisite for a strong product concept. But it takes more than a declaration of being "market driven" to achieve this. It starts with an **institutional mindset**, reinforced by management and embodied by all, **that Market Problems need to be defined before any consideration, discussion, or documentation of features**. Temporarily ignore all other influences such as your product line strategy, your current product's attributes, the capabilities of your engineering team, the technology your company possesses, and your competitor's products. These tend to color your thinking and prevent you from doing Market Problem discovery with a truly open mind.

With this mindset, begin to engage your customer base. But this step is more than just a decision to get on a plane. To be successful, you have to know who to talk to and have access to them. This highlights the importance of having a good network of relationships within your customer base. This is the foundation for all product planning efforts. Conventional wisdom tells us that we need creative marketers and brilliant engineers to help us dream up great products. But in reality, the fundamental basis of value and differentiation is being close enough to your customer to truly understand their problems. The truth is that most problems are relatively easy to understand, and the best solutions are often simple. What prevents a great product is rarely a lack of creativity in coming up with a solution – instead it is often simply ignorance of the real problem to solve. This in turn is usually the result of not having established relationships with customers. It is these relationships, built and nurtured over time, that enable you to get access to key people within your customer base who can give you this information. A picture of innovation in action would not be marketers and engineers huddled in a conference room dreaming up the Next Big Thing; instead, it is embodied in a mundane image of a marketer sitting with his customer having frank, open discussions over a simple cup of coffee. The marketer trolls for information by asking open ended questions about the customer's operating environment. With gentle guidance, this dialogue can reveal challenges, frustrations, and inefficiencies. It is this exchange that is the heart and the start of innovation, differentiation, and product success. In short, **value and differentiation are often enabled more by a network of the right personal relationships than by brilliant creativity**.

The organization needs to make a real commitment to spend time on this process of building relationships. Sales certainly plays an important role – their job is to understand the customer organization and the role of key individuals. The business unit should work with them to find the right individuals and get initial meetings with them (more on this in Chapter 23 "Sales Strategy"). Spend time with them talking about their problems, and seek to understand the environment in which they use your product. Some useful questions to ask are:

- What is the biggest challenge in your environment? (resources, costs, time to market, etc)
- What is the biggest challenge in using my product? (i.e. cost, complexity, performance, availability, etc)
- Explain exactly how my product is used, and the environment in which it is used.
- What other products are used in conjunction with my products? Which are necessitated solely by my product?

As you do this it is important to believe what they say. Here we can take a page from Buddhist philosophy: see the world as it is, not as you want it to be. Drop all pre-conceived notions of what you think the market wants or what is beneficial to you. **Listen to what your customer is saying without filtering**. If they say they need lower costs, don't mentally discard it "because all customers say that" and "they are just trying to get a better price". Amazing and useful insights often occur simply by having this type of conversation. Linkages, opportunities, and so on, are revealed in unexpected ways, simply by understanding the customer environment better through direct, unbiased discovery.

## Conclusion

Beginning all product planning with a focused process of discovery of customer problems is one of the most fundamental tenets of making great products. Too often we fall in love with technology, strategy, and features, such that they dominate our thinking. We lose touch with what we are really trying to do, which is to help the customer. This is not a mistake of incompetence or ignorance; even the most talented individuals or card-carrying members of the "customer focus" club can fall prey. But to sustain product greatness over time, this mode must become part of the organization's culture. Veteran and new marketers alike will know that this is how the organization plans its products; management, finance, and engineering all know the challenging questions to ask to vet out whether they have done this. In the end, it becomes the way of doing business; **no product proposal should ever be put forth unless it represented a powerful solution to real and significant customer problems.**

## The Market Problem: Real World Example

*With the segments initially defined, the task now was to determine how best to appeal to them. The team was well aware that they needed to use the right "reference point" for creating a great product. Some customers had told them that a competitor was adding high-speed encryption technology to their communication chips, and it was rather attractive. There was pressure within the organization to follow suit and add this encryption feature to the product line. But the team was determined to use the right reference point for determining their next great product. For the moment they blocked out any thoughts of what competition was doing and focused on one thing only: the problems that each of the potential target segments was experiencing.*

*In the desktop segment, customers were consistent in expressing that cost was their biggest concern. It was a large but mature market, and so innovation possibilities were rare and commoditization had set in. Even though these machines were packed with technology and features, they were still forced to compete largely on price because everyone had essentially the same offering. So, that cost pressure flowed directly back to their component vendors. The team knew they could never differentiate only on cost, and were disappointed that there appeared to be no meaty Market Problem to attack. The only answer was to keep digging by spending more time with customers. During a subsequent lunch meeting with a customer, it was mentioned that this particular PC OEM was concerned about some of the new EnergyStar regulations from the United States government, which required that computers should consume less than 1 watt of power when in a standby state. Today most PCs consumed nearly 2 watts in this mode. The communications chip accounted for about half of this because it had to be on, waiting for a message from the network to wake up the PC. Most PC makers were lobbying against the regulation because they knew it would be very difficult to meet. They were worried that they could lose government contracts as a result. This was clearly a Market Problem that needed to be solved.*

*The white box segment was even more difficult. The cost pressures mentioned above were greater because these machines were positioned as low-feature, low-cost machines to customers who did not care at all about brand name, service, features, or performance. They only needed the basics. Quality expectations were also lower. Despite a substantial amount of due diligence* with customers, the Marketing team could determine no problems to solve other than cost.

In the laptop segment, the story was much different. Although cost was a factor, there were several other problems on which customers were focused. The first was how to extend battery life. A big buying criterion for a laptop PC was the battery life test rankings performed by the major computer magazines. The PC that won the test would see a big sales boost, even if the margin of victory were only a few minutes. Therefore, short battery life was clearly a problem. On another note, the events of September 11th and the Sarbanes-Oxley regulations in the United States had put renewed emphasis on security and data protection in the market. This was particularly true for laptops, which were easier to steal because of their mobility. The PC OEMs were desperately looking for the right security technology to offer their customers. So there were significant Market Problems associated with battery life and security.

The blade market had its own unique set of problems. Most prominent was the need to reduce heat; with so many blades packed into one chassis, a very large fan was needed in order to keep things from melting. This fan was costly and noisy, both problematic. Also, the blade PC architecture was unique in that it required something known as a serial connection from the communications chip to the rest of the PC. This was in contrast to laptop and desktop PCs, which used a parallel interface. The current solution was to connect the communications chip to another chip, at the cost of several dollars and half a watt of power, which translated the parallel interface into a serial interface. It appeared that customers' desire to reduce the cost of the entire chassis could be addressed by focusing on heat generation and elimination of the external translator chip.

With this analysis in hand, it was time to begin narrowing down the list of all segments into a set of target segments. The team felt that the white box market was definitely out; the overwhelming emphasis on cost left little potential to differentiate. Clearly, the mobile PC market should be a target market segment. The need for low power and high security meant there was plenty of potential for innovation and a willingness to pay for it. The same was true for the blade segment. Although it was small, there was potential to solve some real problems and in the process create strong pricing power. Going forward, much of the analysis would focus on these two segments. The Tier 1 desktop market was a bit of a challenge. It had a large emphasis on cost, *although the need to meet EnergyStar regulations could possibly provide an area for differentiation and value add. But most members of the team were skeptical whether they could extract enough price premium to still compete profitably. They agreed to make it a target segment for now, but scrutinize it carefully. One option was to use Spanning, where a de-featured version of a device for the laptop PC could be opportunistically sold into the desktop market. It would come down to whether the cost structure of the product driven by specialized features for the laptop and blade markets would allow Mason to compete profitably in the cost conscious desktop market.*

# Checklist

## Has Marketing identified real Market Problems?
Amateurs create products around features, but the best organizations strive to make products that solve real and significant customer problems.

## What to Look For:
- Marketing defines the Market Problem before any talk of features or strategy
- The problem is easy to understand, clearly vexing, and currently unsolved
- >3 customers have validated the Market Problem as real and significant

## Are the relationships in place to identify Market Problems?
Innovation does not start with creativity – it starts with relationships. Market Problems are not discovered while sitting inside the ivory tower.

## What to Look For:
- Marketing can list the names of 10 key customers who give them feedback
- Marketing averages >2 hours/week with them discussing their problems

*(Further discussion on this checklist available at www.systemnotcircumstance.com)*

# CHAPTER 8:

## Requirements

*Having vision, great strategy, and a knowledge of the Market Problem is clearly important. But eventually that needs to be translated into a language that Engineering understands: documented requirements. Engineers don't design to PowerPoint, but rather to the Market Requirements Document (MRD). Surprisingly, misexecution of this seemingly simple task damages many product efforts. Marketers love the strategic stuff, but often procrastinate on the tactical grind of putting pen to paper and defining the minute details of a product's attributes. Typically design can't begin until the MRD is complete, so delays at the front can push the entire schedule day for day. The end date doesn't change because market windows don't, and so the schedule gets slowly compressed. The result is that compromises have to be made on the definition (which Marketing always resists), or Engineering gets signed up for serious overtime to catch up. These delays then bleed into the next product, creating a vicious cycle. Companies that are able to consistently repeat their success know the importance of defining products well and early. Management makes it a major focus point, and Marketing knows the right methods of defining the product so that Engineering can execute crisply on it.*

## Types of Requirements

With the Market Problem defined, it is now time to create a solution. This will take the form of product attributes which are defined in the Market Requirements Document (MRD). **In this phase, Marketing must translate the conceptual into the specific.** Of course every product is unique, but we can identify a few common categories of requirements that seem to apply to most:

1. *New Type of Functionality.* This describes something new that the product *does*. It is a behavioral description of how the product will operate. Based on an understanding of the market's problem, the organization will have innovated (or copied from a competitor) to create a new type of functionality which solves the problem.

2. *Integration of Functionality.* Instead of creating new functionality, a product may simply integrate (or eliminate the need for) the functionality of complementary or adjacent products. The obvious benefits are reduced total solution cost, complexity, space, etc.

3. *Improved Performance.* A specific performance parameter is improved upon. This attribute is typically the most easily understood, and thus the easiest to sell. It can be defined in two ways. The first is at the product level, where a target for the product's performance is identified ("this server processor will run at 5 GHz"). Or it can be defined at the system level ("a server based on this processor will process 10,000 database lookups per second"). The latter can often be more effective because users typically experience performance at the system level.

4. *Reduced Cost.* Cost is always king, and customers always want it lower. In terms of feature definition, cost can be defined at two levels. The first is again at the product level, where a specific target is set for the cost of the product itself. The second defines cost at the solution level, including the product itself as well as the cost of all complementary products, training, and so on. It is a broader and more encompassing view, which allows more opportunity to reduce the total cost that the customer pays, even if the price of the product itself doesn't change.

5. *Improved Reliability.* Like product-level cost, this is relatively straightforward. It represents an improvement in the ability of the product

to resist breakdowns. Alternatively, it could also be a reduction of the downtime associated with a breakdown by simplifying the repair procedure.

6. *Interoperability*. This category refers to support for some type of industry standard or other technology scheme which dictates how products from different vendors will seamlessly work together. If the standard is well established or has good momentum, customers may believe that they will eventually need support in order to interoperate with other products in the environment. Thus support for the standard or scheme can provide an effective incentive to purchase the product.

Nearly all features defined in the MRD can probably fit into one of these five categories.

## The Value Hurdle

Let us take a moment to comment briefly on the importance of each category relative to the others. Of particular interest is the comparison of cost versus features. In other words, what is more likely to win: a cost play or a feature play? Conventional wisdom goes both ways. On one hand, there is a commonly held maxim that says "Low Cost Wins" (LCW for short). This means that **the market will always gravitate to the lowest cost solution that addresses the problem *well enough***. Obtaining a premium for solving it to a degree beyond this threshold is difficult. If your competitor comes up with a dirt cheap (relative to your solution) way to solve the Market Problem, even if it is not as elegant as your solution, the market may accept it and your solution will appear seriously overpriced. And it gets worse. A low priced alternative often doesn't even need to solve all the Market Problems that your product addresses. It merely needs to solve the most critical. Customer may be willing to live with some of the usage problems your product addresses, because the competition is offering such an enticing low price. The value of your fancy features can be instantly negated by a price bombing strategy. As we said, low cost nearly always wins. This dynamic suggests a specific relationship between the value of a product and the relative cost of its competition, something called the *Value Hurdle*:

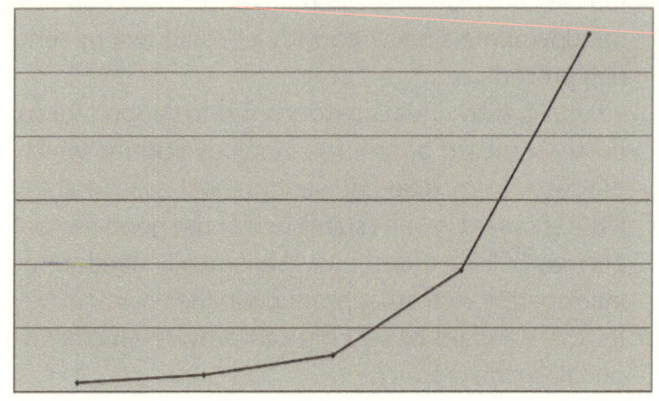

**Price Premium Sought Over Competition**

*Figure 8: Value Hurdle*

Figure 8 graphically shows that as the price gap (from the competition) grows, the amount of value and marketing needed to overcome it grows exponentially. **The extra value you must show to overcome a low price is the Value Hurdle**. Everyone knows that you must exceed a higher threshold of perceived value in order to overcome a low price. But this notion of a Value Hurdle shows that you have to be delivering a *lot* more value if the gap gets large enough. So while it can be stated that it is always better to compete on functionality, you have to make sure the functional value is significant enough to overcome the offering from a desperate competitor engaging in price bombing. You may find significant portions of your target market telling you sympathetically:"I love your strategy, and really wanted to go with your product, but I just can't pass up this price." When you compete on functionality, come strong or don't come at all.

This is not intended to advocate going the cost reduction route, which is a slippery slope that can crater a P&L and the entire market for the product category quickly. Pricing is like a ratchet – it only goes in one direction…down. If you pursue a cost reduction path in order to enable aggressive pricing, a resulting price war can occur, which will only serve to drain the profitability out of the entire segment. You may win in the short term, but you are killing the golden goose in the process. This is always the danger of a cost reduction path. But many forces will push in this direction. The return on investment for a cost reduction project often looks good, as the low cost is coupled with the temporary volume and pricing power earned by earlier products that boasted superior functionality. But that quickly goes away as parity and commoditization result from competitors catching up. Another force pushing you in this direction will be your customers. They usually aren't visionary enough to lead you to innovation possibilities, but they always want things cheaper. They'll also want to commoditize you, knowing that differentiating features limit their ability to make you compete on price. If you find yourself in this situation, chances are you simply haven't worked hard enough to find a real Market Problem. Before committing to a cost reduction project, do another round with your customers to ask the probing questions about their usage environment. **There is always a Market Problem to solve – it is your job to find it** so you can maintain your pricing power.

## Communicating Clearly

The act of translating concepts into documented requirements may seem mundane, but it is important and often done poorly. **Ambiguity in the requirements** is commonly cited (by Engineering, of course) as a **major cause of project delays**. The negative impact to schedule and Marketing's credibility is tangible. Engineers rightfully have little tolerance for this; if Marketing feels a requirement is important, they should be sufficiently motivated to write it down properly so Engineering can act upon it. Yet time and time again this step becomes a major source of friction between the two groups. There is no magic in writing requirements, just a little bit of discipline applied to following four basic principles:

- *Timely*: Engineering always gets squeezed on schedule because the market window doesn't move but Marketing often does procrastinate on the front end. Many product managers may enjoy defining new products, but few are enthusiastic about the grunt work involved in documenting the requirements for Engineering. Inherent uncertainty in the market also causes delays – it induces a strange fear of commitment. The result is that requirements remain as folklore – something talked about a lot but never officially written down. This is clearly unacceptable. Great organizations manage these front end milestones as firmly as they do Engineering schedules. **By using Endpoint Management techniques, the**

**date by which requirements need to be documented is clearly laid out**. The General Manager keeps the pressure on Marketing to hit them, and program managers are employed to track progress.

- *Behavior-Oriented*: A common mistake is to write requirements such that they define the implementation, not the product behavior required by the customer. Product-level performance requirements ("server process will run at 5 GHz") often do this, as they specify a product attribute rather than a system-level performance target ("a server based on this processor will process 10,000 database lookups per second") that the customer actually needs. Marketers sometimes subconsciously apply their own judgment of what the implementation should be. But this is always best left to Engineering and Architecture. Marketing does not stray into implementation space, as it takes away Engineering's opportunity to innovate and find creative solutions to problems. When Marketing oversteps their bounds, it in some ways relieves Engineering/Architecture of any responsibility for the result; they simply implement what Marketing tells them and don't worry about whether it really achieves the goal. Thus, the lesson here is that **requirements should describe product or system behavior, not implementation**.

- *Comprehensive*: For a product to be successful, it must behave exactly as expected and desired. But as products grow more complex, it is increasingly challenging for those who have to define them. Anything left undefined leaves the door open for Engineering to make their own interpretation – right or wrong. Holes in the definition may occur when Marketing relies on the presumed "conventional wisdom" around a particular feature. Because a feature has been discussed at length internally, Marketing may simply assume that everyone understands the requirement. So, the feature is documented with a simple one line description. Yet this can omit important details such as the expected behavior in corner case usage scenarios. Engineering *might* ask for clarification, but they also might simply make their own assumptions. The risk is that their assumptions end up being wrong, possibly resulting in a product that does not meet the market's needs. The lesson to the Marketing team is to "be careful what you wish for because you just might get it". Engineering will design faithfully to your MRD. If a hole in the definition causes a problem, they will be quick to point out that Marketing failed to fully document the requirement. The organization **must recognize the power of an MRD and the importance of making it inclusive of all known behavior scenarios**. In situations where Marketing and Engineering have a healthy relationship, a constructive iteration can take place until both sides are satisfied that all requirements are defined to the proper level of detail and comprehensiveness.

- *Justifiable:* Engineers hate to waste time or expend effort on a pointless goal. Given that schedules are always late and resources are always stretched, they want to know that they are sacrificing for a reason. They need to believe that each feature they are working on is truly necessary for the product to be successful. As such, **Marketing needs to be careful that they can justify every request in the MRD**. Each must be tied back to a specific customer problem, and the case made for a financial return in the form of higher selling price or more customers. If a feature can be taken out, and price or volume doesn't change, Marketing will have a hard time convincing management and Engineering that it is required. This type of skepticism is justified; marketers have developed a bad reputation for themselves by asking for "nice to have" features, inflated performance parameters, excessively low cost, or an artificially early schedule. Even if you have never done this to your engineers, you can be sure that someone has at one point. This is not to advocate that setting aggressive product goals is bad, but rather that there had better be a clear benefit for doing so because it causes the engineers to work much harder. If Marketing is asked to justify the requirements but found to be "crying wolf" on some, their credibility will suffer. Furthermore, **superfluous requirements may hurt the delivery of the real, must-have requirements**.

The organization needs a mechanism to get Marketing, Architecture, and Engineering into an open dialogue on the requirements in the MRD to ensure that they are timely, complete, behavior-oriented, and fully justified. It is recommended that a *Requirements Locking Session* be held, where Marketing, Engineering, and Architecture spend a day or two in a room together reviewing the MRD. The technical teams can point out where they need clarifications or additional information, and Marketing can provide answers in real time or promptly get them from customers. All parties should walk out of that engagement agreeing that they have a final MRD which Engineering can begin scoping.

## Conclusion

Mapping solutions to customer problems into specific, documented features is not a process that the Marketing team should trivialize. In practice it is a common source of project delays and aggravation for Engineering. A **great product concept means nothing until it is properly translated into the language of engineering execution**. The effort spent in this often neglected activity will be handsomely paid back in the positive impact to product schedules and the relationship between Marketing and Engineering. Furthermore, it is important for each feature to be tied back to one of the Market Problems discussed in Chapter 7. It is much easier to convince the organization of the need for a particular requirement if they first understand the underlying problem. Only then will everyone have the proper context to comprehend and value the solution in the form of the product requirements.

# Requirements: Real World Example

*With the Market Problems well defined, attention could then turn to solving them. The laptop segment was considered first. It was clear that reducing the power of the overall system in certain states was an important product goal. Someone suggested a target of reducing the chip's power to 1 watt, a 50% reduction from today's product. But this was quickly challenged as using the wrong reference point – it compares to the last product rather than keeping the focus on the customer's problem. In this spirit, a team member mentioned that a customer had told him that they lived and died on the battery life tests done by major PC magazines. With a little digging, the team was able to figure out the set up with which these tests were performed. In particular, it was noticed that they were done with the network cable <u>unplugged</u>, in order to simulate the usage model of someone in transit with their computer. Thus, the communications chip wouldn't be expected to transmit or receive data in the context of this test. It would only need to be ready to transmit or receive data when a cable was plugged in. The question was asked "what if the chip could sense when the cable was unplugged and transition into an ultra low power mode, then sense a cable being plugged in and move back into full operational mode?" This would reduce power consumption dramatically during the battery life test. A 10 milliwatt power target was suggested. But someone quickly pointed out that this was a product-level performance target, and they should instead define a system-level performance target because it was more meaningful to the customer's environment. So the goal of saving 10 minutes battery life was set.*

*The team then began to consider data protection. Customers were saying that they wanted more security, but in truth they didn't exactly know what form it should take. A competitor to TechCorp had decided that they would offer encryption technology to protect data that was transmitted. But it was not a foregone conclusion that this particular type of security was going to be attractive. The Director of Marketing had been doing research of his own and discovered that a new industry standard had been defined for something called a Trusted Platform Module (TPM). This was a security technology that provided a key hidden in hardware that served as the basis for all cryptography and security in the PC. So instead of being based solely on software, which was inherently insecure, the security was based on hardware. This would fun-*

*damentally make the data on the PC more secure, clearly something that is valuable to a user. However, there was a problem in that this TPM technology was still rather expensive. The cost was prohibiting it from penetrating into the mainstream. But if it were integrated into a larger chip, it could be offered for a small incremental premium. The price elasticity was expected to be high, and thus this strategy could catalyze adoption of TPM into mainstream PCs. It was a prime opportunity to change the game, but was not without risk. The necessary technology and knowledge did not yet exist in the company, so developing it organically would be difficult. But the Marketing team decided to ignore feasibility for the moment and concentrate on what would be successful in the market.*

*Finally, the blade desktop segment was considered. Clearly, power was a consideration because of the problem with heat from so many aggregated blades. Any power reduction would be appreciated, but how much was enough? The team could certainly set an arbitrary target, but again they tried to see things from the eyes of the customer. The typical chassis would likely contain about 100 blades. Using some basic modeling techniques and estimates of power consumption of an entire blade, a typical chassis would require about 10 fans blowing 20 linear feet of air per second to keep the chassis at the desired temperature. Some basic calculations showed that each 50 watts of power consumption required one fan. So, the team decided to see if they could reduce power in the chassis just enough to eliminate an entire fan. At a cost of $120 per fan, and an operating cost of $117 per year in energy costs to run the fan, this represented a real cost saving. So, if power consumption could be reduced by a ½ watt per chip, then the goal could be accomplished. Any less, and that fan could not be eliminated; anything short of doubling this saving would still only reduce the fan count by one. So, this ½ watt reduction in power consumption became the goal. The team also became aware that the interface from the chip to the rest of the PC was a serial interface, in contrast to the parallel interface that the laptop required. Today, this was solved by a $4 external translator chip which sat between the communications chip and the host PC. By integrating this functionality, $4 in solution cost could be saved. Also, this chip consumed about a ½ watt, so integrating the functionality could go a long way towards the previously mentioned power reduction goal. Thus a requirement for this serial interface was added to the Mason definition. There was initial concern because this would be adding* *extra cost to the product, with no benefit for laptop PCs. But it was decided to consider this further only after Engineering had a chance to do their schedule and cost estimates.*

*With this thinking in hand, an MRD was written by the product owner within the Marketing team. In order to make sure that the requirements were clear and comprehensive this document was reviewed with Engineering. There were a lot of requests for clarification in their Requirements Locking Session, but Marketing was able to resolve them after some further consultations internally and with some key customers.*

# Checklist

### Are features defined promptly?

Documentation of a product's requirements must be taken very seriously. Lack of convergence is the most commonly cited cause of project delays.

## What to Look For:

- Requirements are written down in an MRD before engaging Engineering
- A Requirements Locking Session has been scheduled or completed

### Are features defined appropriately?

Extraneous or poorly defined requirements can burn Engineering's valuable time, extending the scoping period and delaying the start of product design.

## What to Look For:

- Features are tied to specific problems and exceed the "Value Hurdle"
- Requirements are behavior-oriented, comprehensive, and justified

*(Further discussion on this checklist available at www.systemnotcircumstance.com)*

# CHAPTER 9:

## Cost Analysis

*Estimating the "cost" of a product sounds like such a simple concept. Add up all the variable components, allocate the fixed expenses, and out pops the number. But the topic is not that simple, nor is it trivial. In a high volume business, particularly for a hardware product, cost can mean everything, so you need to get it right. A primary challenge is to make sure all costs are accounted for upfront, so that the financial analysis is accurate. A secondary challenge is that of justifying the cost targets identified by Marketing. Aggressive targets can generate significant pushback from Engineering, and Marketing needs to prove to the organization that they are truly necessary to compete profitably. Otherwise, the wrong feature-cost-schedule tradeoffs might be made, leading to a suboptimal product definition.*

## The Components of Product Cost

Product cost is important to the profitability of many product businesses. It may not be as important in the software industry where the cost basis can be near zero, but hardware businesses tend to use gross margins as a key measure of success. The scrutiny on cost is most pronounced late in a product's life cycle when commoditization has likely set in – differentiation is low and everyone is competing on price. This can very difficult without the right cost structure. Cost can even be important early in the product's life if Marketing decides to pursue a penetration strategy to quickly drive it into the mainstream. Such a strategy requires healthy margins to generate an adequate return on the initial investment; thus the cost is often critical to the product's success in every phase of its life cycle.

It is very important for the organization to have a good understanding of cost structure – a seemingly simple need, but not always easily achieved. **The most common mistake is a failure to recognize all of the hidden or peripheral costs associated with the product**. Marketing may, for example, fail to include in the financial analysis the royalty for some licensed technology. Or, Engineering might do an incomplete or optimistic assessment of the cost impact of all stated product requirements. This doesn't mean that anyone would do anything deliberately to skew the analysis; let us just say that the omission of any components of the cost makes the overall product cost look smaller, and thus increases the likelihood of an approved project due to an improved financial return. So, the organization's GM should be enforcing a mindset of a complete and thorough cost structure analysis. This means full due diligence and disclosure by Marketing and robust estimation techniques within Engineering. The GM should employ his Finance organization to play the role of bad cop, relentlessly hounding the various functional groups for completeness and accuracy.

Product cost itself is often primarily driven by the Cost of Goods Sold, or COGS. This is the cost of the material and direct labor required to manufacture a single unit of the product. COGS is often a function of the basic architecture of the product, something that doesn't change much over successive evolutionary generations. Thus COGS has a lot of inertia, and the **motivation to optimize cost in the first generation of the product**

**should be high because the organization will be stuck with it for a while**. Unfortunately this rarely happens because first generation products are rushed to market as fast as possible. Cost compromises are often made in exchange for getting the right features to be competitive while still hitting the market window. It may be the right decision at the time, but the consequences eventually start to hurt profitability. Further cost reductions come gradually and are usually asymptotic. It often takes significant time and effort to create radical impact. Furthermore, cost reduction projects are not particularly sexy and don't excite the engineers. So while an organization must make the tough decisions to be successful on the first product, it is important not to undervalue the benefits of optimizing for cost early and from the ground up.

COGS also consists of some other elements identified here:

- *Test Cost:* This is the expense associated with testing each product off of the manufacturing line to ensure proper functionality before shipping to the customer. This cost can be greatly affected by how well the product has been designed for testing. Optimizing the design to reduce test costs is a subtle but fertile area for overall cost reductions.

- *Packaging Cost:* Marketing has a lot of influence on the product packaging and its cost. For retail products, the goal is to make the product more attractive through decisions regarding size, shape, colors, and so on. For commercial products, there are supply chain details that affect the packaging. In both cases, costs are often a function of decisions from the Marketing team about the packaging's attributes.

- *Distribution Cost:* This is the cost of getting the product to the customer. It is typically a function of the channel and supply chain arrangements that the company puts in place.

- *Operations Allocation:* This is the fixed cost of Operations' effort to get the product into production. It may consist of manufacturing line equipment, test equipment, quality engineers, etc. It is usually accrued and then amortized over the cost of each part sold. As a fixed cost, it clearly becomes more dominant if the ultimate sales volume is low.

The organization should have in place a robust method for predicting these costs and including them in the financial analysis done during Product Planning process

## Setting Cost Targets

Marketing will define the cost targets along with the product features in the MRD. There is inherent tension between the two because cost always constrains what features can be delivered. Although this presumably gets resolved in a tradeoff process (discussed in Chapter 10 "Schedule"), it can be a battle leading up to it. Aggressive cost targets only make Engineering's job harder, so they cannot be set capriciously. Nor should they be set simply by what Engineering thinks is possible. Instead they need to be based on the realities of the market. Inevitably this means that the expected selling price should dictate the cost target. A Strategic Pricing Plan (discussed in Chapter 12 "Pricing Strategy") will lay out these expectations. From this, one method can be chosen to make a simple calculation of the cost target. One choice may be to use a desired gross margin: *Price * (1-Margin) = Cost.* Or, the calculation could be based on one of the project's profit metrics (discussed in Chapter 13 "Financial Analysis"), where a cost is determined which makes the metric reach a certain threshold of acceptability. **Whatever the method, it is based on mathematics and a market price, and is completely independent of any internal factor**s. A market-based method creates better targets. It also makes them more defensible against any pushback from Engineering. This approach is the opposite of "cost-plus" pricing, where pricing is dictated by the cost plus a suitable margin.

The role that Operations plays in cost estimates should be briefly examined. They are the true source of the estimates, creating them in response to the product architecture and implementation specification that Engineering provides. Presumably individuals in Operations will work with the factories to get a product cost estimate based on materials, labor, yield, and so on. But there will always be some inherent uncertainty and variability in any such estimate. But given the prominent role that cost can play in profitability, an incorrect estimate could significantly impact financial performance. An initially low estimate that increases later could radically change the financial analysis for a new product. Operations absolutely won't want to be seen as the cause of this negative impact, so by definition **their estimates are likely to be on the high side in the early stages of the Product Planning process**. No Vice President of Operations ever wants to explain why he was the cause of the company's missed financial goals. On the contrary, he will want to be the hero that comes in later and negotiates lower manufacturing costs that ultimately help the company *exceed* those expectations. He can hardly be blamed for operating in this mode. But this can be problematic for the business unit, as conservative estimates could change a "go" to a "no go" for a project with tight margins. This is not a recommendation to systematically second guess Operations' estimates, but rather to conduct deeper discussion with them on estimates that may make a difference in the product decision. They might have suggestions on what can be done relative to requirements or implementation to reduce the cost.

So far the focus has been on product-level cost, but now the attention turns to setting solution-level targets. Remember that from the customers' point of view, they are paying for the entire solution, not just your product. This includes adjacent or complementary products as well as setup, implementation, training, and maintenance costs. The sum of these represents their total solution cost. So while reducing product cost by 50% may seem significant, it may not be if it only represents 5% of the total solution cost. **Finding ways to attack the total solution cost could represent a much greater cost reduction opportunity**. In fact, a cleverly designed product could save a customer real money without having to change the price of the product at all. You obviate or minimize the value of someone else's product in order to protect the value of your own. An example might be a semiconductor product costing $10 that requires an external memory chip costing $5. A future generation of the product is re-designed to process data more efficiently, thus eliminating the need for the memory chip. Without changing the price of the semiconductor chip, the customer's solution cost is reduced by 33%. *Cost burden* eliminated from other products can be claimed (or at least a portion of it) as *additional value* in your product. So, rather than reduce your price to deliver that value, you extract it from someone else's product. This is the power that solution level cost analysis can bring. In practice, this manifests itself as a defined cost target for the whole solution. Marketing is responsible for defining the elements that comprise that solution, while the burden is on Engineering to determine an implementation that reduces that total solution cost.

## Conclusion

In many industries, product cost is a very important part of the organization's profitability, so it is a topic that deserves scrutiny. The Marketing team has the responsibility of making the right tradeoffs around features and schedule in order to optimize the cost and maximize profit. Operations should be applying the necessary effort to give the most accurate manufacturing cost estimates possible so the business unit can properly assess the true product margin and make the right choices. And Engineering is expected to avoid focusing too much on the design of the flashy new features at the expense of cost optimization through design improvements. And behind all of this, Finance has to make sure that costs are being properly accounted for and the cost points are yielding an acceptable level of profitability for the project and business unit. The GM should be coaching his teams to each play their role properly.

# Cost Analysis: Real World Example

The team set out to create cost targets for the product. The initial working assumption was that they wanted about a 10% reduction from the current product's cost of approximately $3.70, either to improve margin or compete profitably in a price war. In fact, this placeholder had slipped out in a casual conversation with the Director of Engineering about Mason a few weeks prior. His response was predictable: "You want to reduce cost _and_ add features? Can't be done!" He questioned the validity of this cost reduction goal. The Marketing team knew that they would have to be able to justify any cost targets they defined, as they would be quite stiffly challenged. But instead of trying to defend the targets, they would just let the numbers speak for themselves. Using information from the pricing strategy and the competitive analysis, they knew that the target price for the laptop market was $7.50, with a worst case pricing of $6.60. In order to be safe they decided to use $6.60 as the price in this analysis so that the project would be financially viable even in a worst case pricing situation. This was an admittedly conservative position, but could be re-evaluated later if it required too many difficult feature or schedule tradeoffs. To determine the target cost, this price was simply multiplied by [1-Desired Margin]. The corporate margin target of 50% was used, which meant that in a worst case pricing scenario the product would still sell at least at 50% margin. This yielded a target cost of $3.30. By basing Mason's target cost on market factors, not arbitrary goals, the team felt they could defend it effectively.

There were two other markets to consider, each markedly different. The blade market was likely to have a higher price point. Any cost that was competitive in the laptop market would certainly be low enough for the blade market. So the blade market was not considered in setting the cost target. However the Tier 1 desktop market segment was just the opposite – pricing would need to be much more aggressive. A $4 price was expected, thus necessitating a $2 product cost in order to confidently achieve 50% margins. This was significantly lower than the $3.30 cost required by the laptop market. The team was concerned that it would be difficult to deliver both the features for the laptop market and the cost for the desktop market in the same product. This analysis made the team start to think that they couldn't successfully attack both the laptop and desktop markets with the same chip. Pending further consideration, the team decided to move forward with two possible cost targets ($3.30 and $2.00) to see what the analysis showed.

Now that product cost targets were understood, the team broadened their focus to look at total solution cost. A networking communications chip is part of a circuit design that includes several other chips as well. A total solution would consist of the costs shown in Figure 9.1 below. (now using the nominal price assumption of $7.50 instead of the worst case $6.60):

| Component | Cost |
|---|---|
| Mason | $ 7.50 |
| Capacitors | $ 0.63 |
| Resistors | $ 0.90 |
| Flash Memory | $ 0.85 |
| **Total Solution Cost** | **$ 9.88** |

Figure 9.1

Ultimately, the customer sees a cost of $9.88 in order to achieve the functionality promised in Mason, rather than just $7.50. The team wondered if there was any way to reduce this number without having to reduce the cost of their chip. So they sat with a few key engineers and brainstormed on this. It turns out that with enough time, Engineering could probably design the chip to require few or cheaper external components. They could also shrink the size of the flash memory needed from four megabits down to two megabits. As a result, solution cost could be reduced as outlined in Figure 9.2:

| Component | Cost | Cost (New) |
|---|---|---|
| Mason | $ 7.50 | $ 7.50 |
| Capacitors | $ 0.63 | $ 0.55 |
| Resistors | $ 0.90 | $ 0.65 |
| Flash Memory | $ 0.85 | $ 0.65 |
| **Total Solution Cost** | **$ 9.88** | **$ 9.35** |

Figure 9.2

So without dropping the price of Mason, the customer could see a savings of $0.53, about 5% of the total solution cost. This would be significant and was immediately put into the requirements document. This perspective was only possible because the team took a more holistic view of the notion of cost.

# Checklist

## Are targets derived from the market or arbitrary judgment?

Cost targets should never be derived from internal factors (such as what Engineering says is feasible), but rather solely on what the market will pay.

## What to Look For:

- Cost targets are derived directly from the Strategic Pricing Plan
- Objective metrics are used to calculate targets, ensuring defensibility

## Is total solution cost being considered?

Product cost is only one piece of the full cost that customers see; rather, it also includes complementary products, training, maintenance, etc.

## What to Look For:

- Marketing can quantify each cost component within the total solution
- Marketing has a target solution cost in the MRD

*(Further discussion on this checklist available at www.systemnotcircumstance.com)*

# CHAPTER 10:

## Schedule

*Engineers will tell you that they can design anything given enough time. Unfortunately time is rarely in abundance in fast, competitive markets. Market windows – that finite time period within which it is most optimal to release the product – can be short and unforgiving of tardiness. Great products will always boast the right features and cost, but they must be delivered at the right time. There is always tension among the "Big Three" of features, cost, and schedule: optimization of one is often at the expense of the other two. Organizations that sustain their success know how to smartly engage in a tradeoff process that yields the best product possible given the circumstances. To do this right, Marketing has to know and defend the schedule dictated by the market, and Engineering has to put enough transparency into their schedules so the organization can have an intelligent tradeoff discussion. Great organizations understand the gravity of this process and will set clear expectations between the two groups.*

## Marketing Defines the Market Window

In general there are two types of market windows. The first can be called static – there is a specific time period in which the customer base will be buying a product in this category. If the product is delivered after a certain end date, it won't be considered and the opportunity will have passed. A good example of this is in the context of selling to a government organization, which usually makes all capital purchases at the end of the year in order to use up the budget. They won't spend earlier, and when the year ends they lose the money. If the product is ready, they may consider it. If it is late, they will not. Another example is a product sold to an Original Equipment Manufacturer (OEM) for integration into a system. The product needs to be available when the OEM is ready to design it in, or else it cannot be used. **Static windows are mostly binary – you are either in or out**. This is in contrast to a dynamic window, where the boundaries are less defined. This is often the case if the customer base is highly diffuse, with a large number of individual buying decisions. In such situations, the market window is likely defined by when competitive products are released.

Missing a market window has serious consequences. Clearly, a business opportunity with a static window will be lost if the schedule is not met. Revenue impact is obvious and reasonably quantifiable. There is also the longer-term issue of giving incumbency to the competition, as it will be harder to win back the business on the next cycle. The additional damage to brand recognition or a reputation as a "technology leader" can be significant. Clearly, it is critical to take a static market window very seriously and have a plan that ensures success in hitting it. **For a dynamic window, the negative effects are more subtle but just as damaging**. The first competitor to market enjoys a period of reduced competitive pressure, which manifests itself as strong pricing power. They also capture a spike in volume from any pent up demand. They'll enjoy a longer period of time until commoditization sets in, as is inevitable in most markets. As a result of being first to market, cumulative profits are higher and the time until breaking even on the investment is much shorter, as shown in Figure 10:

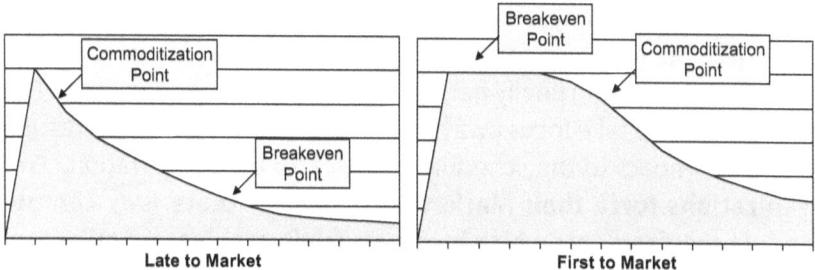

Figure 10: Profitability vs. Time to Market

In his book *Fast Innovation*, author Michael George talks about the significantly greater profit made by early entrants to the market versus those that come later in the market window. As illustrated in Figure 10, he estimates that **by the time commoditization sets in, half the operating profits for a product category have already been earned**. Clearly it is imperative to maximize your time in the market before this point. So although dynamic windows aren't as dramatically defined as static ones, the need to enter the market early in the window of opportunity is just as great.

It is Marketing's responsibility to determine the market window and translate it into a schedule requirement for Engineering. The biggest challenge is, of course, to be intimate enough with the market to get accurate, qualified data. The less obvious challenge commonly faced is the need to define a full set of milestones. There is more to this exercise than just setting a production date. There are a myriad of interim milestones which must be defined and planned for:

- Marketing may want to show an early demonstration of the product in order to prove to customers it is real.
- Customers may need a final (but pre-production) version of the product in order to do their own internal testing.
- Customers will need technical documentation to evaluate the product. This is often needed long before the product is available.
- Marketing will want some literature available in order to help generate interest in the product.
- Customers may need certain ecosystem elements in place before purchasing or using the product.

Unfortunately many schedule definitions overlook some of these milestones. The result is a forced scramble by Engineering or some other group when Marketing finally gets around to recognizing the need. These situations tend to take focus away from the development effort, resulting in negative impact to the schedule as well as a bit of frustration. **Great organizations force their Marketing teams to create *fully* complete schedule requirements which include *all* deliverables and milestones**. They give themselves a chance to plan out a complete project, staff properly, and execute crisply without surprises.

## Engineering Defines the Schedule

Engineering uses the defined feature, cost, and schedule requirements to estimate the schedule to which they can deliver given their resources. The process is always a bit of an educated guess, as the complexities of a product development make for many unforeseen events. This is most evident in the Concept Phase, where the product definition itself is fuzzy. A rather common situation involves Marketing pleading to know the schedule, and Engineering rebuffing them because the product definition has so many undefined areas – "How can we give you a schedule when we don't even know what we are building?" Nonetheless, Engineering will need to use their experience and judgment to account for all uncertainties in order to produce the best schedule they can.

Because of the inherent uncertainty here, some of those assumptions can be frustrating for Marketing. **The wise Engineering manager doesn't simply base the schedule on the time it would take for the *planned* work**. Murphy's Law ensures that there will be some other important factors to consider. The first is extra work created by unexpected technical problems, the kind that can be minimized but not eliminated by careful planning. The second is time spent working on other projects that temporarily become a higher priority. Unless the organization only has one product, one should expect the occasional eruption of urgent issues with existing products which divert resources from the current development project. Even if Management clearly states that the project at hand is the highest priority, it will still happen. Finally, there is the challenge of time wasted due to poor coordination, lack of information, and delayed decisions. Marketing and Management may get frustrated at long or slipped schedules, but sometimes they are the cause when they procrastinate on decisions ("We have seen the enemy, and it is us"). In summary, these are the different types of uncertainty that experienced Engineering managers know can delay a program. They know that they need to include some room in the schedule to account for them, even at the risk of upsetting the Marketing team.

But let's not conclude that adding cushion to the schedule is the best or only way to deal with risk. Although there are always unforeseen events which cause delays, **many risks can be identified and dealt with if addressed proactively**. Engineering can facilitate this by **giving schedules that transparently highlight some of these risks**. This means more than simply saying "here are the dates". It entails providing three separate schedules, each with its own set of assumptions and probability of occurrence. The first is a schedule with 50% probability, which assumes no significant unexpected technical issues, no major execution problems, no product definition changes, no re-prioritizations against other products, and resolution of an identified set of project-specific issues. Clearly this is idealistic, but it helps put bounds on the problem and shows the earliest possible date by which a "truly perfect" project could be delivered. An 80% schedule then better approximates reality by assuming moderate technical, execution, and product definition issues. It also assumes a slightly more pessimistic resolution of some of the identified risks. Finally, the 95% schedule is the one Engineering can safely say they can absolutely sign up to deliver. Although this type of certainty tends to put a program out of bounds relative to the market window, it does a good job of framing the upper bound of schedule for the program.

The value in having these three is to help highlight the risks that differentiate them. The 50% schedule is the benchmark. Although Marketing always wants to believe this can happen, the truth is that it almost never happens. Even giving this schedule creates the risk that the organization will latch on to it as the *real* schedule. But this danger is worth the upside if handled properly. This 50% schedule will be contrasted with the 80% schedule, with Engineering providing a list of specific risks that would prevent the 50% schedule from happening. This is Engineering's chance to get on the table anything they see that would hinder their efforts. If the organization doesn't like the 80% schedule, this is the chance to proactively improve the situation by taking Engineering's list seriously and promptly acting on it. If the proper effort is not applied to avoid the identified risks, then Engineering can essentially say "I told you so". Going further, the risks that differentiate the 80% schedule from the 95% one can be used in the same way. Since these tend to be lower probability risks, they can be harder to identify up front and harder to track within the development phase. Nonetheless, the effort Engineering puts into this risk identification early on brings great benefit to the project, as well as to their own credibility. It helps energize the entire organization to eliminate roadblocks.

This type of schedule creation also helps guide Marketing as to the schedule they can promise to customers. They may choose to communicate the 50% schedule if the market window is tight and winning the business requires it. Although risky, it may be necessary in order to maximize the probability of success. Nonetheless, this is not advised except in extreme circumstances. Typically the 80% schedule would be used as "the" schedule around which to align customers and the organization. Except in certain industries or cultures where on time delivery is absolutely necessary, the 95% schedule is probably too conservative. This is a judgment call by Marketing, with influence from Engineering management. But it is the transparency of risk in the schedules from Engineering that allows this decision process to be an educated one, which enables smarter customer commitment, better staffing plans, and more accurate revenue forecasts.

Part of creating a schedule is also estimating the number of resources necessary to develop the product. These two are symbiotic – obviously the more resources applied, the better the schedule, up until some point of diminishing returns (although most organizations never hit this point, they are always short on people!). The initial resource assumption is usually determined by the number of heads available at the time of the project. The notion of changing this level of resourcing will come later during tradeoff discussions.

## Aligning Schedule with Market Window

Clearly, **you cannot move forward with a project until the committed schedule is aligned with the market window.** The product planning gates provide a nice forcing function for Marketing and Engineering to converge. Life can get tough when there is a gap, with Marketing on one side unwilling or unable to change the product definition and

Engineering on the other claiming their schedule cannot improve. It would be irresponsible of Management to allow the project to continue, hoping the situation works itself out. Engineering starts in a schedule hole and will be under pressure every step of the way. This can be rather demoralizing for them, and they will feel resentment towards Marketing and Management for being put in this situation. It also puts the Sales and Marketing teams in the position of having to lie to customers about the schedule until alignment is somehow achieved. Morale can also suffer due to the obvious ethical issues and potential ill will from the customer. Rather than go down this road, it is better to close the gap upfront. Marketing's usual solution is to simply push Engineering harder, which basically means they end up working long hours for an extended period of time. Of course the ability of the organization to "make a push" at critical times is very important to overall execution, but it is certainly not a sustainable strategy as Engineering quickly gets burned out. It is better to find a plan that works from Day One, rather than trying to squeeze more water from the rock. **Great organizations take definitive action early to get their projects onto a path for execution success**.

There are two ways to do this: increase resources on the project or change the requirements. While attractive, adding headcount can be challenging. It has to be supported by the P&L, and if the operating income picture does not support the new headcount then a strong case has to be made as to why the return is worth the investment. Skepticism usually runs high. It can be even worse if the request creates a headcount bubble – organizations are usually even more reluctant to hire if they know they will soon need a layoff to return to the correct P&L. In such situations, outsourcing is an appropriate alternative if there is a piece of the development program that can be easily carved out. But usually there are concerns about dividing the work, the learning curve, quality, and the ability to provide long-term support for a part of the product developed outside the company. If a bubble or outsourcing are both impossible, then de-prioritizing other projects is a viable option. But remember that other projects also have their own merits and champions, and raiding them would not be a trivial task. This could lead the organization to consider an outside acquisition of a technology or product. This is an effective method but always an expensive one; the need should be strategic enough to justify it.

If adding resources to the project is not possible, then Engineering and Marketing should begin to make some tradeoff decisions to bring the schedule in alignment with the market window. To effectively do this Marketing needs to have a sense for what is must-have versus simply nice to have. They cannot blindly claim that "everything is important" or develop irrational attachment to any particular requirement. **Great but late products make less money than "good enough" products that are on time**. The experienced marketer knows this and is willing to give up those requirements that aren't absolutely fundamental to the product's overall success. Giving up on a requirement is never easy, but there are certain types to look for that may be less painful to eliminate:

- Some features may exist to address certain peripheral markets that are incremental to the core market segments. While such a feature may be absolutely critical to winning a particular market, is that market worth winning if it causes the product to be "out of bounds" in the core market segments? These features may bring incremental revenue, but add real risk, resources, and cost to the entire product. The financial impact of each target market should be quantified in order to give a clear picture of the return from each. This numbers based approach should help guide better decisions regarding the inclusion of features for peripheral markets.

- The same principal applies to a product cost target. In Chapter 6 "Market Segmentation" the Spanning technique was discussed, whereby customized versions of a single product are used to address two or more segments with markedly different price points. The cost point dictated by the lower end segment (to sell profitably at that segment's prevailing price point) may be hard to meet while simultaneously delivering the features needed by the higher end segment. Thus, it may take Engineering a long time to design a product that offers both. There is always the option to forgo the low end market, or simply sell with lower margins. Again, a quantitative approach is recommended to assess the profit increase gained through better margins against the risk and financial impact of causing the program to miss the market window for the core markets.

- There are certain requirements which by their nature require a large amount of engineering effort. Sometimes that effort can be far out of proportion to the requirement's inherent value. Marketing is often unaware of the impact of a particular feature unless they dig deep into Engineering's estimate. The result is that the effort/value imbalance may go unnoticed. Engineering should make extra effort to identify high-effort requirements in their scheduling exercise.

Marketing should be working with Engineering to determine a list of candidate requirements to eliminate or modify. With this in hand, Marketing should then re-validate these requirements with customers. With luck, you will find some which can be delayed until a future generation of the product. You can still derive value from a deferred feature because the buying decision is based not only the product itself but also the strength of the roadmap. This technique, known as *Roadmap Spreading* (instead of trying to deliver everything at once, you spread it over the roadmap like peanut butter on a slice bread), is an effective and mature way for Marketing to achieve alignment of the schedule with the market window. This type of good faith effort on their part is something that goes a long way towards building credibility with Engineering. Compromising on the product definition to achieve the right schedule shows a pragmatism that is much superior to simply demanding superhuman effort from Engineering to achieve the impossible.

## Conclusion

Every organization tries to deliver products with a combination of features and cost that offers the best value to their customers. But in the face of a limited time horizon and resources, this can sometimes be a challenge. Organizations must remember one basic principle: **the market window drives the schedule, not the other way around**. Those who bury their head in the sand regarding a product that is late do so at their own peril. This includes the engineering manager who proclaims from his ivory tower that there is no way he can pull in the required schedule, as well as the marketer who won't make the hard decisions to tradeoff features and cost for schedule. Only a team effort of constructive collaboration on how to align the committed schedule with the market window will lead to product success.

# Schedule: Real World Example

*Marketing now endeavored to define the desired schedule for the product. The PC industry definitely exhibited static market windows. Each had a development schedule and launch date set in stone – a supplier had to line up with the dates or would not be considered. There was little to no latitude given. Complicating the picture was that the various segments – laptop, desktop, blade – each had its own unique schedule. For each segment, a complete set of milestones would need to be mapped out. The owner of the last project had only defined the end date, and the Engineering team was surprised several times with short notice on certain interim deliverables. By spending some time talking with a few customers, they were better able to understand all the necessary milestones. It turned out that the next market window for the laptop market segment was about four months before that for the blade segment, so the former would pace the project schedule. Here is what they defined:*

- *Gold Candidate Product: Date on which hardware and software must be locked. Set at September 30$^{th}$.*
- *Feature Complete: Date on which software needs to have all functions coded and ready for testing, but not necessarily bug-free. Set at August 5th.*
- *1st Samples: Date which initial product could be provided to customer for initial testing. Set at June 15$^{th}$.*

*These represented the development milestones. But the team was aware that there were other deliverables which were necessary but not specifically development milestones:*

- *Demo: Marketing wanted to demonstrate Mason to a few key customers in order to prove the product was real and to generate interest. They knew that Engineering always complains that preparing these demos is a distraction. By identifying the need up front, Engineering could properly staff so it would not detract from the development effort. The required date was set as August 1$^{st}$.*
- *Technical Documentation: PC OEM customers evaluating or designing in Mason would need this documentation to know how the chip works. The team wanted to make sure that the Applications*

*Engineering team started early enough to have this available when customers started asking for it. The most important document was the product datasheet, required on July 1ˢᵗ.*

- *White Papers: The team felt that there were a number of complex technology topics related to Mason which might be difficult to explain. Certainly the topic of security, particularly using the Trusted Platform Module (TPM), was a rich topic that needed detailed explanation. Instead of trying to do this in customer presentations, the team felt that a white paper might help equip customers with a baseline of knowledge which could aid in the selling process. Identifying it upfront would allow the Marketing Communications team ample time to plan this effort. The required date was set at June 1ˢᵗ.*

*With the schedule target defined, as well as the target cost and feature list, the Engineering team then went about creating their initial schedule estimate for the project. When the analysis was concluded, they presented the following:*

*Features:*

- *Cable Sensing Mode (for laptop)*
- *TPM (for laptop)*
- *EnergyStar Mode (for desktop)*
- *Serial Interface (for blade)*

*Cost: $3.10*

*Schedule:*

*50%: Gold Candidate Oct 20ᵗʰ; 1ˢᵗ samples Jul 15ᵗʰ*

*80%: Gold Candidate Nov 20ᵗʰ; 1ˢᵗ samples Aug 15ᵗʰ*

   *-Risk #1: TPM software not licensed and ready to test by May 1ˢᵗ*

   *-Risk #2: MRD is late. Deadline March 10ᵗʰ*

*95%: Gold Candidate Dec 20ᵗʰ; 1ˢᵗ samples Sep 15ᵗʰ*

- *Risk #3: Customer systems not available, leading to system bugs being found late*
- *Risk #4: 4 test engineers not approved and hired by July 1ˢᵗ*

*Demo: September 1ˢᵗ.*

*Clearly the schedule was too late for the laptop market – even the 50% date of October 20ᵗʰ for Gold Candidate did not meet the September 30ᵗʰ requirement. Furthermore, the cost wasn't low enough to compete in the* desktop market with any acceptable level of profitability. It was starting to look like the effort to accommodate the desktop market would prevent the project from hitting the market window for the laptop market. Upon further investigation with Engineering, part of the schedule was driven by the need to spend time on extreme cost reduction as well as the EnergyStar mode. Engineering posed the tradeoff that if Marketing could remove these two requirements, they could pull in the schedule significantly. Marketing ran the numbers; even though the desktop volumes might be high, the low profit margin meant that this segment would only contribute 18% of the overall project profit. This was clearly not enough to justify missing the laptop market window. Thus the team reluctantly agreed to remove the project requirements driven by the desktop market.

Engineering was very happy that Marketing had been flexible enough to offer these tradeoffs. An improved schedule was the result:

Features:
- Cable Sensing Mode (for laptop)
- TPM (for laptop)
- Serial Interface (for blade)

Cost: $3.30

Schedule:

50%: Gold Candidate September 10th; 1st samples May 30th

80%: Gold Candidate September 30th; 1st samples Jun 15th

- Risk #1: TPM software not licensed and ready to test by May 1st
- Risk #2: MRD is late. Deadline March 10th

95%: Gold Candidate Oct 10th; 1st samples Jul 15th

- Risk #3: Customer systems not available, leading to system late bugs being found late
- Risk #4: 4 test engineers not approved and hired by July 1st

Demo: August 1st

This schedule was more in line with the requirements of the program, and the feature set and cost target would still allow the product to compete profitably. But there were still risks, as the September 30th date for Gold Candidate was still only at 80% confidence. If certain events occurred, it could take longer. Since Engineering had clearly identified some of these relevant risks, it made it easier for the organization to prepare for them in order to mitigate them. A plan was put together to reduce the probability of each happening:

- *Risk #1: Development of the TPM portion of the chip was dependent on the company licensing some of the security software that would run on the chip. This was required to offer a full product to the customer, but more importantly was a critical part of being able to test out the chip's TPM features. Without the software, the features couldn't be tested and verified. So it was critical that it be in-house early in the program. A business development person was assigned to find a company that had the software and to promptly strike a licensing deal. The Director of Engineering asked the GM to seek an update on this on a weekly basis in order to ensure it was completed.*
- *Risk #2: Marketing committed to finishing the MRD within three weeks. But more importantly, they agreed to put extra emphasis on their due diligence with customers in those three weeks in order to minimize feature creep later in the program.*
- *Risk #3: The PC OEM customers had traditionally been very stingy in giving prototype systems to their vendors, despite the obvious benefits to testing and quality. The GM agreed to escalate this issue with the customers' executives in order to make sure that enough pre-production systems were available to allow early testing in order to wring out bugs faster.*
- *Risk #4: Part of the plan had involved transferring four test engineers from another organization. But the Director of Engineering knew that this other organization would resist this and try to hold onto their testers as long as possible, despite the fact that the CEO had bought into and mandated the transfer plan. So the Finance Director agreed to talk with his counterpart in the other organization to ensure a firm date that the headcount transfer would happen on paper. The GM also agreed to call his own counterpart and emphasize the criticality of having the transfer happen per the plan.*

*With these measures, the organization was doing its best to head off these risks before they become reality. The Engineering team had done itself a real service. They raised the issues well in advance, when everyone was in the frame of mind to do what they could to make the program successful. They knew that later on, the full burden of success would be on their own shoulders; these risks (and the lack of action on them) would be forgotten and the* finger would be pointed at them in the event of failure. Better to address the risks up front than try to explain them away later.

The organization was now in a good state. They had a feature-cost-schedule definition that Engineering and Marketing could agree on. It was both achievable and would meet the market's requirements. The next step was to analyze this definition to affirm that it would be both competitive in the market and profitable for the corporation.

# Checklist

## Is Marketing defining the market window correctly?
Engineering can only execute flawlessly if they know the target to hit and have time to plan properly. Time to Market (TTM) is a high planning priority

## What to Look For:
- Marketing has identified a complete set of program deliverables and dates
- Marketing can quantify the value of TTM, and set the target accordingly

## Is risk made transparent?
No schedule is deterministic as it is subject to many forces. But the organization can take proactive steps if it fully understands the specific risks.

## What to Look For:
- Engineering gives schedules with 50%, 80%, and 95% confidence levels
- Engineering clearly identifies risk factors that differentiate the schedules

## Is Marketing making the hard tradeoffs?
The organization cannot allow a non-critical requirement to cause the product to miss the market window – the hard decisions must be made.

## What to Look For:
- Marketing decisively separates must-have from nice-to-have requirements
- Engineering can clearly identify high-effort requirements

*(Further discussion on this checklist available at www.systemnotcircumstance.com)*

# CHAPTER 11:

## Competitive Analysis

*There is no greater sin in the world of product marketing than to enter the market without knowing exactly how the product will win against the competition. In the arena of professional sports, an incredible amount of planning goes into how to beat a particular opponent. Victory only comes by knowing exactly how to match up given the opponent's unique characteristics. The world of product competition is no different – to win you have to know exactly how you stack up. And just like no great coach would ever go into a contest resigned to losing, you must never enter the market without a clear competitive advantage. If this edge cannot be clearly stated upfront, no organization should feel comfortable committing resources to the effort. Of anything discussed in this work, this is the single most important factor in creating a great product. Organizations that consistently win in the market have a culture that demands clear competitive knowledge and advantage. They have multiple checkpoints and traps in the process to ensure this is the case.*

## "The Fog of War"

In 1738, a Prussian general named Clausewitz wrote a seminal work on the art of warfare titled simply "On War". For nearly 300 years it has been regarded as a cornerstone of the philosophy of conflict. In it he introduces the concept of "the fog of war". This refers to the uncertainty and chaos in which a general in large scale combat operates, hindering his ability to know the status of his forces, progress of battles, or the intentions and actions of the enemy. Clausewitz writes:

> "...war is the realm of uncertainty; three quarters of the factors on which action is based are wrapped in a fog of greater or lesser uncertainty."

One can visualize the commander inside his field headquarter tent. He struggles to control the campaign, having to piece together disparate bits of information while lacking direct contact with or knowledge of events. With this notion, Clausewitz is trying to convince us that uncertainty and chaos are not exceptions but the norm. Making decisions with imperfect information is therefore to be expected, so a commander had better get used to it. You rely on experience and judgment, and do the best you can.

The business world holds similar challenges. Knowing what competitors are doing sounds easy, but in practice it is not. Scant information is available because rivals are doing their best to conceal their efforts from you. What little you do hear is sparse, infrequent, and sometimes contradictory. And so the organization is forced to make decisions based on information that may be wrong. In the area of product planning, a bad decision can be disastrous in terms of lost revenue, competitiveness, and market share, not to mention the negative impact to morale. It can sometimes take years to recover. Clearly, **the gathering of good competitive information needs to be one of the highest priorities of the organization**.

## The Importance of Competitive Advantage

Good competitive information provides the reference point by which the product's relative advantage can be judged. Let us take a moment to revisit how critical that advantage is to your success. Remember that great products solve real problems, and do so *better than the alternatives*. Strong pricing power and sales volume come to those who earn it by designing fundamental value and differentiation in to the product from the start. There is no business world version of the 'Immaculate Conception' – you simply can't skip this part and still expect a successful product to pop out later in the process. Stellar marketing may bolster a mediocre product, but rarely will it carry the day. Only tangible advantage can form the basis of sustained success. It doesn't matter what form the advantage takes, only that is strong enough to determine the customers' buying decision:

- Functionality which provides real value to the customer and the competition lacks
- Being first to market so that the product captures pent up demand and builds incumbency benefits
- A comprehensive channel strategy that gives the product better access to customers than that of competition
- A fundamentally lower cost structure so that the product can be priced aggressively and profitably (note this is not the same as competing on price; rather, it means having a unique way to design the product such that it has a fundamentally lower cost structure)

If the reader walks away from this book remembering only one thing, let it be this: **great products have a clearly explainable, fundamental advantage over the competition designed in from the start.** The number one goal of any product planning effort is to conceive and define this advantage.

Yet, somehow organizations occasionally forget this important principle. It may be due to incompetence, but the truth is that most key individuals in business are intelligent and capable. There must be another explanation for weak products. **Often the cause is at the institutional level**. An analogy could be that of a mob mentality, where a group of otherwise law-abiding citizens may exhibit irrational or dangerous behavior when part of a large group in an emotional situation. Likewise, normally intelligent business people can make bad decisions in group activities if the organization's institutional norms do not compel them otherwise. The problem is that the chaos and fatigue inherent in an organization in a competitive market, if left unchecked, leads to poor decisions. Marketing and Engineering teams find themselves busy putting out tactical fires and product planning inevitably suffers. The neglect causes planning milestones to approach and pass without a plan being put into place. Everyone starts to feel the pressure to lock on to something – anything. The threshold for the Product Approval gets lower as management bows to the pressure as well. Somehow it becomes more important to have *a* plan than to have a *great* product. Marketing lulls itself into believing they can compete on such soft advantages as incumbency, brand, or customer service. In this delusional state, the organization settles and approves a product that doesn't necessarily have clear, demonstrable advantage. Situations like this happen when the organization doesn't have deeply embedded cultural norms that compel its members to stubbornly refuse to accept any product concept that does not have fundamental advantage. In the absence of this counter-balancing force, the aforementioned **chaos, fatigue, and lack of time cause people to settle and make bad product decisions**.

The frequency with which undifferentiated, me-too products hit the market proves how organizations can easily slide down this slippery slope. Clearly, there will always be time pressures which take attention away from product planning. But it is relatively simple to identify a weak product and make sure it never gets through the process. The litmus test is this: **Marketing should, at any time, be able to state in 25 words or less why the product will win**. The explanation must be clear, succinct, and free of all technical jargon. It must be simple enough that even one's grandmother can understand it. If this can't be done, the organization should question whether the advantage is truly fundamental or simply superficial. Fundamental concepts are easy to explain and understand. If Marketing cannot do this, immediately stop all progress in the Product Planning process until they can. Organizations must avoid the lazy temptation to allow products to pass without demonstration of clear advantage. The short term benefits of achieving a direction for the organization are not worth the risk of long term decline of the business due to a mediocre product. This simple exercise should be the forcing function to make sure that the organization takes a good honest look at the products relative to the competition. Never fight a battle in the market that you can't win – it is better to avoid the losing battle altogether.

Don't assume that a significant improvement over your last product is enough to stay competitive. This would not account for a competitor with a leapfrog or disruptive strategy, nor changes in the market that make current products obsolete. And don't fall into the trap of comparing to the competition's last generation. This is otherwise known as "shooting behind the duck", and fails to account for the seemingly obvious fact that the competition is trying to improve as well. Using either of these reference points to judge the value of your product in lieu of a detailed, honest, and forward-looking competitive analysis can lead to real problems. A deficit versus your competition will never be revealed, so you won't know to take remedial action. The organization will blissfully continue down its path, content with the product, only to find later on that it is inferior to the competition's offering.

## Structure of a Competitive Analysis

There is much that can be documented about competitors and their offerings, but only a certain subset need be characterized and presented. The goal is not to paint broad brush strokes (although in some cases it may be necessary to educate the organization about a new competitor), but rather to focus on those elements that are relevant to the product at hand. Typically there are three main levels of analysis performed. The first is on the *company itself*, starting with how its global strengths and weaknesses might help or hinder its ability to win. Some common elements are:

- *Breadth of IP*. A company that owns a large amount of Intellectual Property (IP) may be able to quickly add new features and functionality without having to acquire or organically develop the underlying technology. This is a big advantage in creating differentiation and reducing time to market.
- *Incumbency*. Being the customer's current vendor means that working relationships already exist, and switching costs help keep the customer from looking elsewhere. Both are a big advantage to maintaining existing business.
- *Distribution*. Channels through which to sell the product are not trivial to build. And they are incredibly powerful because they provide critical access to customers.

- *Market Share.* Owning large portions of the market brings economies of scale which lower costs and increases operational efficiencies. It also helps in terms of credibility in the eyes of the market.
- *Brand Name.* Familiarity and trust are often important buying criteria for consumers and business customers alike. Good brand name is therefore a powerful intangible asset, and one that takes time, patience, and performance to build up.

There are also a number of elements relating to a competitor's financial situation which may be useful to note. First and foremost, a company that is financially unstable is particularly susceptible to FUD (information intended to create Fear, Uncertainty, and Doubt about a competitor). Companies without a solid financial footing may go into bankruptcy, be acquired, have layoffs, cancel products, or be unable to invest adequately in future technology development. All of these notions can be suggested in order to scare customers away from the particular competitor. For instance, the market may be demanding a new technology that requires an investment of tens of millions of dollars and hundreds of engineers to develop. If a key competitor is having cashflow problems, it may be prudent to educate the customer about the financial situation, as well as why it takes a large amount of resources to develop the new technology.

The financial data for a public company can be found easily on the Internet. In particular look at the trend in their earnings and research and development (R&D) expenses. A strong company is growing profit, often an indicator of stable cash flow and the ability to ramp up R&D investment in new technologies. On the other hand, a company showing steady or increasing losses is not sustainable; sooner or later their investors will demand profitability, and cuts in investment and headcount will occur. For a private company, information is harder to find, but some may be publicly available. With a little digging inside the venture capital community, you can typically find out when a startup is going back for more funding. If the funding round is unexpected, or the firm is being entirely re-capitalized and the original investors and executives are being diluted, it can only mean something bad for them.

**Be specific in your analysis, because this is not a data gathering exercise but rather a basis for concrete action.** For instance, if you feel your competitor's incumbency is a challenge, explain exactly why. It may be that customers do not want to change their accounting software vendor because it means large installation costs, a week of downtime, and training costs for employees. If you are able, quantify each of these. By doing the analysis at this level, it makes it easier for you to specifically identify how you will overcome competitors' specific strengths. For the accounting software customer mentioned above, one might offer to pay for the installation and training costs, as well as perform the installation over a four day holiday weekend to reduce downtime. Basically, you are identifying a problem, and creating a proactive, intelligent plan to combat it. But you can't effectively do this if you are simply generalizing by noting that "our competitor is the incumbent, and that will make things a bit harder for us".

With the *company-level* competitive analysis completed, attention can turn to a *product-level* comparison. The first step is to choose some relevant parameters upon which to compare. The obvious examples include:

- Functionality
- Size
- Power
- Price
- Schedule

But don't confine yourself to the obvious. Any facet of a product can be a competitive factor as long as it brings some kind of value to the customer. Ease of use is very relevant. This could be as simple as the usability of the software interface, or more significantly could be the breadth of the ecosystem enabling the use of the product. **Anything that is a buying criterion for the customer can be considered a point of competitive comparison** (and as we've mentioned before multiple times, the only way to know what the customers' buying criteria are is to get out there and talk to them). At the same time, don't clutter the analysis with superfluous data. Only focus on comparison points that highlight a gap (between their product's capabilities and yours) which is worthy of active discussion and action. For factors that are equal, a simple statement of "parity" should suffice, while factors that are not significant should simply be ignored. Keep it simple so that the important differences stand out.

A useful format for displaying the data is a simple table (as shown in Figure 11) that lists the attributes being compared, with the competitors:

| Attribute | Competitor A | Competitor B |
|:---:|:---:|:---:|
| Power | | |
| Cost | | |
| Price | | |

*Figure 11.1: Attribute Comparison Table*

At this point, focus can shift to a *strategy-level* comparison of the product to that of the competition. The goal is to discern the overarching theme on how competitors plan to attack the market. Understanding their overall strategy helps connect the dots on individual disparate bits of information you receive. It also enhances your ability to predict a competitor's future actions. From the collective set of individual actions by a competitor, many things could be inferred about their larger strategy:

- A price bombing action could mean two things. First, the competitor may be desperate and feeling they have no way to compete other than on price. Or, it could suggest a deliberate price penetration strategy to drive a new technology into the mainstream. They may expect that the resultant volume will create economies of scale to reduce their cost structure to eventually achieve profitability.
- Success in certain groupings of customers as a result of some unique features would strongly suggest a segmentation strategy. They are consciously creating customized solutions for subsegments in order to create differentiation.
- Success with one large customer while being absent at others might suggest a strategy of focusing all of their sales, marketing, and feature development onto this customer (while you spread yourself thin over multiple customers), using them as a wedge to enter the market.
- Integration of functionality previously not encompassed in this product category could indicate that competition is trying to leverage their broad IP and expand the scope of the product beyond what you can provide – thereby making your single-function product obsolete.

As this strategy analysis progresses, you will be comparing it to your own in a "what-if" exercise: "If they pursue this strategy, and we pursue ours, what is the likely outcome?" The product-level comparison is important, but **the strategy-level comparison gives you better perspective on how your path will match up to the competition's over the long term.**

It is critical to ensure that any intended advantage is defensible over time. In conducting this competitive analysis, think two steps ahead. Competitors are not static, but rather intelligent entities that will adapt their strategy and tactics in response to your moves. **These actions are called** *Second Order Effects*. If you build a strategy that leverages an advantage in one particular area, what might a reasonably intelligent competitor do to counter it? Suppose the incumbent is pursuing a skimming strategy and you choose a penetration strategy to compete. While the competitor may be initially caught off guard, the second order effect could be that they simply change their pricing and segmentation strategy to compete head to head. If your strategy is to compete on 20% greater performance, the competition may decide in response to make a few small tweaks to narrow that gap, while promising dramatic gains in the next generation product. A strategy to differentiate the product on features may be met with a price bombing strategy. The lure of a rock bottom price often makes customers forget about the value of the functional attributes of another product. That competitor is in effect creating a Value Hurdle for you to overcome. In each case, an intended advantage was immediately countered through a simple strategy change by competition. Some advantages are very significant, and it may take years for a competitor to build the technology, features, or channel necessary to compete. But others are more easily erased through simple reactive moves by the competition. That is why Second Order Effects must be considered to ensure the advantage is defensible. Assume the competition will react, and **base the assessment of competitive advantage on what a competitor will be doing in reaction to your strategy, not what they are doing today**.

## How to Use Competitive Data

The data gathering phase described above should account for the bulk of the time spent on the competitive analysis, but this next stage is by far the most important. Now that you have the data, what do you do with it? Too many organizations treat competitive analysis as an academic exercise. They find and compile the data, present it to the organization in the approval meeting, everyone nods their head, and then the presentation moves on to the product definition as if nothing happened. Competitive analysis basically becomes a documentation exercise. **But the data is only useful if it drives action to compensate for a deficit or exploit a strength**. What follows is a discussion of how best to use competitive data.

First and foremost, you must accept the data. There is a human tendency to focus on that which supports our point of view, and unconsciously ignore that which contradicts it. Educated and intelligent business professionals are not immune to this. They've invested their time, energy, and pride in the product concept. They have visions of market success, growth of the business, and rapid career progression once this product is launched. They may find themselves unconsciously ignoring some competitive weakness in the plan. It is not something that anyone would knowingly do – that would be self-defeating, not to mention a little unethical. But somehow, it happens. Remember what was mentioned earlier about the subtle pressure within the organization to arrive at a plan, any plan, so that everyone can rally around a direction. This pressure and pride mentioned above can both contribute to this "temporary blindness" phenomenon. So **if you are seeing anything that hints at a weakness in your value proposition and competitiveness, take it very seriously**.

With this clear view of the data, you are now ready to act upon it. This is the key word: *act*. Competitive analysis should drive action to maximize advantage and minimize deficits. Don't simply note each point of comparison and then move on. Instead, specifically identify how to compensate for the weakness, or actively exploit the strength. Suppose you've identified that your competition has a feature that your product lacks, but that only a small market segment values this feature. You might suggest one of three concrete responses:

1. Forgo this market segment and reflect that in the financial analysis.
2. Overcome the feature with aggressive pricing in that subsegment, thereby obviating the feature by creating a Value Hurdle.

3. Use creative marketing to re-focus the value discussion away from the missing feature and towards a strength in your product.

What is important here is to lay out concrete, actionable plans to blunt any weakness shown in the competitive analysis. Likewise, it is just as important to plan specific actions to maximize any strengths that are identified. Suppose the product's power consumption is shown to be substantially less than that of the competition. Calculate the exact amount of additional battery life your product allows. Set up demonstrations that graphically show the power consumption of both your product and the competition's. Train your salespeople to deliver this message to the engineers and marketers within the customer company who really care about power so that they advocate internally for power consumption to be a major buying criteria. In general, think of the data in your competitive analysis regarding the relative strengths and weaknesses as the starting point for an entire product marketing plan. The goal is to minimize weaknesses and absurdly magnify strengths. Bring in the relevant technologist, engineers, and marketers to analyze these differences and conjure up powerful ways to mitigate or exploit them. Whether it be through changes to the product, marketing spin, demos, or sales focus, the point is to turn your analysis into action.

## The Fog of War in Action

As we've mentioned, finding competitive data is hard; knowing what to believe is even more difficult. As Clausewitz writes:

*"Many intelligence reports in war are contradictory; even more are false, and most are uncertain. What one can reasonably ask of an officer is that he should possess a standard of judgment, which he can gain only from knowledge of men and affairs and common sense. He should be guided by the laws of probability. These are difficult enough to apply when plans are drafted in an office, far from the sphere of action; the task becomes infinitely harder in the thick of fighting itself, with reports streaming in."*

In this context, it should be helpful to discuss some of the difficulties in interpreting competitive data. **One such challenge is the tendency to**

**underestimate your competition**. We humans tend to believe what we want to believe. Certain factors may exist which cause the competitive data to be taken less seriously than it should:

- You have consistently beaten a competitor, and blindly assume they will continue their record of poor strategy or execution. Yet weak performance is a greatly affected by executive competence, corporate funding and politics, and technology trends – all of which can easily change.
- A competitor may appear to be following a new strategy which is a radical shift from the past, so we resist believing it to be true or that they can execute on it. Yet it is not uncommon for a company to decide to embark on a new and possibly disruptive path in order to re-gain a competitive advantage.
- The competitor may appear to be following a strategy that you have explored yourself and determined to be infeasible or not profitable. Yet your conclusion may be based on a number of factors - such as IP, core competence, market knowledge, and personalities – which are unique to your company but not applicable to a competitor.
- The Marketing team is satisfied with their plan, and not particularly willing to exert the energy to re-think things, even if competitive data suggests it is necessary. Don't think this doesn't happen; it can be a common result of pride or laziness, coupled with the effects of fatigue from a fast-paced job, the urgency to converge on a plan, and the momentum of the efforts so far.

As stated in Andy Grove's now-cliché title, "Only the Paranoid Survive", underestimating your competition is the antithesis of this. **Paranoid organizations work harder and exert more effort to be successful**. Keep this in mind while evaluating your competition.

But while vigilance is important, moderation is as well. **You can, in fact, to your detriment, overestimate your competition**. We return briefly to Clausewitz, who writes:

*"All action takes place, so to speak, in a kind of twilight, which, like fog or moonlight, often tends to make things seem grotesque and larger than they really are."*

The unknown tends to intimidate us out of proportion to the known facts. The enemy sometimes looms large in our mind, and we assign more credit to them than they deserve. For instance, just because a competitor announces they are going to do something, it doesn't mean that it will ever happen. "Vaporware" is a commonly known phrase in the technology industry. It refers to the premature announcement of a product or technology that ultimately doesn't make it to market. It could be that the announcer is simply trying to scare off competitors or influence customers to work with them by giving the impression that they have a big time to market advantage. Or, the announcement may be sincere, but the company or individuals ultimately lose interest or momentum. In some cases, a competitor may promise something exciting to a customer (which then becomes a requirement), but ultimately technical problems delay the offering significantly. Whatever the reason, don't be too quick to believe everything you hear from or about your competitor. Companies are like ducks – calm appearance above the water, chaotic exertion underneath. They will always put a confident face on what they are doing. We may see a competitor with great momentum in the market, but you shouldn't necessarily let this discourage you. Remember that your competitors are often much like your company, warts and all – internal confusion, late schedules, stressed out engineers, management indecision, bad luck, and intractable marketing problems. All of these can lead to that momentum screeching to a halt. Overestimating your competition can lead to damaged morale or an organization abandoning its strategy in panic, **so retain a healthy skepticism in your competitive analysis**.

Another significant challenge, and one that contributes to the two issues above, is **the possibility that the data is corrupted**. Always remember that information you hear is at the end of a long "chain of transmittal":

*What your source tells you → what your source hears or understands → what competitors say they are doing → what competitors are actually doing*

Each link in this chain poses a very real risk of translation error. The onus is on the Marketing team to scrutinize the data they receive. This starts by validating the source. From the person who told you, work backwards as far up the chain as you can. Suppose that one of your sales people gives you a piece of competitive data that she heard from her customer.

You should identify the person who gave it to her. Then ask yourself a few basic questions:

- Do we trust this person?
- What motivation would they have for giving us this data?
- What motivation might they have for misleading us?
- Are they in a position to be getting reliable data themselves?

Also seek to strip away any interpretations that may have been added along the way. Someone in the chain may receive raw data, make their own conclusion, then present that conclusion to you as if it were fact. Be sure to always ask your source to tell you *exactly* what their source said, verbatim. Misinterpretation can often be injected when someone in the chain does not understand the subject matter well enough. They could be confused by jargon or technical information and may miss some of the subtleties in the data.

This suggests the importance of cross-checking your data. Members of governmental intelligence organizations or journalists often only consider information valid if they are able to confirm it from two independent sources. Acting without confirmation is a risk for them, and the same applies to the business world. Luckily, confirmation is not an impossible task. **If a piece of competitive information is truly reflective of reality, then that reality should manifest itself in multiple places**. For instance, if a competitor is telling one customer about their plans, they are likely telling multiple customers. Once you have an initial piece of data, it should be easier for you to skillfully formulate your questions to these other customers in order to confirm.

## Sources of Competitive Data

**Acquiring competitive information is not a passive process**. It takes time to develop the sources and processes to generate it. In this section we discuss some of the more common sources of information.

- *Competitor Website*: Although most companies are careful not to release anything sensitive onto their website, it can still be a source of useful data. Somewhere in the process involving the Marketing and Marketing Communications (MarCom) teams, someone may do a poor job of scrubbing what is posted or not recognize the value of the data. Product briefs are often posted publicly, and can provide insight into the productization and positioning strategies being used. Never underestimate the power of understanding your competitor's positioning. You can use it to craft an effective counter-message; or, you may simply decide to copy it if you find it effective (assuming you believe you can win on other aspects). Press releases can also provide much of this same information (discussed further in Chapter 20 "Press Releases"). Datasheets, although less likely to be available publicly, can be found. They are a good source for technical data about the competitive product. Applications engineers can help scrub them for useful information buried in the detail. Finally, you may be able to find white papers that your competitor has written to help explain the technologies and usage models relevant to their product. Unfortunately for them, these documents also educate you as to the initiatives they are driving or trends they are riding. If they are taking the time to do a white paper on a topic, you can be relatively sure it is central to their strategy and view of the market. You should also feel free to "borrow" ideas and positioning in their whitepapers – no harm in deriving benefit from their efforts.

- *Customers*: This is often by far the best source of competitive information. Customers are motivated to do what is best for their own company, which is to have several suppliers who each offer essentially the same product. This leaves no particular vendor with an advantage, and all with the motivation to compete on price – customer wins. Ironically, they almost have a vested interest in *not* seeing any innovation in the market which might leave a single supplier with enhanced pricing power. This is directly counter to what you are trying to do, which is to build a sustainable competitive advantage in order to *create* pricing power. Leaking a vendor's plans to the competition is a powerful means of ensuring parity. This may sound cynical and unethical, but the motivation for the end result cannot be denied, and thus it does happen. Of course, customers will assuage their moral concerns by obscuring the data with carefully worded statements. Instead of saying "your competitor is doing X", it may be phrased as "if you are not doing X, you won't be competitive". So, it is important to control your own information given to a customer. But the sword cuts both ways, as you can use this dynamic to learn what your competitors are doing. Curious whether your competitor has a certain feature? Ask "We believe this feature is entirely unique in the market", and then wait for their reaction. Want to know your competitor's schedule? Inquire as to "when do I need to deliver the product in order to be competitive?" Of course, these are the type of questions that should only be asked in side meetings with trusted individuals. Never try it in larger open meetings; no individual in the customer company would want to be perceived by their peers as revealing confidential information even though they may be willing to do so in private. But beware of being misled by your customer. It is not uncommon for an unscrupulous purchasing manager to give an artificially low price target which he hints is what the competition is quoting. Or, you may be lead to believe that your "competition" has a certain feature you lack, while in reality this is not a reference to your primary competitor but rather an unproven new entrant who is not established enough to actually win the business. This goes back to the discussion on understanding your source's motivations and validating all data you receive.

- *Trade Shows*: Companies will demonstrate their products at trade shows. Sometimes they have technology demonstrations that hint at future products. Luckily, these demos are not always staffed by people who are savvy enough to hold back on sensitive information. You can learn many interesting things by asking the right questions. Your competitor may also be presenting in topical sessions sponsored by the overall trade show. You can learn much in these sessions as well, particularly during the question and answer sessions afterwards.
- *Job Postings*: As companies embark on new technology and strategy directions, they often need to add headcount and new expertise to their existing team. Sometimes they go so far as to place job posting on their website or through other means in order to attract candidates. Reviewing these can give you a rather good early warning of the nature of their new development efforts.

Gathering information from these sources can be a time consuming job. It takes a real investment of effort to cover everything – the Marketing team cannot be expected to handle it by themselves. Instead, **organizations should strive to make competitive intelligence gathering a part of everyone's job**:

- The Sales team should be asked to continually and proactively search out data and feed it back to the business unit. The Marketing team should be coaching them on specific issues and situations for which they need information.
- Marketing should develop their human network consisting of customers, partners, and vendors. This means developing and nurturing a lot of personal relationships. They need to spend the time meeting with key individuals within the industry and gaining their trust.
- Technologists in the organization who attend conferences or participate in standards bodies should know to be attentive for competitive intelligence. At the risk of stereotyping, individuals from the technical side of the house tend to be less concerned with protecting sensitive information from exposure to the competition. It provides fertile ground for an alert observer.

Proactive efforts can create a network of people searching for competitive information. The next step is to process it. The best way to do so is a recurring meeting solely dedicated to collecting and analyzing competitive intelligence. It allows a central forum for disparate data points to be integrated into a holistic picture. More importantly, it allows focused thinking and discussion on the validity, meaning, and impact of this data. Action plans can be developed for valid data, while invalid information can be discarded so it does not fester within the organization.

## Conclusion

Competitive analysis is an essential part of any product planning effort. If performed diligently and critically, it can ensure that you are defining true competitive advantage into the product from the start. This is critical to being successful in the market later on. But the exhortation to pay close attention to competition comes with one piece of advice: **don't get so focused on them that you abandon your own efforts to**

**understand and solve real Market Problems.** The risk is that the Marketing team unknowingly relies on the competition to do the thinking for them. Action follows focus, and if you are focusing on competition, inevitably your actions will lead you in their direction and me-too products. Observe your competition, but only as a means to find a way to trump them. This requires a unique path based on original thinking about how to solve real customer problems. But however you choose to get there, you must absolutely be able to show specific, overwhelming competitive advantage and how it will enable you to win in the market. If you cannot state this in 25 words or less, get back to work on the product definition until you can.

# Competitive Analysis: Real World Example

*A strawman of the product definition was in place. Now it was time to assess the fundamental advantage it would have over the competition. The Marketing team knew that without a clear, demonstrable edge they would never get approval for the project. So they started by determining which competitors to assess. They decided that there were two companies worth watching – "A" and "B". The analysis of "A" would be handled first, and began with a <u>company-level analysis</u>. "A" was a large company that wielded a lot of power in the industry. Because they sold several high value chips to PC OEMs (not just the network communications chip), "A" had a lot of leverage. They were also the incumbent for the communications chip, and so switching costs to another vendor would be high. Any attempt to dislodge "A" would be made more difficult by these facts. But the Marketing team felt that they could actually use this in their favor. "A" had held this position for several years, and as a result had started to get a little arrogant and complacent. While they had a large support team, they were not always as responsive as they should have been. Their roadmap had also gotten a little stale, something not uncommon for larger companies that have grown satisfied with incumbency. This provided an opportunity to position TechCorp as the more nimble and hungry alternative. Marketing would seek to reinforce the notion that customer problems were taken very seriously and solved quickly by any means necessary. Also, emphasis would be placed on selling a strong roadmap with many exciting technologies coming in the future. Selling the roadmap could combat resistance related to switching costs because customers would see TechCorp as the best long term partner to bring them new technology. If customers were to switch now, they would enjoy many years of cutting edge technology. Positioning TechCorp as an "anti-A" would help counteract the significantly large number of resources that "A" brought to the table.*

*The next phase of analysis was a <u>product-level comparison</u> of Mason to the alternatives. It started with identifying the relevant points of comparison. Cost was of course included, as were multiple items relating to power. The integration of TPM and the serial interface were also added. The Director of Marketing had done a good job of setting up an intelligence gathering network consisting of some sales people, a few trusted customers, and a key player at a software partner company that was relevant in this market space. The team was able to gather some clear information on what "A"* and "B" were offering. The Engineering team also did some cost analysis to predict what their respective product cost could be. The following summary emerged:

| | Mason | Comp A | Comp B |
|---|---|---|---|
| Manufacturing Cost | $3.30 | $3.00 | $3.25 |
| Total Power | 900mW | 800mW | 750mW |
| Cable Sensing Mode | Yes | No | No |
| TPM | Yes | No | No |
| Serial Interface | Yes | No | No |
| EnergyStar Mode | Yes | No | Yes |
| Total Power w/Serial Interface | 1000mW | 1490mW | 1440mW |

*Figure 11.2: Mason Attribute Comparison Table*

There were a few interesting learnings from this data:

- The team was surprised that a competitor would be offering EnergyStar Mode. The initial belief was that this was a differentiator, and thus would enhance competitiveness within the desktop segment. Given the existing concerns about schedule and margin in this segment, losing this advantage only increased the skepticism that this should be a target market.
- Cable Sensing Mode would be a differentiator. Given the value it provided (10 minutes extra battery life), this would be a significant competitive advantage in the laptop market
- TPM would be a differentiator. It was still unclear if the market would accept TPM into the mainstream, but if successful it would provide OEM customers with a strong security story. Given the ever-increasing size and value of sensitive data stored on laptops, offering hardware-based security for a negligible premium should be a tangible a differentiator.
- The integrated serial interface would be a differentiator. Given that it would save $4.00 in solution costs, shrink the footprint by 14%, and reduce power by nearly a ½ watt, the advantage was very solid and compelling.

Overall, the team felt confident they would have a fundamental advantage in the market, one that could be expressed very simply:

*"In the laptop segment, we will win by offering 10 minutes better battery life with Cable Sensing Mode and TPM security priced for the mainstream"*

*"In the blade segment, we will win because we have a 25% smaller footprint, eliminate one fan, and offer a 20% lower solution cost"*

The final phase of the competitive analysis was a <u>strategy-level</u> comparison to "A". Checks with the team's intelligence gathering network revealed that "A" was also focused on power and security. But it was clearly from a different angle. First, their strategy was to reduce total power. As shown in the product comparison, they were at 0.8 watts (vs. Mason's 0.9 watts), and were promising to reach 0.5 watts W within two years. In the security realm, they were also pitching an encryption feature, which would encrypt and decrypt the data to and from the network in real time. With this feature, no one could tap into the network and monitor sensitive data. Over the next few years they would slowly increase the encryption speed up to the maximum throughput of the network. So, in general "A's" strategy was to compete on total power and encryption performance.

To counter this, the team would need to either match these features or find a way to position them as unnecessary. Since neither vector played to TechCorp's nor Mason's strengths, they chose the latter. Regarding power, they would need to make the argument that total power was irrelevant, because most battery drain occurred in specific usage modes such as when the cable was unplugged. Furthermore, the battery tests were performed with the cable unplugged. It would be relatively straightforward to prove that Cable Sensing Mode would be superior to total power in extending battery life. In the area of security, line encryption was important in protecting data being transmitted. But hardware-based key storage was much more important for data at rest (such as on a laptop hard drive). The Marketing team would need to create a story that convinced the customer that the true threat model was that of a laptop being stolen and accessed rather than that of someone hacking into network traffic. This would suggest that line encryption was interesting but not addressing the true threat to laptop PCs.

The team reviewed their competitive analysis. Although they were up against a large and well-funded competitor in "A", they felt confident that they could influence their customers to interpret "big" as slow and complacent. TechCorp would be positioned as the nimble partner who would lead on technology and execution. On a feature to feature basis, they matched up well with features like TPM, Cable Sensing Mode, and integrated serial interface being clear differentiators. And on the strategy level, the Marketing team was comfortable that the emphasis on smart power modes and hardware-based key storage was a better direction than total power and line encryption.

# Checklist

## Does the product have clear competitive advantage?

Strong pricing power is always built on having a significant edge over competition. No organization should let a product pass without it.

### What to Look For:

- Marketing can state a validated advantage in 25 words or less
- The advantage is sustainable, even against 2nd order effects

## Is the competitive analysis actionable?

A competitive analysis is not a documentation tool – it should be a catalyst for action to improve the product's ability to compete.

### What to Look For:

- Marketing has created an action plan to exploit identified strengths
- Marketing has created an action plan to mitigate identified weaknesses

## Is competitive intelligence actively gathered?

Passive gathering never produces enough competitive data to be useful. Rather, the organization must take deliberate steps to extract information.

### What to Look For:

- Marketing has cultivated a list of >5 key competitive data sources
- The organization holds periodic internal meetings to discuss the raw data

*(Further discussion on this checklist available at www.systemnotcircumstance.com)*

# CHAPTER 12:

## Pricing Strategy

*Pricing is one of the more important subjects related to creating new products. Price too low and you leave money on the table; make it too high and you won't sell many units. Yet it is ironic that a task that is so critical is also so subjective. There is no exact science in quantifying the "value" of something. But there are ways to make the process more rigorous. This chapter will discuss a framework which can help guide pricing choices. The challenge is to make the pricing consistent with the rest of the product plan, including the positioning, competition, feature set, and channel strategy. But to do this effectively, the pricing strategy needs to be considered early on, before decisions are finalized on these other items. Pricing shouldn't be determined post facto so that it fits the plan; rather, the product plan should be created in conjunction with the pricing strategy. In this way the plan can be modified if needed to accommodate the realities of the pricing environment.*

## Begin with the End in Mind

One of the key tenets of Steven Covey's book "The 7 Habits of Highly Effective People" is to "Begin with the End in Mind". If you imagine the future you want, it serves to motivate and guide you to that end. This principle applies well to product management. You can look ahead several months or years, and visualize the act of trying to close business with a new product. There are two scenarios that can be envisioned. In the first, you wield strong pricing power as a result of clear differentiation. You are competing on value, not price. The second scenario is at the opposite end of the spectrum, where a poorly defined "me-too" product sits in a crowded field of several similar competitive offerings. Without anyway to differentiate, there is no choice but to compete on price. Your challenge is to make the first scenario a reality. A Sun Tzu maxim comes to mind: "Every battle is won before it is ever fought". The sales cycle can be considered the "battle". Although a great sales effort can help, by this time it is far too late. In fact, the seeds of your fate were sown months or years before when the choices were made on how to define and market the product. The due diligence, sweat equity, and discipline that were applied then are what determine your competitiveness and pricing power, long before the battle ever begins. So **the key to consistently creating great products is executing each of the three facets of the product management process such that you have strong pricing power in the endgame.**

In the *Product Planning Phase*, you are **creating true value**. This is based primarily upon whether the product solves a real problem the customer is having (we call this "value-add"). A product with strong value-add is the result of a product manager who chose to sacrifice and spend significant time on the road with his customers (away from his family and personal life) asking penetrating questions in order to understand the customers' problems. Furthermore, he didn't settle for a me-too product because it was easy; he pushed himself to discover a way to differentiate, and then pushed the organization to execute on it. By demanding true value from the beginning, the product manager greatly strengthens pricing power.

In the *Product Marketing Phase*, the product manager then works to **translate the true value into perceived value in the customer's mind.** Success in this phase comes through focused and creative identification of a product's core strengths, coupled with creative assembling of peripheral facts to further enhance that strength. Too many product managers settle for mundane messaging that consists of nothing more than a feature list, thinking the product will sell itself. It won't. Without good marketing and positioning, a customer won't appreciate the product value and therefore won't be willing to pay much for it.

Finally, in the *Product Management Phase*, you are trying to **preserve the true and perceived value created in the previous two phases**. The goal is to negotiate the final price and close the business. Unfortunately in this very tactical phase, you only have the ability to hurt yourself. A clumsy customer engagement or price negotiation can actually degrade or destroy the pricing power built in the prior two phases. A chapter in the upcoming sequel to this book will discuss how to skillfully handle this phase. For now let it suffice that this is a dangerous phase that must be handled carefully in order to preserve the good work to date.

This entire process is one of creating and preserving value, such that you arrive at the point of closing business with a healthy amount of perceived value. Effectiveness in each phase and an unwillingness to settle or take short cuts will determine your success. Everything you do or don't do comes back to you in the form of pricing power. But this is a long road to travel. It is natural for a product manager to lose faith, motivation, or energy during the whole process when the end-game seems distant. In times like this, look forward to the moment of winning business. Visualize the elation of having strong pricing power and the terror of being commoditized. Let the contrast of these two extreme emotions motivate you to apply the necessary effort at every stage of the game.

## Establishing Strategic Intent

To keep the focus on pricing in the early stages of Product Planning process, a Strategic Pricing Plan is created. At a minimum, this provides the assumptions that are fed into the financial analysis. But the Strategic Pricing Plan is really intended for a more important purpose. **It serves as a forcing function to generate critical thinking about how product attributes and market forces will affect pricing**. We discussed earlier that the true strength of the product will eventually manifest itself as pricing power. Reversing this equation, our predictions of pricing can serve as an early indicator of the competitiveness of the product. Because this is being considered early on, there is still time to modify the product plan itself in order to ensure you have the pricing power you desire. Waiting until right before your launch to determine pricing is a mistake because you've missed most of your opportunities to make necessary changes to the plan.

An important clarification should be made here, although possibly at the risk of splitting hairs. The Strategic Pricing Plan is not a passive task of predicting what the market and other forces will allow you to charge. Rather, **it should be a proactive exercise of stating what you will convince the market to pay**. Of course market and competitive forces are factored in, but so are proactive steps in the product plan that influence the pricing reality. This is a process of establishing a *strategic intent* – what you want pricing to be, and how you will make that happen. If strategic intent deviates from what the market would currently accept, then changes to the product definition or the product marketing plan need to be made in order to close the gap.

## Pricing Framework

As mentioned earlier, pricing is a subjective exercise. But it need not be entirely driven by gut feel. In fact, there are a common set of forces that come to bear on pricing. A valid price is one that is consistent with all of them. This section will lay out that set of forces into a pricing framework.

The process starts with quantifying the value of the product itself. This is essentially **an exercise in translating the product's attributes into a monetary worth to the customer**. In an ideal world, this would dictate the price. But unfortunately, the new product doesn't exist in a vacuum; the customer has alternatives such as buying a competitive product or sticking with existing products. These alternatives set their own price point which becomes a reference point against which your new product will always be judged, whether the comparison is valid or not. A price that is considered too low or too high is only judged as a result of comparison to this reference point, which becomes what customers think they "ought" to be paying. Unfortunately, these reference points become very hard to change. Psychologists call this an "anchor," whereby the human mind will exhibit an irrational adherence to the first value it latches onto when quantifying a concept. This anchor will exert a gravitational pull on your price. The magnitude of this force is directly related to the amount of differentiation you have. If there is none, your price will essentially be set by the anchor and the external forces that create it. The customers are in charge: they can look at you and say "Here's the price, you need to match or beat it to get my business". However, with a product that offers unique value, you are in charge and can exercise your pricing power. You have the ability to look at the customer and say "That anchor doesn't apply to my product because it offers you value the other guys don't have". The product rises above the fray of similar competitors battling it out on price. Then, the challenge is to define what your product is worth, by quantifying your value proposition and positioning it such that the customer accepts it.

So, to supplement the value analysis, you must factor in the effect of alternatives. The competitive analysis and a comparison to last-generation products (with their existing, accepted price points) should help you understand the incremental value the product provides. If that is small, expect your price point to migrate towards the reference point. If large, you can make the case that the product can support a price based mostly on your value analysis. Finally, you will finish this process by factoring in other elements such as macroeconomic conditions and the market's price elasticity. Let us get started with examining each step in creating the Strategic Pricing Plan.

## Step 1: Quantify the Value

Marketers often use the concepts of "value" and "differentiation" in discussions of marketing and pricing. These terms are overused to the point that the real meaning gets lost. Let's keep it simple: **value is simply a measure of the usefulness of a product to a certain market segment**. If your product solves a certain problem that the customer base is having, then it has value for them. If the problem is particularly vexing, then your solution offers a *lot* of value to them. But value alone is not enough to achieve strong pricing power. If multiple products all solve the same problem, then the vendors offering them must resort to competing on price. To extract a premium for your product's value, it must be the only product that can solve the problem (or solves it in a unique way that is desirable). This is known as differentiation. Unfortunately, marketers tend to use the terms value and differentiation interchangeably.

Quantifying value is difficult. The problem is that value is often based on functionality, while pricing is spoken in the language of money.

Therefore, functionality has to be translated into dollars. You cannot rely on the customer to make the translation. **Performing this translation, and convincing the customer of its validity, is the essence of product marketing**. The key to success is to bring all elements of value into the equation so that they feed into the monetization. Any benefit the product brings should be claimed as part of the product's value and in order to support a higher price. Here we discuss some common value vectors:

- *Performance*: This is probably the most common value proposition for technology products. The speed of PCs, database software packages, and compact disc drives all increase with each product generation, and are a central part of the marketing message. Performance can be translated into dollars in the following ways:

  o *User idle time*: Slow performance may cause a user to sit idle waiting for the product to execute a particular function. Assuming that users are employees, their value per time unit can be monetized using their loaded cost (salary plus cost of benefits). Using time-motion studies or estimations, determine the idle time reduction (relative to alternative products) attributable to higher performance. Multiply this by the loaded cost per time unit to calculate the value of the cost savings. If an engineer has a loaded cost of $300K per year, then the cost of 1 minute of an idle engineer is $2.50.

  o *Lost opportunity cost*: Users who sit idle may be stalled on performing revenue-generating activities. So there is an opportunity cost associated with idle time. Quantify the revenue potential of a single employee over a unit of time. For instance, a 100 person salesforce for a $100M company would have a revenue potential of $1M per person per year, or about $8.33 per minute. Every minute of a salesperson's idle time eliminated is worth $8.33.

  o *Aggregate performance*: If multiple units of the product are required to provide an aggregate level of performance, increasing the performance of a single product may mean the customer can purchase fewer units of the product. Although this may seem counterintuitive, in a competitive market it could mean the difference in winning the business. Calculate the reduction in units of the product required to deliver the requisite aggregate performance levels. The amount of money saved is the value of increased performance.

- *Integration of peripheral functionality*: A common strategy in the technology industry is to integrate the functionality of other products used in conjunction with one's own product. Quantifying the value proposition is relatively straightforward – the price of the product being integrated represents the value of the additional functionality in your product. You could further make the case that there is additional value from any other synergies generated by the integration, such as reduced complexity, increased reliability, or better security.

- *Uniquely new functionality*: A new product may provide new functional capability not previously available from any product in the market. Thus, there is no established reference point for the functionality as there would be in the above vector. The task is to quantify the value of a "capability". There are a few common categories of functionality:

  o *Security*: The value of any security measure is proportional to the value of the asset, the costs of a breach, and how often an incident could be expected to occur. You may attempt to find industry data on the value and frequency of security incidents relevant to the product category. This data can be used to quantify the value of security features that reduce the occurrence of such breaches.

  o *Simplification*: Some features can reduce the number of steps necessary to complete a certain task. Quantifying the value of this involves quantifying the reduction in idle time and loss of opportunity cost (described above). You can also include the cost of any equipment (or other outlay) that is made obsolete by the simplification of the task.

  o *Convenience*: Making a product more convenient usually means making some type of functionality available anytime, anywhere. Unfortunately, the value of this is quite difficult to quantify, and may best be handled using your judgment.

- *Elimination of peripheral costs*: Because of the competitive nature of the technology industry, most product managers will be under pressure to reduce product cost. You lean on Engineering to do so, but eventually reach the point of diminishing returns. It is then important to consider ways to reduce the cost of peripheral products used in conjunction with your own. Engineering may be able to architect your design such that it mitigates or eliminates the need for these peripheral products. The resultant savings can be claimed as value in your product. Consider the example of a communications processor priced at $40. All such products also require $25 in external memory chips for storage of data used by the processor. Total solution cost is $65. The next generation product is designed with better code density and more efficient algorithms such that all the data can be stored on-chip, thus eliminating the need for the external memory chip. Solution cost is reduced from $65 to $40. Without changing the cost of the product itself in order to enable a profitable reduction in your price, you have provided $25 in cost savings to the customer.

- *Reliability*: Product reliability is a chief concern of most customers – it needs to simply work so they can concentrate less on your product and more on what they do. By estimating the mean time to failure and average product lifetime of both existing and new products, you can define value based on:
  - o Less down time, in the form of both the loaded cost of a user and the opportunity cost of their activities.
  - o Less service cost, in the form of the cost of an individual with the necessary skills to service the product.
  - o Less frequent replacement cost due having to purchase new products less frequently

An illustrative example is that of a $5,000 product which typically requires two repair visits per year to replace a component. Each of these visits costs about $500, and user downtime is estimated at $1,000 per occurrence. Over the three year life of the product, the total cost of ownership is $14,000. A new product is designed to require, on average, only one service visit during the product entire operational life. The value of this increase in reliability can be reasonably claimed to be $7,500.

It should be clear to you that in order to price on value, you must have intimate knowledge of the customers' usage environment. Without this knowledge, it is very difficult to quantify how much a customer would value the product's attributes. The solution is simple: spend lots of time with your customers asking probing questions about their usage environment. Don't be afraid to appear uninformed. Let them know that you are looking for ways to give them a better product. They will often open up to you once they understand there could be benefit in it for them.

## Step 2: Factor in Alternatives

If products could be priced solely on their own value, this exercise would be much easier. Some truly revolutionary products can achieve this. With a very high level of value and differentiation, the pricing exercise can, to some degree, begin with a clean sheet. But rarely will you find such a situation – there is nearly always some alternative to your product to use as a reference point that needs to be factored in. The most obvious alternative is a comparable product from the competition. If it offers roughly the same attributes, its price will often set the anchor. Another alternative for a customer is simply to stick with existing products rather than up-selling to the new product you are offering. Existing products are stable and prices are often declining due to multiple competitors catching up. In either case, there is a baseline of functionality offered by the alternatives. The total value of the new product being offered is the value represented by the baseline functionality plus the value of the new, unique functionality. Thus, the price of a new product is determined by the price point set by the alternatives plus the price premium commanded by the product's new and differentiated attributes.

To accurately factor in the alternatives, you must first estimate the price curve for the base level of functionality available today. Ask yourself, "If today's product continued to be sold as-is, what would it have to sell for in order to continue to win business?" Expect this curve to show a downward slope as commoditization sets in over time. You should also factor in new entrants to the market, especially if there are few barriers to entry such as intellectual property, capital investment, or sales channels. Also expect these new competitors to lead with price to overcome obvious deficits such as lack of incumbency and field testing. Even at the risk of draining the profitability out of the entire market, like moths to a light they will still try. Each new competitor entering the market can reasonably be expected to impact the prevailing price point by 10-30%. They need not even have a credible product – customers often just form an anchor on the lowest price they hear from the vendor base. Finally, consider the Second Order Effects of your own eventual pricing strategy – would competitors drop their price even further to combat your value story? With all of these considerations in mind, map the anticipated price curve as shown in Figure 12.1:

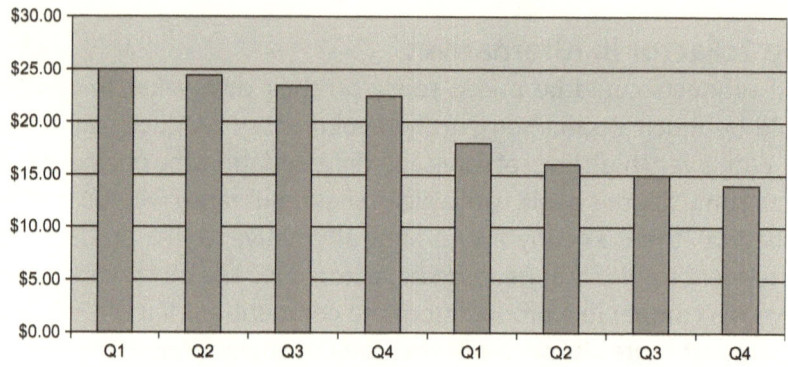

*Figure 12.1: Price Curve for Baseline Functionality*

Next, quantify the specific value assignable to each new feature (i.e. a price premium over baseline functionality) per the discussion in the previous section. But be aware of a key principle: your price premium will always be less than the value you calculated for the feature. Assuming the customer agrees with your quantification, they'll likely expect to share at least half the savings with you.

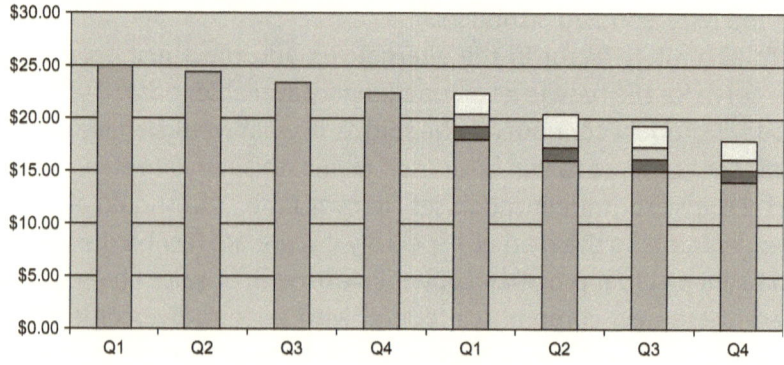

*Figure 12.2: Price Premium for New Features*

Note that there is a maxim that states that within a given product category, **it can be very difficult to charge more for new technology. Often, the best you can do is charge the same for new technology or less for the same technology**. If you are assuming that your incremental value raises the price of the new product significantly above that of the old, you'll need to make doubly sure that the value is significant enough to justify it because customers will automatically resist it.

There are a number of benefits from this graphical approach:
- It clearly shows how the next-generation product will be price positioned versus today's alternatives.
- It drives critical thought on how customers value each of the new features.
- It shows the construction of the price from the bottom up, instead of just a single number which represents the product manager's "guess". This makes for a more defensible pricing plan.
- It allows easier tradeoff analysis between features, schedule, and cost. If a particular feature drives little price premium, but is causing significant cost or schedule impact, this graphical approach can help you spot that quickly.

## Step 3: Consider Other Factors
Value and alternatives (in that order) should always play the dominant role in determining your pricing plan. But of course there are other relevant factors:
- *Price Elasticity*: this is the degree to which sales volume increases as pricing is reduced within a certain market segment. **It is important to understand the purchase barriers within a particular segment**. If price is the barrier, it suggests that elasticity is high and customers would start buying if price is reduced (causing volume to go up). The "buy" threshold for each individual buyer may be concentrated on natural price points, leading to step function curves; or it may be spread over a range of prices, leading to a smooth curve. As Figure 12.3 shows, reducing the price leads to a steadily increasing sales volume. Although the buying threshold is diffuse, it appears that the $6 price point is significant, as the slope of the curve increases below it.

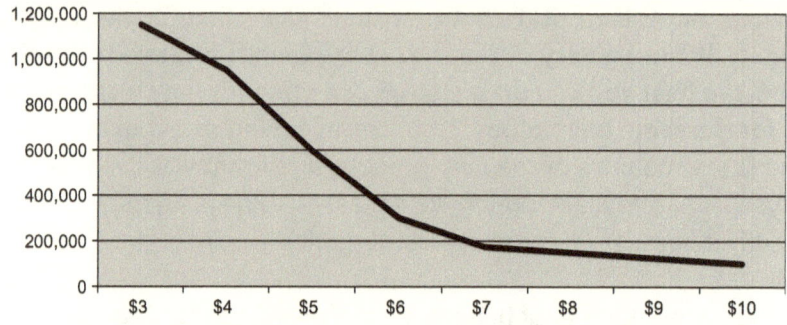

*Figure 12.3: Sales Volume vs. Price for Elastic Market*

This is in contrast to a non-elastic market, where price drops will not cause a corresponding increase in sales volume. This is shown in Figure 12.4. This is usually the case when price is not the last major barrier to a buying decision. Either the product or technology is not applicable to the market segment, or the customers in that segment simply haven't begun to appreciate the usefulness and applicability of the technology.

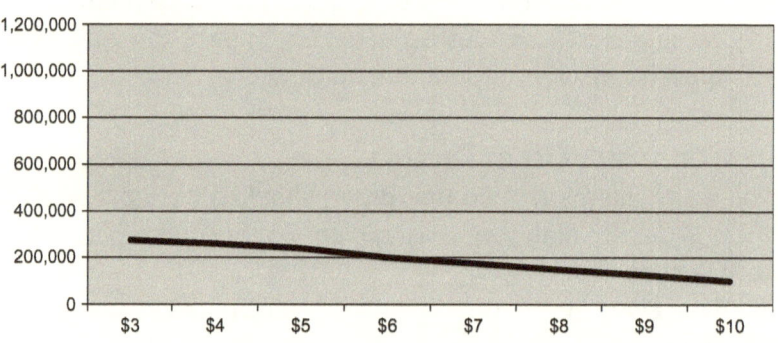

*Figure 12.4: Sales Volume vs. Price for Inelastic Market*

As you introduce new technology into your product, one choice to be made is whether to position it as a premium feature, or try to drive it into the mainstream. Your choice must be consistent with the elasticity characteristics of the market segment. **Positioning new technology at a premium is known as a skimming strategy.** It targets a market segment which both understands and values higher performance, functionality, or reliability. You harvest (or skim) profit from a premium segment that is willing to pay for the technology. A skimming strategy can be effective in a market segment with low elasticity. Price is not the last barrier to adoption; rather, the mainstream of the segment does not yet value the technology. Stable, premium pricing can often be achieved because competitors are not motivated to bomb pricing in order to drive volume or gain market share; instead, the game is played on premium technology.

In an elastic market, the dynamic can be different. Competitors are rewarded for driving down the price point because it can drive higher volume. They are willing to trade lower margins for increased volume or market share. This motivates competitors to use a particularly effective offensive tactic: driving premium technology into the mainstream market segment at a mainstream price. The effect can be highly disruptive; customers can now have next-generation capabilities for what they are paying today. Competition can be made obsolete very rapidly. Those caught unprepared for this disruptive change could require an entire product design cycle to catch up. In a highly elastic market, your pricing assumptions should account for the fact that someone may try this tactic; you may even be the one to initiate it. If this is the case, assume that prices can freefall rapidly.

- *Schedule*: The first product to market can often enjoy monopoly status until competitive products are available. Pricing pressure is minimal due to the lack of competition. In contrast, a product that is late relative to competition or the market window may have to lead with price in order to gain a foothold in the market and overcome a lack of incumbency, field testing, and brand name. Those evaluating your product for their company know that their reputation is on the line with the purchase decision. Therefore, they have little personal incentive to choose your late product, even if it is superior. Differentiated and valuable features may help, but what will really overcome being late is a lower price. Thus, a product's schedule relative to the alternatives is an important factor in the pricing picture.

- *Macroeconomy*: The marketing of a product always takes place against the backdrop of the overall spending environment. Macroeconomic conditions are very relevant, whether on a global, regional, industry, company, or personal level. In tough times, budgets for product purchases will dry up. Marketing will need to assess where the product fits into the customer's "budget hierarchy". If it is a luxury or discretionary item, chances are it will be the first type of purchase postponed. Premium pricing strategies may be hampered in such an environment. These conditions are also less conducive to revolutionary products, as purchasers tend to get more conservative during times of tighter spending. Such economic conditions typically require more aggressive pricing in order to stimulate sales.

- *Product Cost*: Marketing all too commonly uses their product cost as a prime determinant of pricing decisions. The target price is simply calculated using the cost estimate from Operations and the corporate margin target from Finance. This straightforward yet unsophisticated method is not recommended because it is completely disconnected from the market. Product managers strive to create value such that they can exercise strong pricing power. Why settle for a cost-based method that has no connection to that value? One is tempted into this path out of pure laziness. It takes hard work to quantify the value of a product and then market it to customers. The easy way out is to make a simple calculation, then win business by offering a low price. There may seem to be little downside – the process doesn't require much effort and it makes the finance community happy by hitting the target margins. The problem is that is does not maximize the return on the company's investment in the product. **A cost-based price is nearly always going to be lower than a price based on a strong value proposition coupled with a strong marketing effort.** This may not hold for fully commoditized markets, but until that point is reached one should continue to strive for a value-based pricing strategy. In fact, in his book "Marketing High Technology", William Davidow goes so far as to say that Marketing shouldn't even be told what their product cost is. They should focus on establishing value in the customer's mind, and setting pricing based on what the market will bear. While this is likely difficult in practice – the central role of the product managers makes it hard to isolate them from cost information – it does emphasize the need to exert yourself in the pursuit of value-based pricing.

## Conclusion

Establishing pricing intent early in the process, in the form of a Strategic Pricing Plan, is very important. Not only does it produce defensible financial analysis assumptions, but it helps crystallize the value proposition of the product. **Money is the truth serum of business – if you believe something has value then you should be able to demonstrate why people would pay for it**. By translating features and value into the language of pricing, you help justify the need for certain product requirements. And by going through this process early, you can still make the necessary changes to the product definition or positioning necessary to support this pricing plan. A plan which comprehends all of the various factors discussed above should be quite defensible against the scrutiny of a tough audience during the Concept and Product Approval presentation meetings.

## Pricing Strategy: Real World Example

With the product definition settled and a good picture of how it stacked up against the competition, the team considered how to price the product. They knew that pricing power was everything – without it they were doomed to commoditization, and without overwhelming advantage in the product definition they would never get it. So creation of this pricing analysis would be an early indicator of their fate. They decided to start with the product that would be targeted at the laptop segment.

Mason was not creating an entirely new category of product. It was building on an existing product line and adding features and functionality. So there was certainly an anchor that would exist in the customer's mind – the price of the existing product. They would need to map the price that today's baseline level of functionality could command going forward. Because new competition would be entering the market with this set of functionality and existing competitors would continue to add new functionality, this price curve would drop precipitously. In fact, they predicted that when a new market window opened up in five quarters, the product category would experience an approximate 20% price drop across the board for today's functionality. This was significant because the typical price drop from quarter to quarter was about 2%.

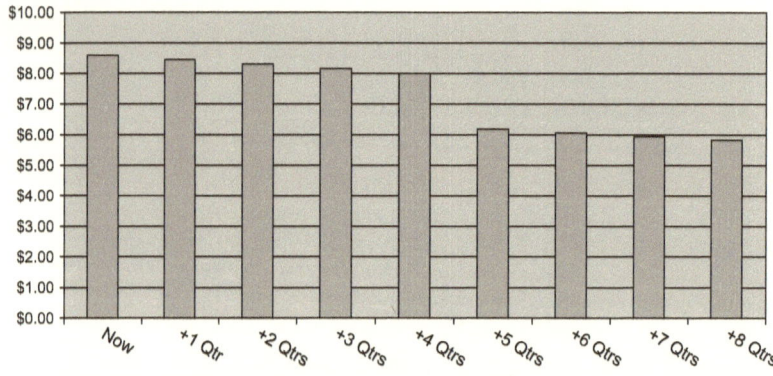

*Figure 12.5: Pricing for Today's Functionality*

With this baseline established, the incremental value of the product could be assessed. One item that was relatively straightforward to quantify was the value of reducing the external components used along with Mason. Earlier analysis had shown a reduction of $0.53 relative to the current product and

174

*that of the competition. One can never claim the entire savings in their price, but it was decided to try to claim half of it. This represented a $0.26 premium.*

*The evaluation of the TPM was next. There were external TPM chips that could be used, but they cost approximately $4.00. This price was essentially prohibitive to mainstream deployment. So integration of the functionality didn't necessarily represent a $4.00 savings because it wasn't being deployed at that price. So a different logic would need to be used. What was important was to assess the price point that would enable mainstream adoption. After talking with customers and doing some analysis on previous technologies, it was determined that at $1.00 TPM would be deployed widely. Not exactly scientific, but the value of TPM was thus established as a $1.00 premium.*

*Finally, the value of Cable Sensing Mode, or Intelligent Power, was analyzed. This would be tricky. There was no direct metric for the value of a minute of battery life. But one could make an indirect quantification. It turns out that most PC OEMs offered both six cell nickel-cadmium batteries that typically last four hours, but had a more expensive option for a nine cell lithium-ion battery that lasted six hours. Some research showed that the latter cost $7.50 more to the PC OEM. So it could be asserted that the value of a minute of battery life was $0.06. Thus a full ten minutes of battery life would be worth $0.60. Mason could possibly claim half of that value for a premium of about $0.30. There was also strategic value of the positive exposure of winning a PC magazine battery life test against other PCs, but that would be nearly impossible to quantify. So, the proposed price curve was now as follows:*

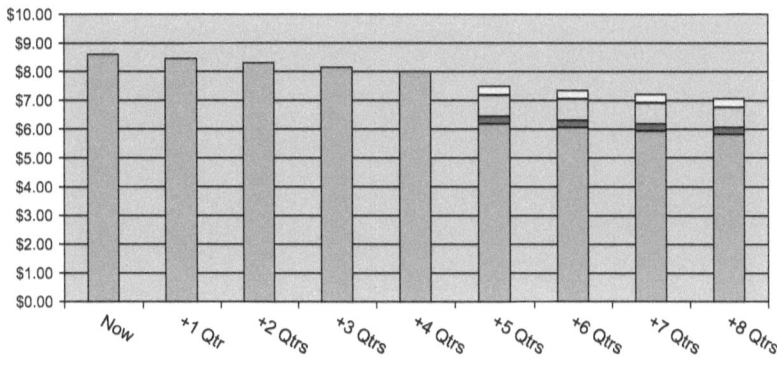

*Figure 12.6: Price Premium for Mason*

Although pricing was coming down, the new features would help keep it stable even in the face of strong competition. And decreases were still being offset by cost reductions and volume growth in the market, so this was still a profitable market going forward.

There were other factors to consider as well. Would a lower price create any elasticity effects that might increase volume and overall profitability? The answer was no. Price would have to be dropped rather sharply to open up a new tier of customers, but gross margin at that point would be wholly unacceptable. Regarding schedule, it appeared that Mason would line up with the market window, and so there would be no need to price aggressively to encourage customers to wait. And finally, the macroeconomic picture needed to be considered. The global economy and PC sales had been strong for three years, but talk of recession loomed. This would surely depress PC sales and cause OEMs to look for greater cost concessions from their vendors. In response, Marketing decided to lower their worst case pricing scenario and the low end of the sensitivity analysis from -8% to -12%.

# Checklist

## Does pricing power dominate every product decision?

Differentiation and value (or lack thereof) directly determine pricing power. Smart organizations use a Strategic Pricing Plan as an early check.

## What to Look For:

- A Strategic Pricing Plan is used to give early indicators of pricing power
- Projects are not approved if they cannot show defensible pricing power

## Is the Pricing Strategy value-based?

Pricing based solely on cost or external reference points is always a poor strategy; pricing based on value tends to be higher and more justifiable.

## What to Look For:

- User benefits and value have been quantified into monetary terms
- Effects of alternatives, schedule, elasticity, etc on pricing are factored in

*(Further discussion on this checklist available at www.systemnotcircumstance.com)*

# CHAPTER 13:

## Financial Analysis

*The basic nature of a product company is simple: money is invested in those projects which are expected to produce the best returns. Since great products make great companies, the viability of an organization rests on making the right investment decisions. Projects are judged on their financial merit, relative to specified metrics and other potential projects. The secret to doing this process well is three fold. First, great organizations exercise discipline in their assumptions, questioning and validating them until confidence in accuracy is high. Second, they know which tools to use and how to do so properly, combining the rigor of analysis with experienced judgment. Finally, they make use of tools that account for the inherent uncertainty in any prediction of the future.*

## The Input Variables

Every financial analysis tool consists of three elements: the input variables, the model, and the output variables (also referred to as metrics). A big part of the input variables are the profit being made (inflows) as well as the money being spent (outflows). The constituent parts of the inflows are:

- *Volume*: The market segmentation analysis (discussed in Chapter 6 "Market Segmentation") will have yielded volume estimates.
- *Price*: The pricing strategy (discussed in Chapter 12 "Pricing Strategy) will have yielded pricing assumptions.
- *Cost*: The cost analysis (discussed in Chapter 9 "Cost") will have yielded product cost assumptions.

These three items can of course be used to calculate the profit inflows for the project. But to correctly model these inflows, **you have to recognize the risk that they may never actually materialize**. There are two primary types of risk: execution risk that the company cannot deliver the product on time, and market risk that the business cannot be won. A project with a $20M return and low risk is clearly more attractive than a project with a $25M return but a 50% chance of failure. So a characterization of risk must be attached to the inflows being modeled. The method that the business world accepts is to model risk in terms of a percentage (this will be discussed below). By doing so, it allows the income flows across projects of differing risk level to be accurately compared to one another. Therefore, risk is the fourth variable necessary to model inflows.

Next, the outflows – the costs of developing and marketing the product – will be modeled. Some are obvious, such as the R&D costs. But sometimes significant costs are overlooked and omitted, causing Profit and Loss (P&L) spending surprises down the road. The Finance team needs to play a strong role in pushing Marketing and Sales to account for all costs upfront. With everyone playing by the same rules, no single project is disadvantaged simply because its proponents did a more thorough job of anticipating and modeling their costs. Here are the typical outflows identified in financial analysis:

- *Development Costs*: Otherwise known as R&D costs, this is what it costs Engineering to develop the product. These are mostly driven by the cost of people, or headcount, but may also include equipment purchase costs. Engineering will create an estimate based on the product definition given to them.

- *Sustaining Costs*: R&D costs get the product to production, but often overlooked are the significant amount of resources to sustain and support the product after launch. In practice this can be as high as 25% of the total project cost. **Omission of sustaining costs is a common cause of underestimation of project costs**. It can also cause bigger problems. A business unit's headcount tends to be estimated as the aggregation of the headcount estimate of all active projects. Some projects are concurrent, but others run serially; the headcount from one project rolls off onto the next program. If sustaining support is overlooked, headcount will not be reserved for it. This means that sustaining engineering work will force engineers to support a program for longer than expected, meaning they cannot roll off onto the next one. This results in delays for the next program. If sustaining costs are consistently left out of the headcount analysis, the result is systemic misexecution due to chronic resource limitations.

- *Marketing Costs*: These are all of the expenditures that Marketing will need to effectively bring a product into the market. Examples may include advertising, market development funds (MDF), channel programs, literature, sales training, sales tools, demos, and tradeshow presence. These also tend to be underestimated, because most organizations don't demand that their Marketing team look that far ahead. These can range from small for an established product to enormous when seeking to unseat an incumbent or creating an entirely new product category.

- *Operations Overhead*: The Operations team performs a valuable function in support of the business plan. They put in place the manufacturing capacity (internal or external), supply line, order fulfillment, and product quality infrastructure necessary to deliver the right quantity of product at the right time. This doesn't come for free. Most Operations groups will charge their overhead as a percentage of revenue, based on historical data compiled over time. Most companies account for it in COGS (and thus reflects

in the gross margin), while some may allocate pre-production expenditures to R&D expense.

## The Models

The input variables are entered into various financial models which
will yield output variables, or metrics. Each of these will help characterize
different aspects of the project's financial viability. Each type of model
tells a different part of the story. None is perfect, but companies typically
use more than one to give a holistic picture. Here we review several common models.

Nearly every company uses a type of analysis called Net Present
Value, or NPV. It calculates the profit to be made by summing the inflows
and subtracting out the money spent to make and market the product.
Simple addition and subtraction of these monetary flows could be used if
not for two elements. First, it would not account for the risk of the inflows
not materializing. You know the outflows are going to happen *now*, but
there is inevitable execution and market risk that could prevent money
being made *later*. Second, it does not account for a concept called the
*time value of money*. This dictates that $10 today is not the same as $10
tomorrow. Let's say that instead of investing $10 today in the proposed
project, it could be invested in an alternative investment vehicle (with
a risk profile similar to the proposed project) at a 20% rate of return. It
would thus grow to $12 a year from now. In this example, $10 today is
worth $12 tomorrow, and thus $10 tomorrow is worth less than $10 to-
day. So, the inflows tomorrow need to be converted into "today's value".
This is more commonly called Present Value. The rate of growth of investment dollars (20% was used above) is called the Discount Rate, because
this is the rate at which dollars tomorrow are discounted back to today's
value.

Suppose a particular investment of $100 today could generate a
$100 per year cash payment each year for five years starting two years
from now. This can be as shown in Figure 13.1:

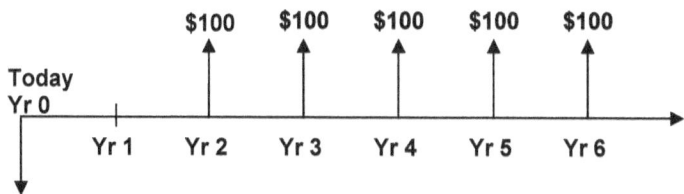

*Figure 13.1: Modeling Outflows and Inflows for NPV Analysis*

How would one determine if this is a good investment? One can't simply sum up the inflows and outflows because this wouldn't account for risk of inflows not appearing, nor the *time value of money*. So the discount rate would be used to convert future inflows into their present value. This is a relatively straightforward calculation. Apply the following formula to any in or outflow ("DR" is the Discount Rate):

$$NPV = NetDollars_{Today} + \frac{NetDollars_{Year1}}{(1+DR)^1} + \frac{NetDollars_{Year2}}{(1+DR)^2} + \frac{NetDollars_{Year3}}{(1+DR)^3} + ...$$

*Figure 13.2: Present Value Calculation*

This equation continues for as many years (or any time period chosen) as the cash flow continues. It applies both to inflows and outflows, so one would find the present value of all inflows, do the same for outflows, then subtract the latter from the former. The result is the Net Present Value. Note that this calculation can be done more easily using the NPV function available in most spreadsheet packages (in Microsoft Excel click on the "Insert" menu and choose "Function…"; select "NPV" and click on "OK"). The sum across all inflows and outflows is the NPV. Let us look at an example using various discount rates (all dollar units are in thousands):

| Project 1 | Now | Year 1 | Year 2 | Year 3 | Year 4 |
|-----------|-----|--------|--------|--------|--------|
| Revenue | | $ 8,000 | $ 11,550 | $ 2,000 | $ 450 |
| Product Cost | | $ 3,600 | $ 5,198 | $ 900 | $ 203 |
| Profit Inflows | | $ 4,400 | $ 6,353 | $ 1,100 | $ 248 |
| Expense Outflows | $ (3,000) | | | | |
| Net Cash Inflows | $ (3,000) | $ 4,400 | $ 6,353 | $ 1,100 | $ 248 |

| | |
|---|---|
| NPV @ 15% Discount Rate | $ 6,494 |
| NPV @ 25% Discount Rate | $ 5,250 |
| NPV @ 35% Discount Rate | $ 4,266 |

*Figure 13.3: NPV Calculation with Various Discount Rates*

From Figure 13.3, it is clear that a higher discount rate makes the present value smaller. Note that most of the modes in this chapter are available for download at www.systemnotcircumstance.com.

The calculation itself is relatively simple, but it is more important to understand how the model works. The first element is the nature of the discount rate and how it is chosen. The explanation starts with the concept that **risk and reward are inextricably linked** – the more risk you take, the more reward you expect if it turns out well. Companies that deal in risky technologies and markets are expected by their investors to yield a high rate of growth. The measure of risk and reward is the same – a percentage representing the expected growth rate in the company's value. Thus, the Discount Rate is the quantification of the company's or project's inherent risk. In exchange for exposure to the risk posed by an investment, investors expect the company to deliver or exceed returns commensurate with that risk. On the inside, this translates into a minimum level of return for an investment in a development project. Therein lays the reason why future cash flows are discounted back to a present value. Yes, the company could invest $100 today in the project at hand and make $120 in one year, but it could also simply invest that money in another vehicle with the same risk level and it would grow to $120 in that time frame. So that growth rate is assumed as a baseline, and thus the NPV calculation shows the value generated *over and above that*. Most companies have determined their own standard discount rate that accounts for the risk associated with its relevant technologies and markets; all projects within the company use it. Low risk industries might use 15%, high growth industries might use 25%, and more speculative ventures might use 35%. The discount rate chosen can have a great effect on the NPV of a project. That's the intent – **the NPV model allows the probability of success to be factored into an assessment of the attractiveness of a project**.

But what does this number, "NPV" really mean? Consider a project that requires $1M initial investment and shows an NPV of zero when using a discount rate of 25%. Does this mean the project is not profitable? Not at all. Rather, it indicates that given the level of risk inherent in this project (characterized by the 25%) the project exactly meets the company's growth goal of 25%. On the surface, this might appear to be a good thing. But remember that stock price and private company valuations are all based on expectations. Meeting those expectations means that you will simply maintain the present stock price or valuation. But the goal is always growth in these metrics, so the best projects are those that exceed expectations. If the aforementioned $1M investment were to yield an NPV of $2M, this would be accomplished. An NPV of zero is the equivalent of today's investment growing at the discount rate; the same result could be achieved by investing the money in the alternative investment path mentioned earlier rather than investing in the proposed project at hand. An NPV of $50 is the equivalent of $50 appearing 'magically' today and growing alongside the initial investment. By investing in a project with NPV greater than zero, the company is producing new value incremental to the expected returns.

We must also factor in the concept of opportunity cost. Even after all the projects with positive NPV are funded, one might make the argument that even projects with NPV of zero are beneficial because they are in fact making money. In a world of limitless resources, this would be possible. But in the real world the logic is flawed because it does not account for the fact that **resources are always limited and companies cannot grow headcount without bound**. The first limit is the organization's P&L, which will only support a certain number of people. The second is the fact that hiring takes time, especially if the skillsets are specialized. The third is that any geographic area will only have a finite number of workers skilled in the appropriate industry. Eventually the companies in that area consume most available workers and further growth of headcount is very difficult. So companies need to assume that there is a somewhat fixed headcount possible – the hard choices need to be made to allot them to the highest value projects. Executives are obligated to apply the company's limited resources to projects that will show extraordinary growth. Sometimes the organization simply needs to walk away from some projects, even if they are projected to be profitable.

NPV does a great job of accounting for risk and value of a project. However, **it doesn't tell the whole story on whether the required investment was appropriate to achieve that value**. There are two simple additional tools which can help. The first is *Revenue Turns*. This is simply calculated as total revenue (not discounted) divided by the total fixed expense (R&D, marketing, sustaining, but not COGS) of the program. It is a characterization of the revenue that can be generated relative to the money spent to get it. Unlike NPV, the absolute value of this number does not mean anything. It is only meaningful relative to a corporate bench-mark. This benchmark is good at highlighting the *relative* worth of the project. Let's say there are two projects, each with an NPV of $5.25M, as shown in figure 13.4:

| Project 1 | Now | Year 1 | Year 2 | Year 3 | Year 4 |
|---|---|---|---|---|---|
| Revenue | | $ 8,000 | $ 11,550 | $ 2,000 | $ 450 |
| Product Cost | | $ 3,600 | $ 5,198 | $ 900 | $ 203 |
| Profit Inflows | | $ 4,400 | $ 6,353 | $ 1,100 | $ 248 |
| Expense Outflows | $ (3,000) | | | | |
| Net Cash Inflows | $ (3,000) | $ 4,400 | $ 6,353 | $ 1,100 | $ 248 |

| | | |
|---|---|---|
| NPV (@25%) | $ | 5,250 |
| Total Revenue | $ | 22,000 |
| **Revenue Turns** | | **7.3** |

| Project 2 | Now | Year 1 | Year 2 | Year 3 | Year 4 |
|---|---|---|---|---|---|
| Revenue | | $ 4,253 | $ 7,000 | $ 6,000 | $ 1,000 |
| Product Cost | | $ 1,914 | $ 3,150 | $ 2,700 | $ 450 |
| Profit Inflows | | $ 2,339 | $ 3,850 | $ 3,300 | $ 550 |
| Expense Outflows | $ (1,000) | | | | |
| Net Cash Inflows | $ (1,000) | $ 2,339 | $ 3,850 | $ 3,300 | $ 550 |

| | | |
|---|---|---|
| NPV (@25%) | $ | 5,250 |
| Total Revenue | $ | 18,253 |
| **Revenue Turns** | | **18.3** |

*Figure 13.4: Comparison of Revenue Turns*

Using NPV, it would be difficult to determine the better project. One could look at revenue, possibly preferring $22.0M to $18.2M. But this doesn't show the whole picture. You would need to dig deeper to dis-tinguish between the two. Notice that the first project requires a $3M investment to generate $22M of revenue and an NPV of $5.25M, while the second only requires a $1M investment to generate the same NPV, albeit with less revenue. Now which project is better? Most would conclude that the smaller investment is better – less outlay to create just as much value. The NPV number alone would not have highlighted this, but the Revenue Turns metric would have (18.3 vs. 7.3, with higher being better). This sim-ple indicator provides a sanity check on the absolute numbers involved, before they get a bit more obscured by the NPV formula.

Similar to this is the metric known as *Gross Margin Turns*, or GM Turns. This is calculated by dividing the total gross margin (revenue minus the COGS) by the expense number. This is a characterization of the amount of profit that can be generated by spending a certain amount of money. It provides further insight over and above that of the prior two metrics. Let's again look at our original Project 1, but now compare it to another project with higher revenue and NPV, as shown in Figure 13.5:

| Project 1 | Now | Year 1 | Year 2 | Year 3 | Year 4 |
|---|---|---|---|---|---|
| Revenue | | $ 8,000 | $ 11,550 | $ 2,000 | $ 450 |
| Product Cost | | $ 3,600 | $ 5,198 | $ 900 | $ 203 |
| Profit Inflows | | $ 4,400 | $ 6,353 | $ 1,100 | $ 248 |
| Expense Outflows | $ (3,000) | | | | |
| Net Cash Inflows | $ (3,000) | $ 4,400 | $ 6,353 | $ 1,100 | $ 248 |

| | |
|---|---|
| NPV (@25%) | $ 5,250 |
| Total Gross Profit | $ 12,100 |
| GM Turns | 4.0 |

| Project 2 | Now | Year 1 | Year 2 | Year 3 | Year 4 |
|---|---|---|---|---|---|
| Revenue | | $ 18,000 | $ 20,000 | $ 11,000 | $ 4,500 |
| Product Cost | | $ 11,700 | $ 13,000 | $ 7,150 | $ 2,925 |
| Profit Inflows | | $ 6,300 | $ 7,000 | $ 3,850 | $ 1,575 |
| Expense Outflows | $ (6,500) | | | | |
| Net Cash Inflows | $ (6,500) | $ 6,300 | $ 7,000 | $ 3,850 | $ 1,575 |

| | |
|---|---|
| NPV (@25%) | $ 5,636 |
| Total Gross Profit | $ 18,725 |
| GM Turns | 2.9 |

*Figure 13.5: Comparison of GM Turns*

Project 1 again shows a $3M investment yielding an NPV of $5.25M with a gross profit of $12.1M. Project 2 uses a $6.5M investment to generate an impressive NPV of $5.6M and a gross profit of $18.7M, about 50% higher than that of Project 1. The latter is clearly superior, right? Not necessarily. The ratio of profit to expense – the GM Turn – is significantly lower (2.9 vs. 4.0). The profit generating power of a dollar of investment for Project 2 is less, mainly because it is being invested in a lower margin product as can be seen in the numbers in Figure 13.5. Many corporations don't solely look at the absolute profit dollars, but also at how hard it is to generate that profit. GM Turns help highlight this attribute by quantifying it in a simple metric. It is a useful tool to identify where spending is too high relative to the resultant profits.

**Both of these "turns" analyses tend to put a lot of focus on the expense portion of the project**. If either is below the corporate threshold, it should be an indicator for the team to circle back and re-examine the expense. The Engineering team may want to run the estimates again to make sure they are correct. The Marketing team may also want to consider removing features that are significant drivers of the development cost.

## Accounting for Uncertainty

In each of our models so far, a set of static input variables has produced a set of static metrics which are used to make conclusions about the project. But the input variables are only best guesses. What happens when reality turns out much differently, as is likely in most cases? Could the decision on the project change? Yes, it could, and so **the modeling effort must be able to account for this inherent uncertainty**. Relevant scenarios can be characterized with simple questions: "What if you only achieve 50% of your volume targets?" "What if you can't charge as much as you estimated?" "What if the competition comes out with a similar product?" Each of these questions will need to be modeled in terms of changes to the input variables and subsequent changes to the output metrics.

There are four primary methods of doing this, each displaying increasing level of detail and accuracy. Early in the Concept Stage, uncertainty is high. The situation only calls for gross indicators of a project's viability. This is where the first type of our tools, *Breakeven Analysis*, comes in handy. This tool is used to determine the specific value of a particular input variable which makes a particular metric reach the stated threshold of unacceptability (the term "Breakeven" is not used literally). Let's suppose that the corporate minimums for output metrics are as follows:

- NPV: $10M
- Revenue Turns: 10
- GM Turns: 5

Let us further suppose that we have a product that will sell for an initial price of $17.00 (dropping 9% per year), yielding an NPV of $15.8M and strong Revenue and GM Turns. A likely question to be asked is "At what starting price does the NPV become unacceptable?" You can do this by changing the initial price in the model until the NPV hits the designated threshold, in this case $10M. The analysis shows that if the initial Average Selling Price (ASP) turns out to be $14.41 (a drop of about 15%), then the project would begin to look unattractive according to the NPV variable (although other variables should be analyzed as well).

| Nominal ASP | Now | Year 1 | Year 2 | Year 3 | Year 4 |
|---|---|---|---|---|---|
| Volume | - | 1,000 | 1,250 | 1,563 | 1,953 |
| ASP | | $ 17.00 | $ 15.47 | $ 14.08 | $ 12.81 |
| Revenue | $ - | $ 17,000 | $ 19,338 | $ 21,996 | $ 25,021 |
| Product Cost | | $ 6,800 | $ 7,735 | $ 8,799 | $ 10,008 |
| Profit Inflows | $ - | $ 10,200 | $ 11,603 | $ 13,198 | $ 15,013 |
| Expense Outflows | $ (7,000) | | | | |
| NPV (@25%) | $ 15,794 | | | | |
| Total Revenue | $ 83,355 | | | | |
| Total Profit | $ 50,013 | | | | |
| Revenue Turn | 11.9 | | | | |
| GM Turn | 7.1 | | | | |

| Breakeven ASP | Now | Year 1 | Year 2 | Year 3 | Year 4 |
|---|---|---|---|---|---|
| Volume | | 1,000 | 1,250 | 1,563 | 1,953 |
| ASP | | $ 14.41 | $ 13.11 | $ 11.93 | $ 10.86 |
| Revenue | | $ 14,407 | $ 16,388 | $ 18,642 | $ 21,205 |
| Product Cost | | $ 6,800 | $ 7,735 | $ 8,799 | $ 10,008 |
| Profit Inflows | $ - | $ 7,607 | $ 8,653 | $ 9,843 | $ 11,197 |
| Expense Outflows | $ (7,000) | | | | |
| NPV (@25%) | $ 10,000 | | | | |
| Total Revenue | $ 70,643 | | | | |
| Total Profit | $ 37,301 | | | | |
| Revenue Turn | 10.1 | | | | |
| GM Turn | 5.3 | | | | |

*Figure 13.6: Breakeven Analysis*

Thankfully, Microsoft Excel provides us a useful tool to perform this analysis. It is called Goal Seek, found in the "Tools" menu. You simply highlight the cell showing the NPV value, select the "Tools" menu, and click on "Goal Seek". In the field labeled "To Value", enter the NPV threshold value (in this case, $10M). Move the cursor to the next field down, "By Changing Cell", and click on the cell containing the starting price variable (the prices in subsequent years are tied to the starting price in the spreadsheet). Then click "OK". Excel will quickly calculate the price which makes the NPV reach $10M (this is much easier than manual trial and error).

The specific value $14.41 is not so important at this early stage where accuracy is low. More interesting is how far the nominal assumption needed to change in order to hit this "breakeven point". If price only had to drop by 10%, it is an indication that the plan is not very robust to errors in your price assumptions. In contrast, if NPV reaches the threshold only after a 50% reduction in price variable, you know that your financial picture is not particularly sensitive to changes in price. In general, you are looking for sensitivities to particular variables that could cause certain metrics thresholds not to be met. Your Breakeven Analysis then concludes with the following question: "Do I expect the input variable to ever reach this breakeven point?" **This type of binary inquiry relieves you from necessarily having to guess the specific values at this early, hazy stage.** If the answer is no, then you can demonstrate confidence in the plan. If your answer is yes or maybe, then it is an indication that the plan may need some more work.

As the project proposal moves into the Product Definition Phase, greater levels of accuracy are possible (and required). An appropriate tool is *Scenario Analysis.* Here, you construct a small set of possible values for each input variable of interest, typically consisting of nominal, worst case, and best case assumptions. Using the same example as in Figure 13.6, we can construct tables for each input variable being changed as shown in Figure 13.7:

| ASP | | | |
|---|---|---|---|
| Scenario | Yr 1 ASP | NPV | GM Turns |
| Worst Case | $ 12.00 | $ 4,620 | 3.6 |
| Nominal | $ 17.00 | $ 15,794 | 7.1 |
| Best Case | $ 22.00 | $ 26,967 | 10.6 |

| Volume | | | |
|---|---|---|---|
| Scenario | Yr 1 Volume | NPV | GM Turn |
| Worst Case | 700 | $ 8,956 | 5.0 |
| Nominal | 1,000 | $ 15,794 | 7.1 |
| Best Case | 1,250 | $ 21,492 | 8.9 |

| Expense | | | |
|---|---|---|---|
| Scenario | Expense | NPV | GM Turns |
| Worst Case | $ 9,000 | $ 13,794 | 5.6 |
| Nominal | $ 7,000 | $ 15,794 | 7.1 |
| Best Case | $ 6,500 | $ 16,294 | 7.7 |

*Figure 13.7: Scenario Analysis*

For even further granularity, *Sensitivity Analysis* can be used. Instead of input variables taking on discrete values associated with scenarios, they are varied over a continuous range of values. The result is total visibility

of how the metrics will change as a result. Performing this analysis manually would be quite tedious; luckily, Excel saves us again with the "Table"
feature. Begin by deciding which input variable you would like to vary, as
was done in the example shown in Figure 13.7. Then decide the metrics
of interest. Create column headers with the name of the metrics. Below
each, enter an "=", then click on the metric in the model (to create a reference to that cell in the model). Now, down the left side of your table,
create a list of the values for the input variable of interest. Highlight the
entire table (which is currently empty) from the "Data" menu select "Table".
A dialogue box will open. Place the cursor in the field labeled "Column
Input Cell". This is asking you to identify the cell containing the input variable of interest in your model; click on this cell and press "OK". Your table
will immediately populate with values of the metrics which correspond to
each value of the input variable ("Yr 1 ASP"), as shown in Figure 13.8:

| Yr 1 ASP | NPV | Rev Turns | GM Turns |
|---|---|---|---|
| $ 15.00 | $ 11,324 | 10.5 | 5.7 |
| $ 16.00 | $ 13,559 | 11.2 | 6.4 |
| $ 17.00 | $ 15,794 | 11.9 | 7.1 |
| $ 18.00 | $ 18,028 | 12.6 | 7.8 |
| $ 19.00 | $ 20,263 | 13.3 | 8.5 |
| $ 20.00 | $ 22,498 | 14.0 | 9.2 |
| $ 21.00 | $ 24,732 | 14.7 | 9.9 |
| $ 22.00 | $ 26,967 | 15.4 | 10.6 |
| $ 23.00 | $ 29,202 | 16.1 | 11.3 |
| $ 24.00 | $ 31,436 | 16.8 | 12.0 |
| $ 25.00 | $ 33,671 | 17.5 | 12.7 |
| $ 26.00 | $ 35,906 | 18.2 | 13.4 |
| $ 27.00 | $ 38,140 | 18.9 | 14.1 |
| $ 28.00 | $ 40,375 | 19.6 | 14.8 |
| $ 29.00 | $ 42,610 | 20.3 | 15.6 |

*Figure 13.8: Sensitivity Analysis*

Sensitivity Analysis is very powerful – you have total control over the
mathematics. Yet, **it stills leave out one element: *probability***. While you
can vary the input variables over an expected range, it treats each value as
equally likely. But this is not reflective of reality. Presumably the nominal
value is most likely, while probability drops as the variable's value devi-

ates farther from it. To accurately model this, you could represent an input variable as a probability distribution instead of a one-dimensional range of values. This would reflect the probability of occurrence of each value within the range. With the right tool, those probabilities would cascade through the mathematical model and create an output metric that is also a probability distribution. Such a tool does exist: it is called *Monte Carlo Simulation*. Returning to the example above, the two main input variables of interest were price and volume. These were fed into a model to produce NPV and GM Turn metrics. If volume and price were instead expressed as probability distributions as shown in Figure 13.9, then a Monte Carlo simulation would produce an NPV that would also be expressed as a probability distribution.

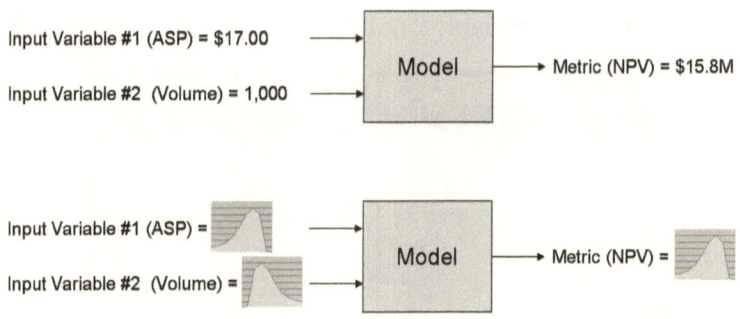

*Figure 13.9: Monte Carlo Simulation*

If only one input variable was modeled as a distribution, this could be done manually. Each value of the input variable would have an associated probability, and that probability would be directly assigned a resultant output metric value. But when two input variables are represented by distributions, the combinatorials get too large to handle manually. This is where Monte Carlo simulation comes in. It works as follows: a value for each input variable is chosen at random from the distribution (with, of course, higher probability values more likely to be chosen), and a value for the metric is calculated. This is then repeated some statistically significant number of times – assume 100,000 iterations (thankfully there are some Excel plug-in software packages, such as *@Risk*, which will perform this analysis). The result will be a distribution for the metric which reflects the unique probability characteristics of the input variables. **This type of**

**characterization of a metric gives a more insightful and realistic representation of the probabilities and risks associated with the project.** But be warned that many in the audience may not understand how this works or what the results mean. Be sure to explain it carefully so the message is not lost on them.

## Conclusion

Financial analysis is such an important part of the product planning effort because it is *the* litmus test for the project's viability. All personal feeling about the product and its merits take a back seat to dispassionate, rigorous analysis. Quantifying a complex situation and accounting for natural uncertainty both help support the making of a good investment decision. But this comes with a word of caution. These numbers can become like the siren's song, tempting us into using them with overconfidence. **The precision of a number should never be confused for its accuracy.** Numbers provide a crisp representation that makes the decisions easier to make; yet they can just as easily mislead if they are wrong. Sometimes this is the case simply out of sloppiness. In some cases Marketing so badly wants the product to happen that they unconsciously bias the numbers to the positive side. That is why it is so important for an organization to have proper checks and balances on the financial analysis. A healthy but skeptical interplay between Marketing, Engineering, Finance, and Sales on the assumptions and analysis can help vet out the myths and inconsistencies before the project goes before Management.

# Financial Analysis: Real World Example

*The final phase of the analysis involved evaluating Mason's financial viability. Luckily most of the information required was already in place. Cost and price estimates had already been made by Marketing. The R&D expense was also known because Engineering had completed their resource planning. Just a few more data points remained to be determined. The first was the estimate of sales volume for Mason. The target market segments were highly concentrated among approximately 10 PC OEM customers, so the best type of volume forecast would be bottoms up. The TAM analysis was relatively straightforward, as the volumes of each PC OEM were available from market research firms and also relatively stable. This was the easy part – the hard part was to estimate a share of market. At the most basic level they would simply assume which customers they would win. But because the market was so concentrated, any changes to these assumptions would cause large swings in the financials. This would need to be considered later, but for now, the nominal assumptions were created as shown in Figure 13.10:*

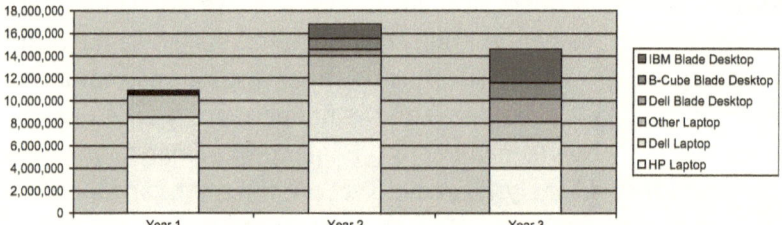

*Figure 13.10: Mason Sales Volume Assumptions*

*Next, the team needed to characterize the risk level of the program. If they were to do this "from scratch" it would be a very complex exercise. But the corporation had already determined that the standard risk rate was 25% – a return that TechCorp's investors felt was commensurate with the risk of a semiconductor company in these particular markets. This didn't necessarily account for Mason's specific risk profile, but the corporation felt that using different discount rates across projects would be too hard to manage.*

*The Engineering team had provided their R&D expense estimate. It was a large number – $21.3M over three years. Much of this was driven by the need to develop the TPM technology from scratch, making this expense number larger than for a typical project. It was also necessary to include a full* estimate of marketing expenses for the life of the program. The Finance Director was adamant that these be forecasted up front. He was frustrated because this hadn't been done on the last project, and there had been nearly $1M in surprise expenditure requests from Marketing. The following was estimated:

1. TPM software licensing ($590K)
2. Two white papers ($12K)
3. TPM certifications ($42K)
4. Four tradeshows ($48K)
5. Performance testing ($8K)

These marketing expenses totaling $700K were added to the development expenses, making a total of $22M.

Now that the input variables were all quantified, it was now time to run the models. The standard NPV, Revenue Turns, and GM Turns models were completed, yielding the following:

- Revenue: $291M
- NPV: $84.3M
- Revenue Turns: 13.2
- GM Turns: 7.3

Now, they needed to analyze these numbers. The Marketing team sat down with Finance and tried to make sense of them. The NPV was a clear winner relative to other projects being considered – $84.3M certainly looked very healthy. The company standard of 11.0 for Revenue Turns was also easily exceeded – so far, so good. GM Turns were also greater than the required threshold, but not by much. This would warrant further scrutiny.

The marketers were feeling rather proud of themselves for having such a promising opportunity in front of them. But it was the Finance analyst's job to burst their bubble. He asked a very simple question: "What happens if some of your assumptions are wrong?" Could it make some of the metrics drop below the target value? Marketers never like to admit this is the case, but they grudgingly agreed to perform some Scenario Analysis to prove that the business case would still be robust even if some assumptions were wrong. Although they could do this on every output variable, they decided to focus on a few. They chose NPV because it is the most comprehensive metric (corporate threshold was $20M), and GM Turns because the nominal value of 7.3 was so close to the corporate threshold of 7.

*The input variable examined was volume. Although macroeconomic conditions might depress sales a bit, the far more significant risk was that of not capturing one or more of the customers they assumed they would. The Marketing team determined that a reasonable risk was not winning the Dell laptop business. Another risk was that the blade market would not grow as rapidly as predicted. Both events together would represent a worst case scenario for volume. The analysis yielded the following:*

| NPV on Volume Scenarios | | |
|---|---|---|
| | *Volume* | *NPV* |
| Nominal | 42,320,000 | $ 84,323,592 |
| Worst Case | 29,000,000 | $ 51,682,166 |
| Breakeven | 16,071,445 | $ 20,000,000 |

| GM Turn on Volume Scenarios | | |
|---|---|---|
| | *Volume* | *GM Turn* |
| Nominal | 42,320,000 | 7.3 |
| Worst Case | 29,000,000 | 5.0 |
| Breakeven | 40,555,589 | 7.0 |

*Figure 13.11: Scenario and Breakeven Analysis on Mason Volume*

*The analysis showed that NPV would still look reasonably healthy even in the event of a worst case volume scenario. The breakeven volume for NPV was also much lower than the worst case volume, indicating that the plan was robust to any reasonable changes in volume. But the GM Turn would fall short of the threshold if volume fell a mere 5% to 40.5 million. This was interpreted as meaning that if volume dropped sharply, the amount of gross profit generated would not justify the amount of R&D expense. The team would need to work on this to make this metric more robust to changes in volume. More on that shortly.*

*The Average Selling Price (ASP) assumptions were examined next. A worst case scenario could result if a new competitor entered the market and bombed the price of the baseline functionality. Although Marketing was very sure that no one would be able to match the differentiating features such as Cable Sensing Mode, this would still have some compression effects. A weak macroeconomic situation could apply some downward pressure as well. It was estimated that $6.60 in the laptop segment would represent a worst case pricing scenario. Little change to the blade segment pricing was expected, so it was left static in the analysis. The results were as follows:*

| NPV on ASP Scenarios | | |
|---|---|---|
| | *Year 1 ASP* | *NPV* |
| Nominal | $ 7.50 | $ 84,323,592 |
| Worst Case | $ 6.60 | $ 66,483,148 |
| Breakeven | $ 4.26 | $ 20,000,000 |

| GM Turn on ASP Scenarios | | |
|---|---|---|
| | *Year 1 ASP* | *GM Turn* |
| Nominal | $ 7.50 | 7.3 |
| Worst Case | $ 6.60 | 6.8 |
| Breakeven | $ 6.92 | 7.0 |

*Figure 13.12: Scenario and Breakeven Analysis on Mason ASP*

*Again, the NPV showed itself to be robust against changes in the assumptions. But GM Turns still looked suspect; it would fall below the corporate threshold if the ASP were to drop a mere 8%. Clearly the GM Turns were not robust to uncertainty, and deserved some attention. The team looked at how GM Turns would change if the R&D expense number were modulated:*

| GM Turn on Expense Scenarios | | |
|---|---|---|
| | *Expense* | *GM Turn* |
| Nominal+10% | $24,200,000 | 6.6 |
| Nominal-10% | $19,800,000 | 8.1 |
| Breakeven | $22,956,931 | 7.0 |

*Figure 13.13: Scenario and Breakeven Analysis on Mason Expense*

*So GM Turns would drop below the target if expense later rose by only 4% – not an uncommon scenario. Coupled with the strong NPV picture, the Finance manager concluded that Mason was a healthy project but needed to have its expense number reduced slightly. Marketing was a bit surprised that anyone would feel the need to make changes to a project with such a healthy NPV. But the Finance analyst held his ground. His reasoning was pragmatic – making a lot of money is good but the investment required to get it must be appropriate. And for better or for worse, the GM Turn was a major component of how the corporation determined what was appropriate. Better to meet the target than have to explain and justify it to senior management during the approval presentation. So Marketing and Engineering got together to brainstorm. Three ideas were put forth:*

1. *There were a few other groups in the company that would benefit from some of the technology building blocks that would be developed for the TPM. A cost-sharing agreement was negotiated such that three business units would each contribute to the funding of the TPM block and the other two business units could use the technology in their own products. This reduced the project expense by $650K.*
2. *Instead of hiring eight test engineers domestically, it was decided to hire them overseas where headcount costs were roughly 50% less. This saved another $450K.*
3. *Marketing agreed to drop some of the requirements to work with the Linux operating system. This reduced the software development and test time by about 10%, leading to a savings of approximately $150K.*

The team was thus able to reduce the project expense from $22M to $20.7M. This had the effect of raising the nominal GM Turn from 7.3 up to 7.7. Although not drastic, it did provide a bit more margin to make Finance feel comfortable. The new scenario analyses were as shown:

| NPV on ASP Scenarios | | |
|---|---|---|
| | Year 1 ASP | NPV |
| Nominal | $7.50 | $85,573,592 |
| Worst Case | $6.60 | $67,733,148 |
| Breakeven | $4.19 | $20,000,000 |

| NPV on Volume Scenarios | | |
|---|---|---|
| | Volume | NPV |
| Nominal | 42,320,000 | $85,573,592 |
| Worst Case | 29,000,000 | $52,932,166 |
| Breakeven | 15,561,357 | $20,000,000 |

| GM Turn on ASP Scenarios | | |
|---|---|---|
| | Year 1 ASP | GM Turn |
| Nominal | $7.50 | 7.7 |
| Worst Case | $6.60 | 7.3 |
| Breakeven | $6.12 | 7.0 |

| GM Turn on Volume Scenarios | | |
|---|---|---|
| | Volume | GM Turn |
| Nominal | 42,320,000 | 7.7 |
| Worst Case | 29,000,000 | 5.3 |
| Breakeven | 38,251,294 | 7.0 |

Figure 13.14: Scenario and Breakeven Analysis with Reduced Expense

The GM Turn was now much more robust to changes in the ASP, meeting the corporate threshold even in a worst case situation. The same was not quite true for changes to volume, but at least the situation was improved. The team went ahead with the numbers as they were, but the action item was taken by Marketing to work with Sales to better hone the volume assumptions to see if worst case assumption (29 million units) was too pessimistic.

# Checklist

## Have a variety of metrics been used properly?

The organization should never rely on a single metric, but rather multiple models that each gives its own perspective.

### What to Look For:

- Risk, return, time value of money have been reflected in an NPV analysis
- Expense vs. return has been assessed using Revenue and GM Turns

## Is the plan robust to all foreseeable risks?

All investment decisions are made with imperfect information, but the organization can use modeling techniques to make the best decision possible.

### What to Look For:

- Marketing has identified and quantified the program's market risks
- Sensitivity analysis shows acceptable return in all reasonable scenarios

*(Further discussion on this checklist available at www.systemnotcircumstance.com)*

# CHAPTER 14:

## Presentation Fundamentals

*In ancient Greece, the art of rhetoric was an important skill for anyone seeking to rise to a position of power. Although talent certainly helped, a large component of it was considered to be a learned ability. The same applies to one taking a product into an approval meeting. Certainly the plan must be sound, but the presentation of it is a critical part of passing. And like rhetoric, there are a known set of skills which can be learned to improve one's chances of success. Sustained success in product planning requires that products pass their approval meetings the first time – trying and failing creates too much delay and loss of confidence. Great companies use a common formula to ensure this: a consensus exists among key players before the meeting ever starts, the presentation itself is succinct and focused, and a clear decision is reached. The result is a Product Planning process which proceeds quickly and enables faster time to market.*

## Before the Presentation

Approval meetings for a product are the most important events in the planning process – but also the most stressful. This is a complex process involving numerous variables, uncertainties, and contradictions. The phase-gate process brings structure to the analysis, setting the stage for an organized approval meeting to determine if the project has enough merit to proceed. Properly conducting them and obtaining prompt approval to move ahead is critical to the organization executing its strategy. Here, some of the important principles involved in this effort will be reviewed.

Nothing derails an approval meeting faster than to have unresolved issues and debate during the meeting. This happens when all key members of the team are not fully bought into the entire plan prior to the meeting. Since Marketing usually leads the Product Planning process, it means that members of Engineering, Finance, Operations, Sales, or Applications Engineering might not be fully in the loop. Any one of these groups has the power to derail the process. Inadequate preparation beforehand to achieve consensus is the most common factor that prevents approval of a project. Again referencing the Sun Tzu quote, "Every battle is won before it is ever fought". This suggests one of the most important principles in product planning: **You must have full implicit agreement <u>before</u> the meeting, such that the meeting itself is just a formality**. There should be no suspense as to the meeting's outcome. No new information should be revealed during the meeting, nor should unresolved issues exist walking in. If these conditions are not met, then issues have to be worked out during the meeting. But product planning issues are often too complex to be resolved in a single session, so the meeting usually devolves into animated debate. This phenomenon is commonly called "thrash" – substantive arguments that crowd out remaining discussion of the project and thus prevent approval.

This phenomenon should not be much of a surprise. The poor human mind is unfortunately wired to initially resist new concepts. Surprise someone with new data in the meeting, and their natural reaction is to think of all the reasons why it is wrong or won't work. It is not malicious, it is just natural. One needs time to ponder a concept, consider its merits, and ask clarifying questions to obtain all the contextual data. At that point a reasonable mind may come to appreciate a good idea. But rarely is there enough time for this in an approval meeting. Surprise your audience with new information – even something you consider entirely appropriate and correct – and you risk forceful pushback leading to thrash. Certain members of the organization may also have a need to feel like they contributed to the formation of the plan, rather than having it dictated to them. Some would rather blow up the meeting rather than let things proceed with them as a bystander. And finally – backing away from human foibles for a moment – there is the plain fact that the audience may think of issues or solutions that the core team did not. Leveraging the collective experience of the organization can be incredibly powerful. A few individuals simply can't find all the answers for such a complex task as product planning. For all of these reasons, the pre-meeting convergence is very critical to success.

Some companies may be mature enough to have official cross-functional teams that meet regularly to conduct the Product Planning process. Others may handle it through more informal means. In either case, the process won't always touch every single stakeholder in the organization. The solution is simple, and very human-oriented. **The product manager needs to go meet with key employees face-to-face to discuss the plan**. It is a Kissinger-esque type of shuttle diplomacy, an iterative process to work through the kinks in the plan (at least as they are perceived by these individuals) and solicit feedback. The benefits will be immediately apparent. Key individuals in the organization will have the chance to ask their questions in private, rather than as "look smart" questions in front of an audience. You can solicit their feedback, both to leverage their experience (and make it look like your own in front of your audience), and to make them feel as if they contributed to the plan (making them an ally). They can find any holes in the plan in private, rather than in front of an audience, allowing you time to address them before the meeting. Finally, they can vent any frustrations they are having to you in private, not in public. The end result is a better plan, and a more supportive audience – both key factors in getting an approval.

Each individual must be approached in a uniquely appropriate way. We begin with an assumption that the Marketing team is all on the same page about the strategy – a clear prerequisite. Beyond this, the senior Engineering managers should be engaged based on their personality. Some are very aware of the business side of things, and know how to spot a weak or strong product strategy. So Marketing must first convince them of the strategic merits of the plan. This starts with helping them understand the Market Problem and the benefits of solving it. An Engineering manager who understands the impetus for a certain feature is much more supportive than one who is simply told "this is what we are designing, go do it". The former approach acknowledges the intelligence and experience of these individuals instead of pigeonholing them as "technical types" who wouldn't understand the business side of things. Work diligently to address their concerns and incorporate their feedback. This respectful and thorough approach makes their support much more likely. Their energy can be disruptive if ignored, but incredibly powerful and helpful if harnessed in a collaborative way. Other Engineering managers may have more tactical concerns, whether because they are second line or that is simply their personality. They'll want clarification on feature, schedule, and cost requirements. These details are important – it only takes a single incorrect one to invalidate key assumptions and consequently unravel an entire plan. This attention to both the strategic and the detail is what is required to bring the Engineering team into the fold.

The Operations team will want to understand issues related to cost and capacity planning. Don't assume that they will find a way to hit an aggressive cost target. Engage them early and convince them why it is imperative to do so. The same applies to a particularly aggressive volume ramp.

The Sales team also plays an important role. If key sales managers and salespeople on large accounts do not believe in the merits of the plan (specifically that it addresses their customer's needs), then there is a problem. No salesperson wants to sell a losing product. Their support is critical, because you will soon be asking them to head to the front lines to sell it. If they are not bought in and excited, you won't get their best effort (or any effort if they have other, more promising products on which to focus). Marketing's job is to convince Sales that the strategy is strong and the product plan is sound, and hence worthy of their precious time.

The last category of individuals to seek out is the "snipers". These are individuals who are not necessarily managers or even key contributors. But they are typically experienced (though not necessarily highly competent), vocal, and opinionated. During the approval meetings they can be expected to raise tangential issues and generate some thrash. Sometimes their points are valid, but as often not. You may think they don't "get a vote", but their shots can be disruptive nonetheless. Every organization has a few individuals in this category. A natural reaction is to ignore them and be frustrated that they are asserting themselves. Instead, try to embrace them. Treat them as you would any of the key managers and spend time with them. Give them the chance to exhaust their arrows in your private meeting. Seek as best you can to incorporate their feedback (even if only superficially…it is not a democracy). While this may seem a drain on precious time, it is simply the pragmatic way to ensure that the approval meetings go smoothly.

The strength of your approach with all of these groups rests on how well you have validated your facts and clearly identified your assumptions. We've mentioned that product plans are complex, with many moving parts to coordinate. Marketing's credibility requires that they know what they are talking about. This doesn't mean they need to know everything. But it does mean that every assertion they make falls clearly into one of two categories. The first are facts that have been validated using reliable sources. The second are statements clearly identified as assumptions. **A sloppy organization sometimes confuses the two, and decisions end up being made using assumptions that were thought to be facts**. As long as there are enough confirmed facts to move forward with a reasonably solid plan, a product plan can live with a few assumptions that can be validated later. Decisions often have to be made with imperfect information. This tolerance of assumptions allows the organization to continue making progress on the project, even in the face of some uncertainty. From a more tactical level, it allows the presenter to get through a presentation without having to debate or be absolutely right on every facet of the program. As long as assumptions pass a basic reasonableness test, you can resist the temptation to take on a questioner head-to-head on whether it is true. You simply state the reasons for the assumption, and promise that it will be an area of focus for the next phase of analysis. This aikido-like approach helps maintain harmony in the meeting, while correctly documenting the area of concern for later action.

## The Slides

We now take a look at the slides themselves, and how to make them effective for your purpose. In Chapters 15 "Concept Approval Presentation" and 16 "Product Approval Presentation", the content is specifically discussed; here we'll examine the stylistic concerns. First and foremost, **it is critical to settle on the right level of detail for your presentation**. In most cases, your audience will appreciate brevity. They want the presenter to get to the point quickly. Curiously, experience shows that most presenters don't seem to understand this. Too many presentations become an expose on everything the presenter knows about the topic. The usual result is that the audience gets bored and key messages are obscured by the volume of information. It also raises the likelihood of thrash; the more information you present, the larger the "target" for a feisty audience member to question a particular data point. Discussion on critical topics is good, but pointless thrash about peripheral topics is detrimental.

This is the "push" model of presenting, where the presenter gives a lot of information and expects the audience to choose what to engage on and retain. It is in contrast to the "pull" model, whereby the presenter presents only the high points, and then places the detail into backup slides. In those places where the audience has questions, more detail can be presented via the backup slides. While a good presentation should anticipate where the audience will want to see detail, this method alleviates the need to perfectly predict it. The pull model lets the audience control the focus. The presenter is able to present a "small target", and only wade into messy detail on those topics the audience specifically asks about. Presentations organized in this manner tend to be shorter and exhibit less thrash. The audience stays more interested and key messages are retained. The speaker is better able to control the meeting and gives the appearance of greater clarity of thought.

**Keeping the content of each slide simple will help in the audience's understanding and retention of the information**. This starts with properly organizing the slide. The human mind best retains three ideas at one time, so organize the information into three main bullets which support the slide's main thesis. Keep each of these three primary bullets simple, basically in soundbyte form. You can include more detail in the sub-bullets. But strike a balance between clarity and overload. The more text on the slide, the less they will be listening to you. If you keep it sparse, they will better understand the main idea – you can verbally add more color as needed. For the three primary bullets, it is also good practice to use symmetry of grammar. For instance, consider the bullet "Provides wire-speed performance". It starts with a present tense verb follow by an adjective and noun. So, bullet #2 should also start with a verb and follow with an adjective and noun: "Offers lower power in the industry", instead of "Industry's lowest power". Although subtle, this uniformity makes the information feel more natural to the audience. Finally, it is wise to keep the graphics simple. While sometimes useful to add flash to bland text, they can also be distracting if too elaborate. You don't want to leave the audience wondering why you have so much time on your hands that you can create flashy animations and builds. They will appreciate succinct information and analysis far more than a visually stimulating presentation.

## Conducting the Presentation

With preparation done and slides in hand, it is now time to conduct the meeting. There are some basic principles which you can follow to improve the experience for all:

- *Schedule enough time.* It is likely you will run short on time, forcing you to compress the latter part of the presentation in order to finish. This rushes communication and prohibits discussion, both undesirable states. Worse yet, you may run out of time and not be able to get a decision from Management, thus defeating the purpose of the whole meeting. So be sure to allot enough time to give the topic meaningful consideration – conservatively you might schedule twice the time it takes to give the presentation without interruptions. The worst that can happen is you will finish early.
- *Eliminate thrash.* Ensure the requisite level of coordination beforehand. Thrash is an exponential source of time-consuming discussion. You can easily derail an entire meeting with a single controversial topic that has not been settled beforehand.
- *Control the discussion.* The presenter must know when to facilitate a debate and when to put a stop to it. This requires the ability to distinguish between critical gating issues, and those which can be solved outside the meeting and need not delay approval of the project. It can be helpful to create a running "Bin List" of

topics that need to be addressed but not necessarily *right now*. This technique allows the presenter to defer non-critical items without offending the questioner or making him feel his concerns are being ignored.

   **These techniques can help the presenter achieve the most important goal:** *get a decision*. This may seem rather obvious, but it is a hallmark of poor organizational execution to delay project decisions because of an inability to solve the controversial issues and converge on a single plan. There will always be tough issues to sort out in product planning. Organizations that execute well have product champions who push through these obstacles using sheer willpower, creativity, and compromise. They walk into the meeting confident they have consensus. The downsides of not getting a decision are painful. Getting the calendars of all key participants aligned for a follow up meeting is difficult, thus injecting weeks of delay into the process which eventually manifests itself at the *end* of the program. It also means delays in engaging customers on the next round of either validation or marketing of the product. Overall, it makes the Marketing team (especially the presenter) look bad. Thus, it pays big dividends to do this meeting once by doing it right the first time.
   Yet there will be times when you simply can't get approval for a project in the meeting. Despite the best efforts of a dedicated team, items sometimes get overlooked. A well designed and executed Product Planning process reduces the chances of this, but it happens. Don't take it personally; pride will cloud your judgment and make you defensive in the face of constructive input (if it was easy to create a great product and plan, everyone could do it). Do your best to recognize and avoid it. Be open to the input of others and ready to regroup and replan in order to reach convergence. But be smart about this. If you can't get full approval, ask for conditional approval based on successful closure of a few key action items. And try to schedule the follow up while in the meeting, while everyone is present and focused on this project. This mitigates any loss of momentum. And in the event that the project is simply well out of bounds in terms of convergence and satisfaction of the corporate criteria, don't be afraid to kill it. You can't fall in love with a program so much that you cannot let it go if it just doesn't make sense.

## Conclusion

It would be hard to overstate the importance of having the approval meeting go smoothly. It represents a critical opportunity for the organization to finally converge on a product direction. This paves the way for proper staffing, prompt execution, and healthy morale. The basis of this is, of course a great product and a solid plan. But as simple as it sounds, the execution of the meeting also plays an important role. **A great plan can grind to a halt because of a poorly executed approval meeting.** Don't think that your exciting features or a massive financial return will carry the day. Always keep in mind that the organization is composed of intelligent and opinionated professionals that need to be gently and skillfully brought onto the same page. The preparation done in advance to achieve convergence and create a good presentation will pay dividends many times over.

# CHAPTER 15:

## Concept Approval Presentation

One of the challenges related to approval meetings is simply deciding on which analysis to perform and how to present it. Team members can waste a lot of time trying to figure out what the audience needs to see. And if the analysis and presentation isn't consistent from project to project, the lack of familiarity with the format can be distracting for the audience. The solution is the same for both: a standard template that is proven and "field tested" within the organization. The same analysis is performed and presented each time in the same way. Everyone knows what to expect in terms of format. This ensures that the focus stays on the product and that the Product Planning process proceeds efficiently, as this is a cornerstone of being able to execute on great products over time. What follows is such a template for the Concept Approval presentation. An example of each type of slide used for the Real World Example project (Mason) is shown and the content explained. This particular format need not be followed rigorously, but it does represent the types of analysis to be performed, and one proven way to present it. What is important is that the organization creates a template that works for its own business, industry, and management preferences, and then uses it consistently. Note that these slides are available for download at www.systemnotcircumstance.com.

---

## Executive Summary

- **Mason will be targeted at the Laptop and Blade PC segments**
  - Laptop PCs value battery life and data security
  - Blade PCs value low heat generation and a serial interface
  - Desktop PC will be a secondary, opportunistic market

- **Mason will:**
  - Reduce cost to enable aggressive pricing
  - Dramatically increase battery life by sensing when the cable is plugged in
  - Offer high security by integrating TPM
  - Eliminate the external serial chip to reduce the power and solution cost for a blade desktop

- **We expect Mason to be very competitive**
  - Cable Sensing Mode, TPM, and serial interface should create strong differentiation in laptop/blade markets
  - Big assumption that customers buy into TPM, which is not yet proven in the mainstream market

- **Revenue and NPV are strong, but GM turns are a concern**
  - Lifetime 42M units; $291M revenue; ~$85.6M NPV; 7.7 GM Turn

- **Main concerns to be addressed before PA**
  - Can we meet the cost targets?
  - Can we convince the market to embrace TPM as a mainstream technology?
  - Can we achieve significant battery life savings with Cable Sensing Mode?

*TechCorp Proprietary & Confidential*

---

*Figure 15.1: Executive Summary Slide*

### Key Questions the Slide Should Answer:
- What problems does the product solve, and how?
- Does this project make sense to pursue?

### What the Slide Shows:
Don't keep the audience in suspense about the product's features or results of the financial analysis. Delaying this basic information until later in the presentation tends to make them restless and more likely to quibble over details. The Executive Summary (Figure 15.1) removes the suspense right away, leaving the audience more receptive to the rest of the presentation. Typical information would include:

- *Key Attributes:* What is new and notable about this concept? In CA, this is often a functional description of what the product will achieve
- *Competitiveness Statement:* Will the product win and why? If this can't be expressed in 25 words or less, it's an indication of a problem.
- *Financials:* If the financials are strong, the audience tends to be more open to the product definition. Make this clear upfront.
- *Key Challenges:* Good projects always face difficulties. Identifying them upfront preempts the audience from having to point them out.

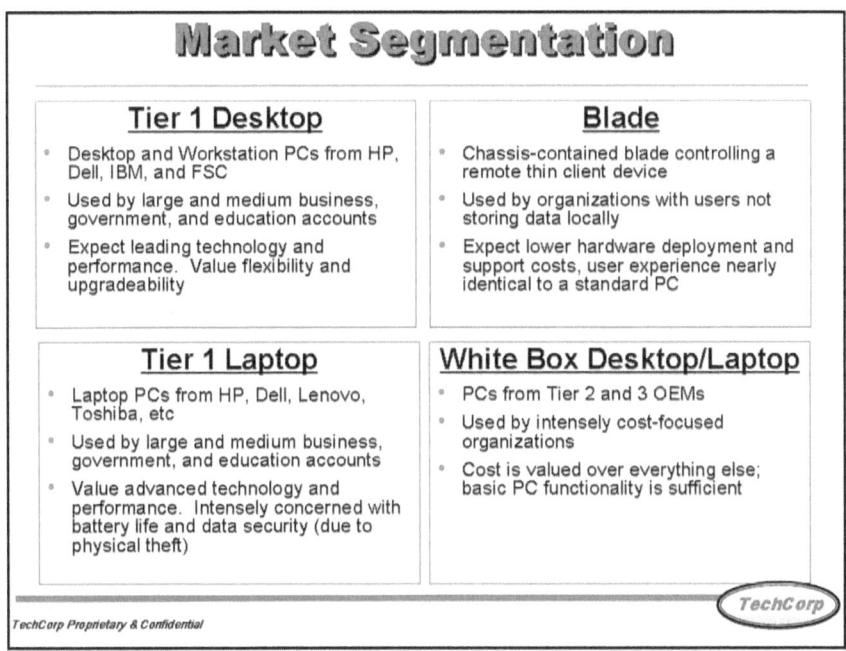

*Figure 15.2: Market Segmentation Slide*

### Key Questions the Slide Should Answer:

- What market segments are being considered for the product to address?
- What are the general characteristics of each segment?

### What the Slide Shows:

Here you will show all of the market segments under consideration. Some will be designated primary or secondary targets. Others may eventually be eliminated, but showing them anyway allows you the opportunity to present your underlying reasoning for doing so. A high-level characterization of the segments is presented in order to educate the audience about each one's boundaries. Specific requirements or Market Problems are not presented (that will come in a later slide), but rather the general characteristics that make each segment unique. For instance, Figure 15.2 states that "Tier 1 Laptops" are "intensely concerned with battery life…" This is in contrast to customers in the "Tier 1 Desktop" segment, who are more concerned with "flexibility and upgradeability".

213

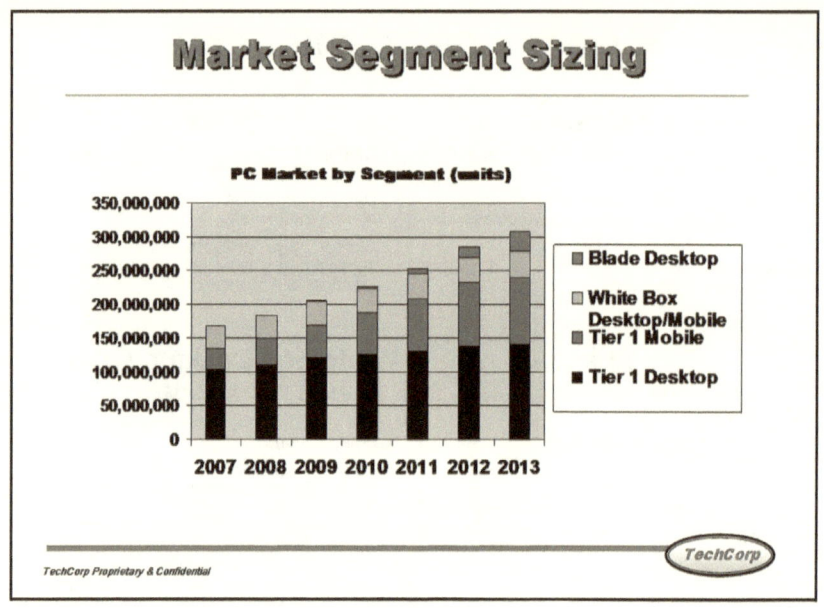

*Figure 15.3: Market Sizing Slide*

<u>*Key Question the Slide Should Answer:*</u>
- What is the size of the opportunity that each segment represents?

<u>*What the Slide Shows:*</u>

Sizing your segments is a fundamental part of the analysis. The stacked bar graph (Figure 15.3) is useful for presenting this data because it all fits on a single chart. But the story behind the numbers is as important as the chart itself. The presenter must be able to point out the relevant trends, i.e. why a particular segment is flat or growing, why a small segment may be strategic, and so on. This type of information helps set the stage for later discussion of strategy and tradeoffs. For instance, an audience looking at this slide may question why any effort or product costs should be wasted in the tiny blade desktop market instead of optimizing for the massive desktop market. In this case, the presenter would make the case that since there are a lot of competitors in the desktop market and cost seems to be the dominant requirement, it will be very hard to differentiate, hold pricing power, or extract much profit. In contrast, the blade desktop market has some very unique requirements that allow a product to add significant value. Also, the price point is higher, so a healthy profit per unit can be extracted at this early stage in the market's development.

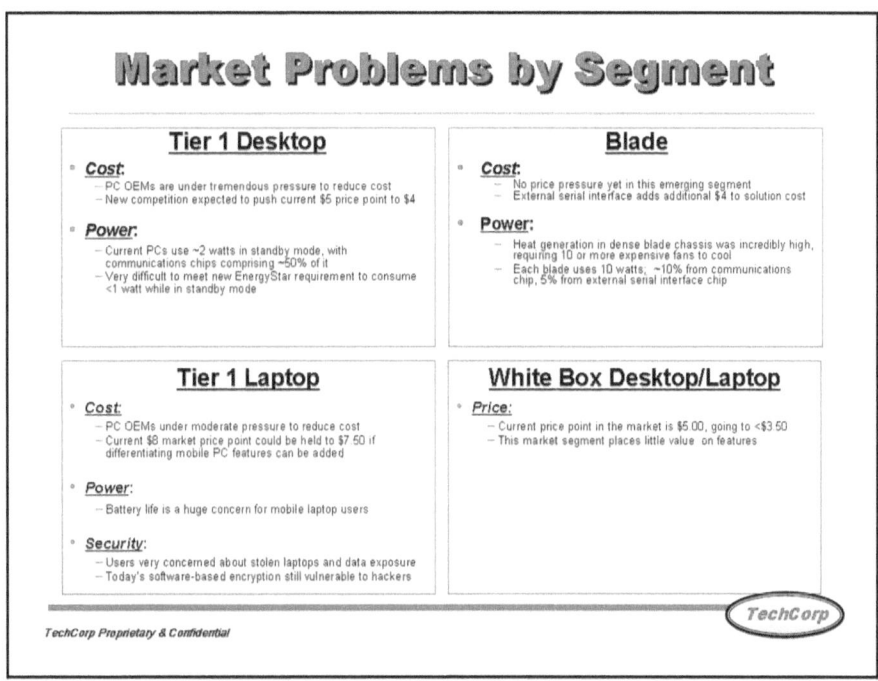

*Figure 15.4: Market Problem Slide*

## Key Question the Slide Should Answer:

- What are the relevant Market Problems in each segment?

## What the Slide Shows:

Relevant problems for each segment are identified. In Figure 15.4, note the usage of categories such as "Power" and "Security" to organize them. The focus should be on identifying a segment's unique problems, thus setting the stage later for a customized product to solve them. Note that there is purposely no mention of solutions here. This enforces the discipline of leading with problems, not features. It gives the presenter a chance to get consensus that these are in fact the right problems to attack. With this established, the audience tends to be more open to the solution. Presenting both problem and solution at the same time tends to cause more thrash. Problem statements should be as concise as possible, and the magnitude or effects of the problem should be quantified as much as possible.

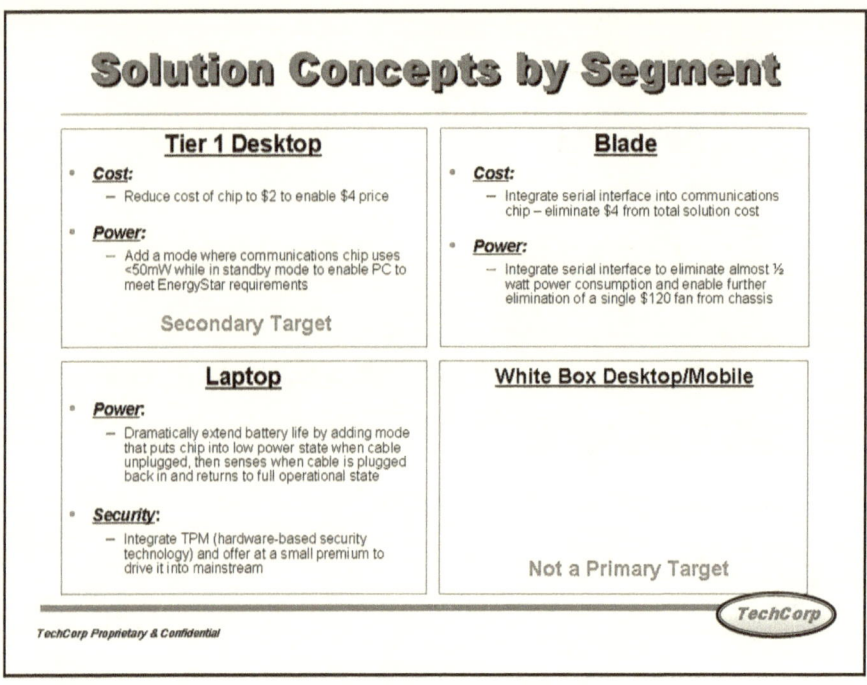

Figure 15.5: Solution Concept Slide

<u>*Key Question the Slide Should Answer:*</u>
- How does the product solve each segment's problems?

<u>*What the Slide Shows*</u>

The slide in Figure 15.5 communicates two categories of information. First, it establishes which segments will be designated as "Primary Targets" (Laptop and Blade), which means that product definition choices will be shaped specifically to address those segments' needs. A "Secondary Target" designation could also be applied, which means that the segment would be pursued opportunistically but it would not drive the product definition.

Second, this slide should list the concept for how the product could solve each segment's problems (as stated in Figure 15.4). Because this is the Concept Phase, the focus of these solutions should be more on what satisfies the market and less on what is feasible (although it must pass a basic sanity check).

## Competitive Comparison

|  | Mason | Competitor A | Competitor B |
|---|---|---|---|
| Manufacturing Cost | $3.30 | $3.00 | $3.25 |
| Total Power | 900mW | 800mW | 750mW |
| Cable Sensing Mode | Yes | No | No |
| TPM | Yes | No | No |
| Serial Interface | Yes | No | No |
| EnergyStar Mode | Yes | No | Yes |
| Total Power w/Serial Interface | 1000mW | 1490mW | 1440mW |

| How We Win | |
|---|---|
| Mobile | **Power:** <br> • Cable Sensing mode saves more battery life than does the lower total power approach of Competitors A and B <br> **Security:** <br> • TPM protects data on stolen laptop; bulk encryption does not and thus is less attractive <br> • Competitors A and B require $4 external TPM; Mason will push price to $1 (which will drive it to mainstream) |
| Blade | • Integrated serial interface saves $4 solution cost, eliminates a $120 fan (relative to Comp A and B) |
| Desktop | • PC OEMs can't win government accounts without EnergyStar mode (Comp A does not have it) |

TechCorp Proprietary & Confidential

TechCorp

Figure 15.6: Competitive Comparison Slide

### Key Questions the Slide Should Answer:
- How does this product compare to its competition?
- Why will the product win?

### What the Slide Shows

The slide in Figure 15.6 starts with a simple competitive analysis. It identifies a small set of relevant attributes and compares the product to that expected from the competition. But while this information is helpful, your "How We Win" statement is by far the most important part of the presentation. It is critical for this to be clear and convincing. Your audience wants to know exactly why customers will choose this product over the competition. The statement needs to be simple and specific. Does it solve a problem in a better way? Is there a fundamental cost advantage? Does the product have a superior distribution strategy? This slide is the litmus test on whether the product possesses clear competitive advantage. If it doesn't convince the audience, you are not likely to obtain approval to pass this Concept Approval gate.

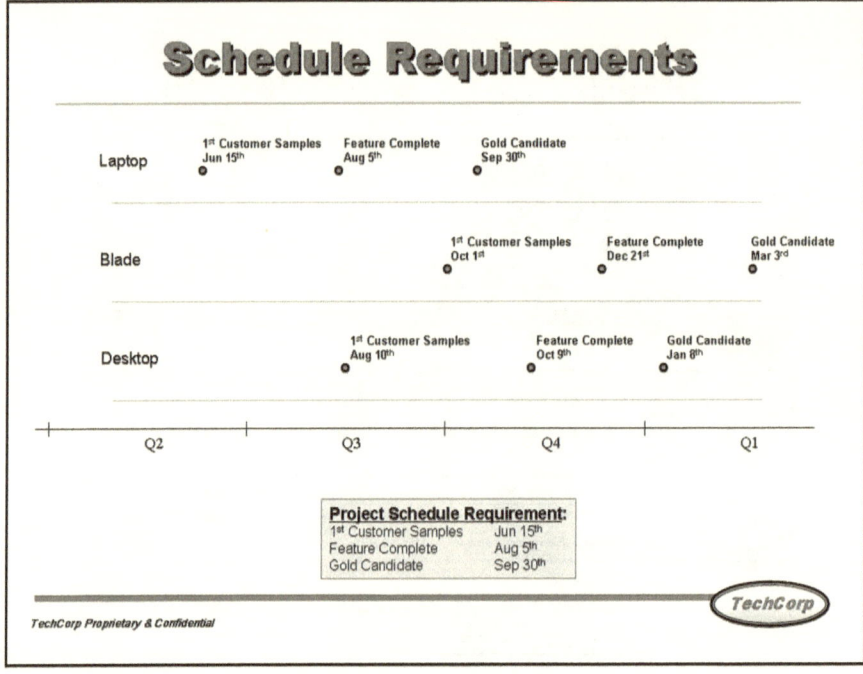

*Figure 15.7: Schedule Requirement Slide*

<u>*Key Question the Slide Should Answer:*</u>
- What key schedule milestones must the project meet?

<u>*What the Slide Shows*</u>

The slide in Figure 15.7 shows the critical milestones and deliverables for the project. Since this is the Concept Phase, it need not be an exhaustive list – just the major ones. It can be particularly informative to break down the information for each segment. This helps the audience understand how each one affects the overall project schedule. This provides important context for some of the choices made in the project. For instance, the schedule may be tight because Marketing is trying to meet the early market window for a niche segment, while the most profitable market segments have market windows farther out in time. Trying to hit the early window may require extra resources or painful feature tradeoffs, which ultimately are more detrimental to the product. This graphical approach helps highlight issues like this. At the bottom of the slide, the aggregated schedule is shown – the official target for the project.

218

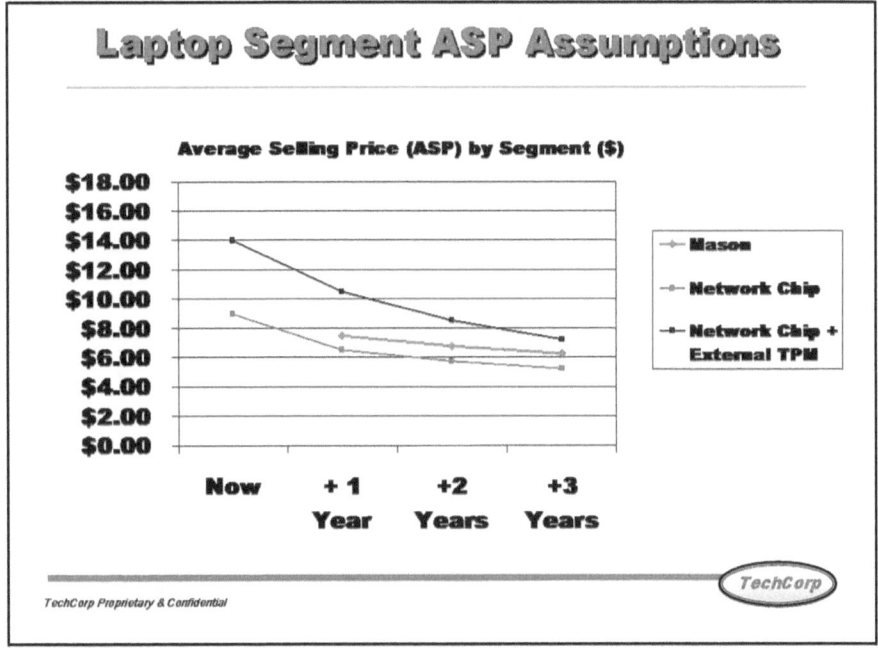

*Figure 15.8: ASP Assumption Slide*

<u>Key Questions the Slide Should Answer:</u>
- What is the price point over time for this product category?
- Is it consistent with the feature set, market dynamic, competitive dynamic, market segment size, and product cost?

<u>What the Slide Shows</u>

A simple line graph as shown in Figure 15.8 is the preferred format for showing the ASP projections. This allows the presenter to convey trends over time, rather than simply a single-number snapshot. Be sure to include actual pricing within the product category to date. This helps highlight any discontinuities between current reality and forward looking projections.

As with other elements of the Concept Approval, the numbers need not be 100% accurate, but simply representative of the dynamic in the market. The presenter most certainly needs to be able to defend the reasons for the expected pricing. A good basic (need not be complete) Strategic Pricing Plan should provide the necessary information to competently defend these assumptions.

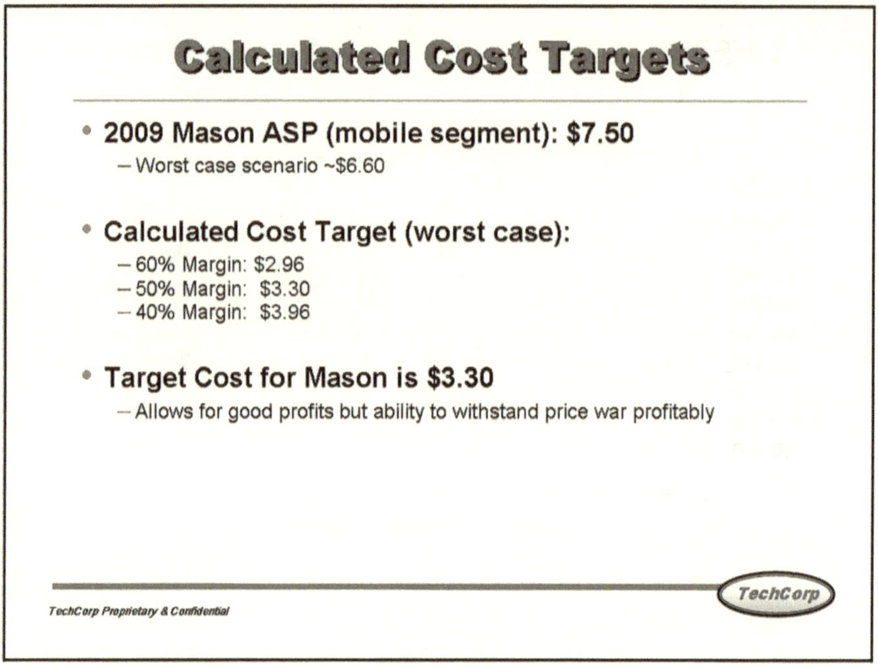

---

# Calculated Cost Targets

- **2009 Mason ASP (mobile segment): $7.50**
  - Worst case scenario ~$6.60

- **Calculated Cost Target (worst case):**
  - 60% Margin: $2.96
  - 50% Margin:  $3.30
  - 40% Margin:  $3.96

- **Target Cost for Mason is $3.30**
  - Allows for good profits but ability to withstand price war profitably

*TechCorp Proprietary & Confidential*                                     *TechCorp*

---

*Figure 15.9: Cost Target Slide*

*Key Question the Slide Should Answer:*
- What product cost is required to compete profitably?

*What the Slide Shows*

The slide in Figure 15.9 shows the derivation of the cost target that Engineering needs to achieve. It is calculated by working backwards from the market price (from the Strategic Pricing Plan) rather than being arbitrarily created. If you can justify the ASP assumptions, then the cost target simply falls directly out. You might calculate this based upon margin targets, as it does above. But one may choose to use other metrics, such as profit dollars per unit, or overall profitability of the program (i.e. price needs to be such that the product earns $20M in gross profit over its lifetime). Whichever metric is chosen, it can be helpful to show a desired, acceptable, and minimum target and the corresponding product cost. This helps the organization to better understand how much effort to apply in optimizing the product's cost.

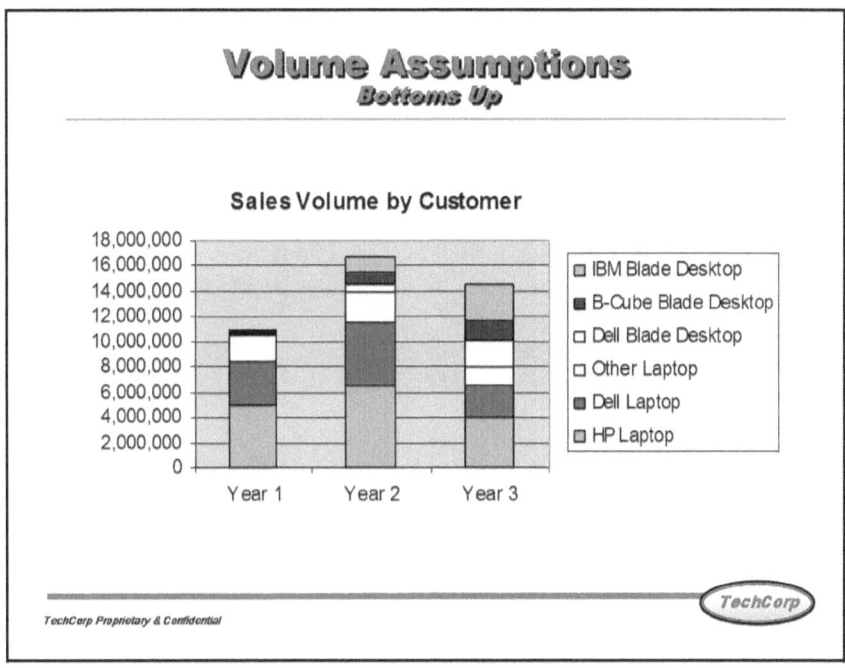

*Figure 15.10: Volume Assumptions Slide*

### Key Questions the Slide Should Answer:

- What business will be won with this particular product?
- Are the assumptions consistent with the product definition and market environment?

### What the Slide Shows

A stacked bar chart, as shown in Figure 15.10, is used to show a bottoms-up forecast of the expected sales volume. This is appropriate given that this PC OEM market is concentrated on a small group of large customers.

The audience will be looking for a basic threshold of consistency with some of the other elements of the plan. Is a premium-priced product showing mainstream volumes? Do the assumed volumes represent a reasonable share of the TAM shown in Figure 15.3, given the number of competitors and the product's level of differentiation? Are the volumes a drastic change in market share from today's market? In general, the audience will want to see that the volume assumptions make sense given the other elements of the product, plan, and market situation.

221

# Engineering Resource Estimates

| Resource | +1Qtr | +2Qtr | +3Qtr | +4Qtr | +5Qtr | +6Qtr | +7Qtr | +8Qtr | +9Qtr | +10Qtr | +11Qtr | +12Qtr |
|---|---|---|---|---|---|---|---|---|---|---|---|---|
| Chip | 8 | 10 | 12 | 18 | 16 | 10 | 8 | 2 | 1 | 1 | 1 | |
| Software | 2 | 4 | 8 | 14 | 6 | 6 | 6 | 6 | 2 | 1 | 1 | 1 |
| Hardware | 1 | 3 | 3 | 3 | 2 | 1 | 1 | 1 | | | | |
| Test | | | 1 | 1 | 14 | 18 | 18 | 18 | 10 | 2 | 2 | 1 |
| Total | 11 | 17 | 24 | 36 | 38 | 35 | 33 | 27 | 13 | 4 | 4 | 2 |

*each number represents man-quarters

**Total R&D Expense = $20M**

TechCorp

*TechCorp Proprietary & Confidential*

Figure 15.11: Resource Estimate Slide

## Key Question the Slide Should Answer:

- What headcount is required to execute this project?

## What the Slide Shows

The slide in Figure 15.11 comes from Engineering and shows their headcount requirements for the project. In the Concept Phase, these estimates need not be highly accurate. This slide's value is mainly the gross characterization of the effort required for the project. What is needed is an approximate expense number for the ROI, as well as a general skillset mix so Engineering can assess if they are appropriately staffed. It may be only a guess, but at least it is an educated guess. It is also a forcing function to make sure every group involved in the program is being consulted to help scope the total effort. A chip company like TechCorp is very good at estimating the required hardware engineers, but they often forget some of the effort needed from software and applications engineering. This slide helps highlight any unaccounted headcount requirements.

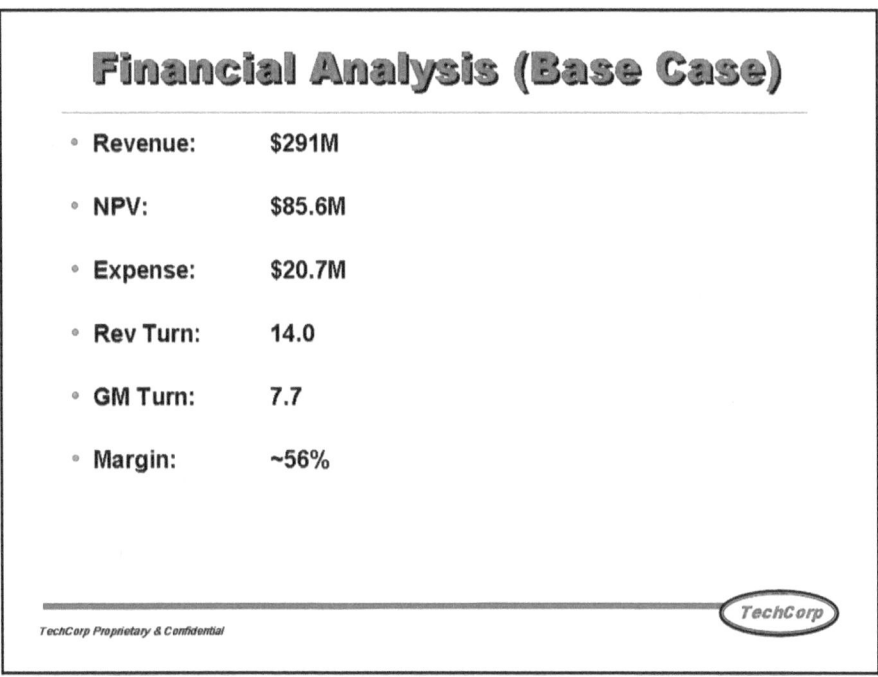

Figure 15.12: Financial Analysis Slide

## Key Question the Slide Should Answer:

- What would be the financial return from investing in this project?

## What the Slide Shows

Figure 15.12 is a simple but important slide showing a summary of the financial parameters of the project. It should include only those metrics that Management and Finance care about. Presumably, the corporation will have set a standard for the metrics of interest. Adding more is not helpful as it distracts from the core information being presented.

The nominal values of each metric are shown. A Scenario Analysis will be shown in later slides. This slide should be kept simple to establish the baseline values.

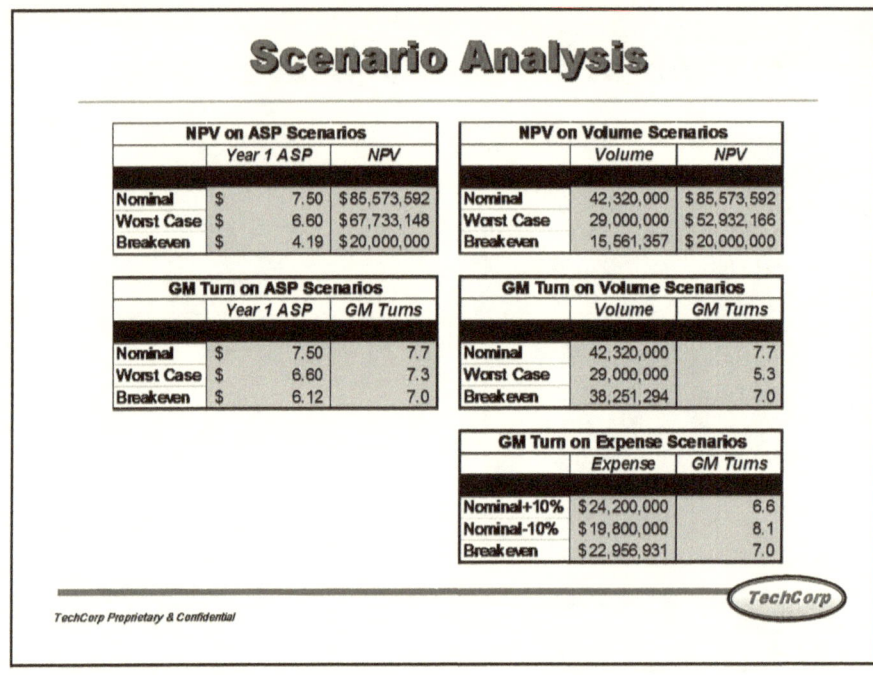

*Figure 15.13: Scenario Analysis Slide*

### Key Questions the Slide Should Answer:

- What happens if any of the ROI assumptions are wrong?
- Could moderate changes to the input variables reverse the project decision?

### What the Slide Shows:

Figure 15.13 shows some of the Breakeven and Scenario Analyses undertaken to account for uncertainty. The presenter has chosen two output variables to test: NPV and GM Turns. The first is a common choice, while the second was presumably chosen because the baseline values are close to the corporate target and bear some scrutiny. A table for each shows the effects of changes to the input variables upon the output variables. This is high level analysis – not intended to be exact. But, the presenter should be capable of describing a set of circumstances which would lead to the Nominal, Worst, and Breakeven scenarios.

## Key Assumptions To Validate

### Market

- What ASP can we achieve?
- Which customers do we think we can win?
- Can customers be convinced of the value of TPM? How much will they pay?
- Can we license the software needed for TPM?

### Technical

- What cost point can be achieved?
- What is the cost adder for the integrated serial interface?
- How will the Cable Sensing Mode work?
- What power level can we achieve when a cable is not plugged in?
- Can we successfully integrate TPM?
- Will TPM core be ready for integration on our schedule?

TechCorp Proprietary & Confidential

*Figure 15.14: Validation Plan Slide*

### Key Question the Slide Should Answer:

- What are the major assumptions that must be validated before Product Approval?

### What the Slide Shows:

Given that this is the Concept Phase, everyone should understand that assumptions have to be made in advance of the full due diligence. Figure 15.14 is intended to capture both market and technical items that need to be explored further. Identifying them here serves three purposes. First, it diffuses any tension in the audience about the plan being based on a solid foundation; important assumptions are clearly labeled and a commitment is made to validate them. Second, it helps guide the team's efforts in the Product Definition Phase. Third, it allows Management to circle back in the Product Approval to check if these assumptions have in fact been validated.

## Conclusion

An important take-away from this chapter and Chapter 16 "Product Approval Presentation" is that an effective and proven template for approval meetings is very helpful. It saves a lot of time for those preparing, because the target is clear on what analysis needs to be presented. It increases the probability of a well-thought out plan with no omissions of critical data. For these reasons, the use of a template increases the likelihood of approval for projects at the Concept Approval stage. This helps the organization execute more efficiently on its overall Product Planning process. Great organizations will have such a template and demand its use. However, it is not an instrument of dogma; the spirit of each analysis should dominate rather than the exact recommended format of each individual slide.

# CHAPTER 16:

## Product Approval Presentation

What follows here is a template to be used for the Product Approval presentation. Most of the analyses are the same as in the Concept Approval stage, but with a higher expectation of detail, validation, justification, and decisiveness. A few new types of analyses will also be necessary. This chapter will focus on those areas that require incremental information; slides that would be largely similar to those from Concept Approval are not covered. These slides are also available at www.systemnotcircumstance.com.

---

# Executive Summary

- **New features in Mason:**
  - Cost reduction
  - Cable Sensing Mode
  - Integrated TPM 1.2
  - Integrated serial interface

- **We expect Mason to be very competitive in laptop and blade segments**
  - Laptop: *Intelligent Power* saves 10 minutes battery life, TPM is a compelling security capability
  - Blade: integrated serial interface saves $4, eliminates one fan in chassis, reduces footprint 20%

- **Revenue and NPV are strong, GM Turns under control**
  - Lifetime 42M units; $291M revenue; ~$85.6M NPV; 7.7 GM Turn

- **Areas of immediate focus**
  - Aggressive hiring ramp required to meet schedule is a concern
  - Must begin TPM marketing campaign to drive perception of value; partner with SW companies
  - Must begin technical analysis of TPM to understand implementation challenges; high risk to schedule

*TechCorp Proprietary & Confidential*

---

*Figure 16.1: Executive Summary Slide*

<u>Key Questions the Slide Should Answer:</u>

- What are the new attributes of this product?
- Is the product competitive?
- Is the project financially viable?

<u>What the Slide Shows:</u>

The format and content of this slide in Figure 16.1 are similar to that in Concept Approval. The most noticeable difference is that this summary is making very definitive statements. Unlike the CA, which dealt with assumptions and the need to validate them, the Product Approval is making firm statements about a real go-forward plan. The feature set is locked, and the next steps, as mentioned in "Areas of Immediate Focus", are actionable items with which to kick off the project.

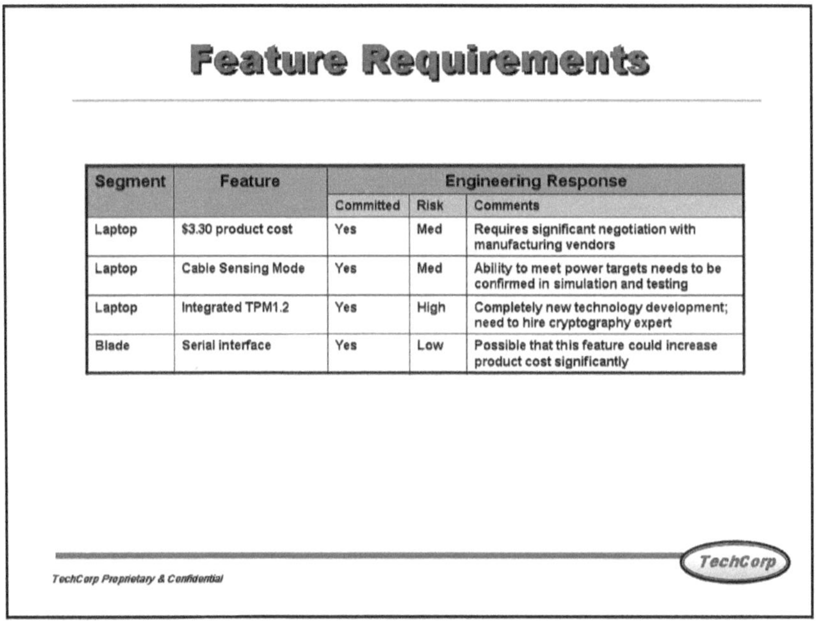

**Feature Requirements**

| Segment | Feature | Engineering Response | | |
|---|---|---|---|---|
| | | Committed | Risk | Comments |
| Laptop | $3.30 product cost | Yes | Med | Requires significant negotiation with manufacturing vendors |
| Laptop | Cable Sensing Mode | Yes | Med | Ability to meet power targets needs to be confirmed in simulation and testing |
| Laptop | Integrated TPM1.2 | Yes | High | Completely new technology development; need to hire cryptography expert |
| Blade | Serial interface | Yes | Low | Possible that this feature could increase product cost significantly |

TechCorp Proprietary & Confidential

TechCorp

*Figure 16.2: Feature Requirements Slide*

<u>*Key Questions the Slide Should Answer:*</u>

- What are the committed features of this product?
- Are any of them segment-specific?

<u>*What This Slide Shows:*</u>

Figure 16.2 is based on a "request-commit" format. The requests from Marketing are in the "Features" column. In the "Committed" column, Engineering states whether or not they can deliver the feature within the cost and schedule boundaries defined by Marketing, and the resource constraints dictated by the organization's P&L. There may be cases where Engineering and Marketing jointly decide to eliminate some requirements in the tradeoff process; this format helps document that.

There is also other useful information here. The "Segment" column notes which segment drives a particular feature. There is also a column for Engineering to highlight the risk any particular feature adds. Together both of these help the audience understand the tradeoffs and resultant risk profile of the product definition. For instance, if multiple risky features are being added for a segment which comprises a small portion of the product's profit, that would be something the audience might want to question. This format helps highlight such a situation.

**Schedule Requirements**

| | Market Req't | ENG Commit | |
|---|---|---|---|
| • **Documentation** | | | |
| – Bill of Materials | Apr 20th | Apr 30th | |
| – Product Specification | Apr 20th | Apr 30th | |
| – Design Guide | May 15th | May 15th | |
| – Datasheet | May 15th | May 15th | |
| • **Hardware** | | | |
| – First customer samples | Jun 15th | May 15th (50%) | Jun 15th (95%) |
| – Production samples | Aug 30th | Aug 10th (50%) | Sep 5th (95%) |
| – Production volume | Dec 10th | Dec 1st (50%) | Dec 15th (95%) |
| • **Software** | | | |
| – Bring up drivers | Jun 20th | Jun 15th (50%) | Jun 25th (95%) |
| – Alpha drivers | Aug 5th | Jul 15th (50%) | Aug 10th (95%) |
| – Gold drivers | Sep 30th | Sep 10th (50%) | Oct 10th (95%) |

TechCorp Proprietary & Confidential

TechCorp

*Figure 16.3: Schedule Requirements Slide*

*Key Question the Slide Should Answer:*

- Does the committed schedule meet the market window?

*What the Slide Shows:*

The CA schedule slide tried to show the market window for each of the target segments. In the PA, you can dispense with that detail and simply boil it down to one target set of deliverables and milestones for the organization to hit. At this stage, seek to define every important deliverable and date rather than simply the major milestones. In Figure 16.3, requirements for hardware, software, and documentation are all listed.

Multiple confidence levels are shown for Engineering's commit dates. Clearly the audience will be assessing whether the project can hit the market window. Engineering and Marketing must be in agreement that the committed project dates are acceptable. In cases where a date doesn't exactly meet the market requirement (such as some of the 95% confidence dates above), the Marketing team would need to be ready to explain why they believe they can tolerate the gap and still succeed in winning and holding the business. The project should not enter the PA meeting unless this convergence has been reached.

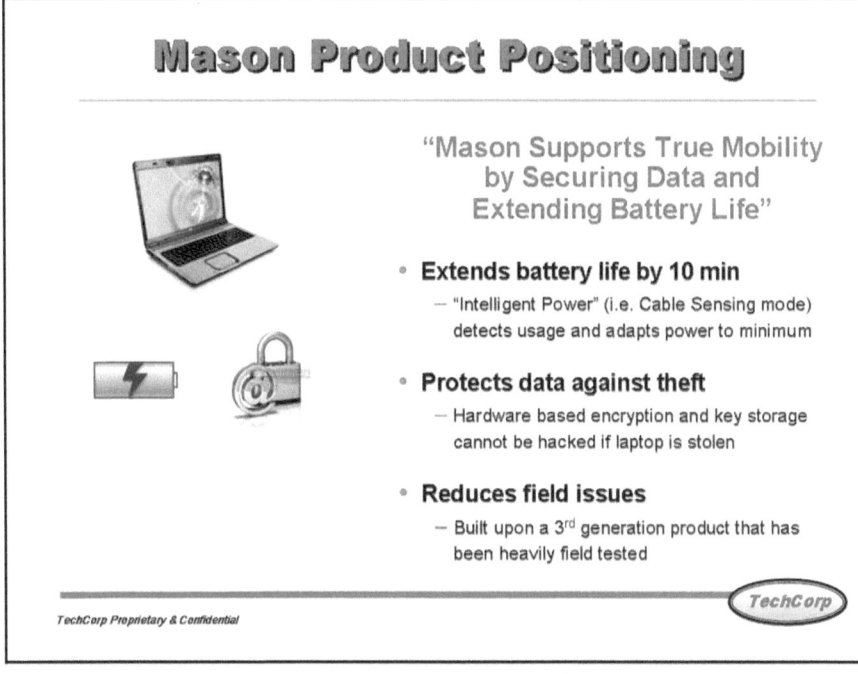

*Figure 16.4: Product Positioning Slide*

<u>*Key Question the Slide Should Answer:*</u>
- How will these features be positioned to customers?

<u>*What the Slide Shows:*</u>
During the Product Planning process, participants mostly deal with features and attributes. The danger is that the organization begins to lose sight of how this gets mapped into the language of the market. This slide should show how the product and its attributes will be marketed to customers. It helps the audience understand why certain features are being requested and the value they provide. This exercise is also quite good as a "smell test" for the product definition. If any particular requirement can't be tied to a real customer problem and explained in layman's terms, it could be an indication that it is not as valuable as originally thought.

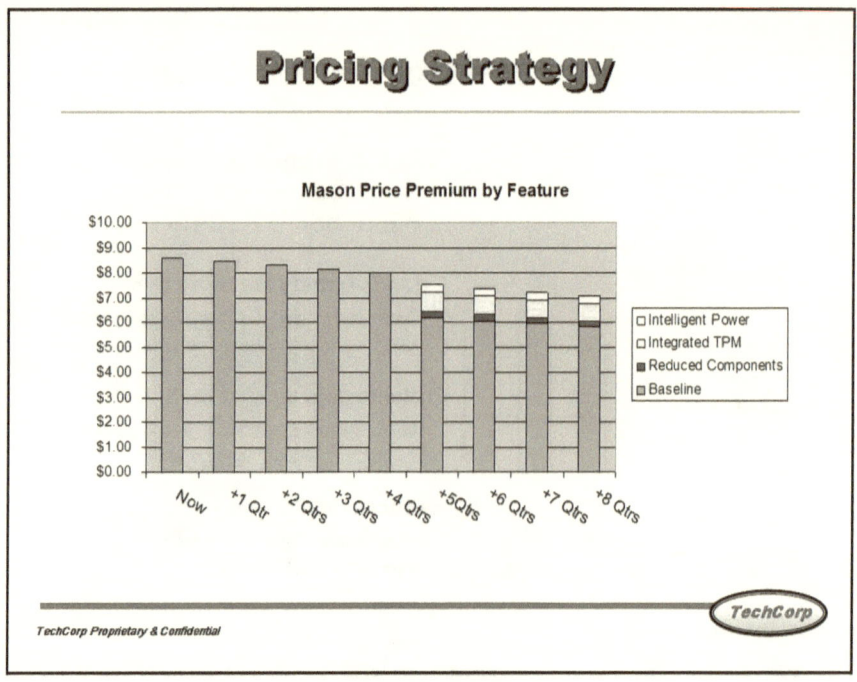

*Figure 16.5: Pricing Strategy Slide*

<u>*Key Questions the Slide Should Answer:*</u>
- What price can the product command in the market?
- What is the value contributed by each new feature?

<u>*What This Slide Shows:*</u>

Figure 16.5 is similar to the pricing slide shown in the CA, but with more detail. An estimate of the value of each particular new feature is shown, helping the audience understand their relative importance. This provides good context for demonstrating why each feature is included in the product definition.

## Required Resources

| Resource | +1Qtr | +2Qtr | +3Qtr | +4Qtr | +5Qtr | +6Qtr | +7Qtr | +8Qtr | +9Qtr | +10Qtr | +11Qtr | +12Qtr |
|----------|-------|-------|-------|-------|-------|-------|-------|-------|-------|--------|--------|--------|
| Chip | 8 | 10 | 12 | 18 | 16 | 10 | 8 | 2 | 1 | 1 | 1 | |
| Software | 2 | 4 | 8 | 14 | 6 | 6 | 6 | 6 | 2 | 1 | 1 | 1 |
| Hardware | 1 | 3 | 3 | 3 | 2 | 1 | 1 | 1 | | | | |
| Test | | | 1 | 1 | 14 | 18 | 18 | 18 | 10 | 2 | 2 | 1 |
| Total | 11 | 17 | 24 | 36 | 38 | 35 | 33 | 27 | 13 | 4 | 4 | 2 |

*each number represents man-quarters

- Incremental Hiring Required
  - 1 TPM architect
  - 2 firmware engineers
  - 1 software engineer
  - 1 chip engineer
  - 8 test engineers (overseas)

- Total R&D Expense = $20M

TechCorp Proprietary & Confidential

TechCorp

*Figure 16.6: Resources Slide*

## Key Question the Slide Should Answer:

- What headcount is required to execute on this project?

## What the Slide Shows

Rather than just the estimate shown in the CA, Figure 16.6 now shows the official headcount required for the project. This funnels up into the P&L and Portfolio Analysis planning for the entire business unit, and so is very important. Additionally, this slide identifies any new hiring that must take place in order to properly staff the project and achieve the committed schedule. This information is specifically raised in the PA because an approval of the program is an implicit approval to fund these new heads.

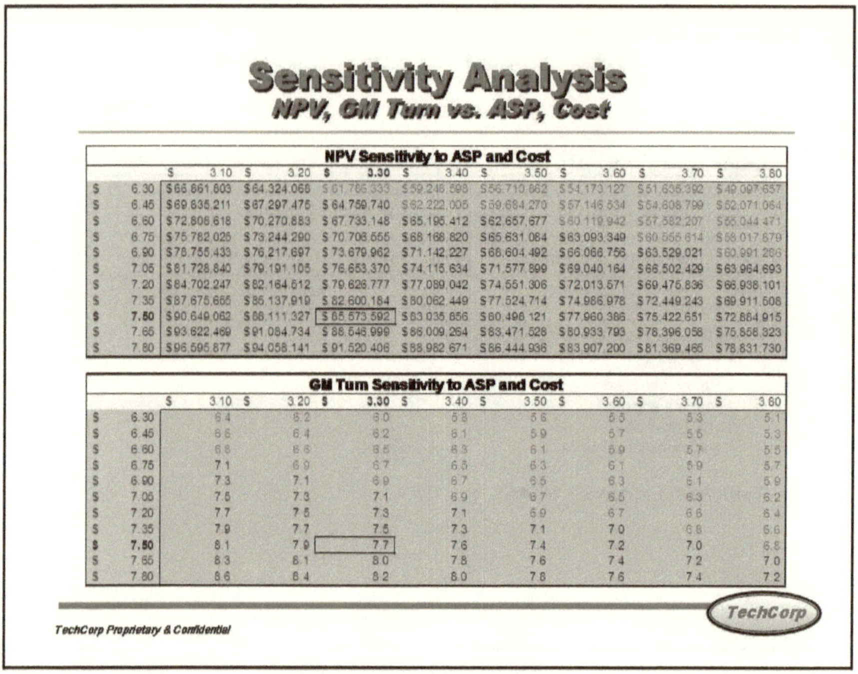


**NPV Sensitivity to ASP and Cost**

| | $ 3.10 | $ 3.20 | $ 3.30 | $ 3.40 | $ 3.50 | $ 3.60 | $ 3.70 | $ 3.80 |
|---|---|---|---|---|---|---|---|---|
| $ 6.30 | $66,861,803 | $64,324,068 | $61,786,333 | $59,248,598 | $56,710,862 | $54,173,127 | $51,635,392 | $49,097,657 |
| $ 6.45 | $69,835,211 | $67,297,475 | $64,759,740 | $62,222,005 | $59,684,270 | $57,146,534 | $54,608,799 | $52,071,064 |
| $ 6.60 | $72,808,618 | $70,270,883 | $67,733,148 | $65,195,412 | $62,657,677 | $60,119,942 | $57,582,207 | $55,044,471 |
| $ 6.75 | $75,782,026 | $73,244,290 | $70,706,555 | $68,168,820 | $65,631,084 | $63,093,349 | $60,555,614 | $58,017,879 |
| $ 6.90 | $78,755,433 | $76,217,697 | $73,679,962 | $71,142,227 | $68,604,492 | $66,066,756 | $63,529,021 | $60,991,286 |
| $ 7.05 | $81,728,840 | $79,191,105 | $76,653,370 | $74,115,634 | $71,577,899 | $69,040,164 | $66,502,429 | $63,964,693 |
| $ 7.20 | $84,702,247 | $82,164,512 | $79,626,777 | $77,089,042 | $74,551,306 | $72,013,571 | $69,475,836 | $66,938,101 |
| $ 7.35 | $87,675,655 | $85,137,919 | $82,600,184 | $80,062,449 | $77,524,714 | $74,986,978 | $72,449,243 | $69,911,508 |
| **$ 7.50** | $90,649,062 | $88,111,327 | $85,573,592 | $83,035,856 | $80,498,121 | $77,960,386 | $75,422,651 | $72,884,915 |
| $ 7.65 | $93,622,469 | $91,084,734 | $88,546,999 | $86,009,264 | $83,471,528 | $80,933,793 | $78,396,058 | $75,858,323 |
| $ 7.80 | $96,595,877 | $94,058,141 | $91,520,406 | $88,982,671 | $86,444,936 | $83,907,200 | $81,369,465 | $78,831,730 |

**GM Turn Sensitivity to ASP and Cost**

| | $ 3.10 | $ 3.20 | $ 3.30 | $ 3.40 | $ 3.50 | $ 3.60 | $ 3.70 | $ 3.80 |
|---|---|---|---|---|---|---|---|---|
| $ 6.30 | 6.4 | 6.2 | 6.0 | 5.8 | 5.6 | 5.5 | 5.3 | 5.1 |
| $ 6.45 | 6.6 | 6.4 | 6.2 | 6.1 | 5.9 | 5.7 | 5.5 | 5.3 |
| $ 6.60 | 6.8 | 6.6 | 6.5 | 6.3 | 6.1 | 5.9 | 5.7 | 5.5 |
| $ 6.75 | 7.1 | 6.9 | 6.7 | 6.5 | 6.3 | 6.1 | 5.9 | 5.7 |
| $ 6.90 | 7.3 | 7.1 | 6.9 | 6.7 | 6.5 | 6.3 | 6.1 | 5.9 |
| $ 7.05 | 7.5 | 7.3 | 7.1 | 6.9 | 6.7 | 6.5 | 6.3 | 6.2 |
| $ 7.20 | 7.7 | 7.5 | 7.3 | 7.1 | 6.9 | 6.7 | 6.6 | 6.4 |
| $ 7.35 | 7.9 | 7.7 | 7.5 | 7.3 | 7.1 | 7.0 | 6.8 | 6.6 |
| **$ 7.50** | 8.1 | 7.9 | 7.7 | 7.6 | 7.4 | 7.2 | 7.0 | 6.8 |
| $ 7.65 | 8.3 | 8.1 | 8.0 | 7.8 | 7.6 | 7.4 | 7.2 | 7.0 |
| $ 7.80 | 8.6 | 8.4 | 8.2 | 8.0 | 7.8 | 7.6 | 7.4 | 7.2 |

*Figure 16.7: Sensitivity Analysis Slide*

*<u>Key Questions the Slide Should Answer:</u>*

- What happens if any of the ROI assumptions are wrong?
- What would cause the investment decision to change?

*<u>What the Slide Shows:</u>*

This slide in Figure 16.7 accounts for uncertainty with greater granularity than the Scenario Analysis did in the CA. The Sensitivity Analysis shows how the output variables are affected by changes (along a continuum of values) of the input variables. The presenter has chosen to demonstrate how the NPV changes with both ASP and cost simultaneously. The NPV values falling below the corporate target are highlighted in gray. This highlights where the decision on the product might change with any of several combinations of ASP and cost. The gap between these values and the nominal assumptions will be of great interest to the audience. A small gap conveys that the project is risky, vulnerable to even small changes in the relevant input variables. The presenter will need to be able to explain why the input variables are not likely to migrate to the values which put the metrics into the "gray zone".

## Conclusion

The Product Approval presentation can be a very intense experience. The threshold of detail and validation is very high. You have to be absolutely right, and be able to withstand a fair amount of scrutiny. Furthermore, you'll need to have a complete go-to market plan that is fully consistent and aligned throughout. The last thing the presenter needs is to be wondering what to present. The use of a template by the organization keeps the team focused on the substance of the analysis rather than the format.

# PART 2: PRODUCT MARKETING

# CHAPTER 17:

## Creating Complete Products

*There is a line from a popular movie that says "if you build it, they will come". It may apply to baseball fields, but not necessarily products. Many organizations fall into this trap, thinking that if they create something that has superior power, performance, features, or cost, then winning is a foregone conclusion. Unfortunately it is not. There are many examples of products with great attributes that failed for other reasons: customers didn't understand the product's value, were not aware of the product, or found the product hard to use. The game is not always about faster, better, cheaper; sometimes it is won or lost based on how well these adjacent issues are addressed. Truly successful organizations define products with great attributes, but they go further to create truly complete products which also address these other elements.*

## Create Products, Not Devices

Most companies have a reasonable grasp of the basics of product marketing. They define something that the market wants, codify a message, and train the salesforce and Marketing Communications (MarCom) teams to deliver that message. Once the world understands the offering's benefits, they buy it and revenues start to roll in. That is product marketing in a nutshell. But underlying too many product efforts is the "if we build it, they will come" mentality. Whether arrogance or naiveté, it is based on an overestimation of the market's awareness and understanding of the product or ability to easily use it. The organization may believe they've created a great product, yet something is still preventing it from becoming a market success. This gap between intent (to make a great product) and reality (failure) was explained by William Davidow in his book "Marketing High Technology". **He observed that "great devices are invented in the laboratory, while great products are invented in the Marketing department."** Using his naming convention, a "device" is the entity defined in the MRD and designed by Engineering. As it sits on a table in the lab, it can exhibit all the specified requirements, including features, functionality, form factor, and cost. These attributes may be clearly superior to that offered by competition. But at the moment this device is simply an inanimate object sitting on a lab table. It takes an effort by the Marketing department to turn it into a complete product that can exploit all the potential of its attributes.

Problems arise when marketers believe that buying decisions are based solely on which product has the better performance, functionality, quality, and cost attributes. In fact, there are a number of other powerful factors involved. To illustrate, let us take a simplistic view of the buying process:

1. Customer becomes aware of the product
2. Customer sees enough to want to learn more about the product
3. Customer studies product in detail
4. Customer validates claims about product
5. Customer decides to buy the product
6. Customer uses product

The superior attributes of a product would come into play primarily in Step 3 as an influencer of Step 5. But in this context, we ask a very simple question: what about the other four steps? Is it possible that within them there are pitfalls that would prevent a buying decision in your favor? A product may have superior attributes, but what if customers aren't even aware of them? Or, at the moment they do become aware of them, could they fail to grab the customer's attention such that they want to learn more? Could the non-availability of some basic product information prevent an initial analysis? Might there be serious uncertainty about whether the product will work in the customer's usage environment, or significant work required to make it happen? Any of these outcomes could halt this six step buying process, completely independently of the attractiveness of its attributes.

The organization's attention must be on more than just the device characteristics. It has to be a broader view which considers all of the scenarios above. Specifically, **a complete product addresses the following in addition to the attributes of the device**:

1. *Channel*, which provides access to the target market segment in order to make them aware of the product
2. *Positioning*, in order to grab potential customers' attention and make them want to learn more
3. *Product information*, so that basic information is readily available to satisfy the customer's desire to do a quick initial evaluation
4. *Ecosystem*, which identifies, integrates, and tests all adjacent entities with which the product must work so a potential customer knows it will work "right out of the box".

**Failure to address each of these four areas can create what we call "hidden inhibitors" to the buying process** – no matter how good the device is, unseen blockers will arise. Customers sometimes won't even be able to verbalize why their interest waned. The rest of this chapter will look at each of these elements in depth.

## Channel

The first step in any buying decision is to become aware of the product. A company could create the most delicious cookie ever made, but if your supermarket did not carry it, you are not likely to buy it. Even if you find out about it through other means such as a direct mail piece, you probably still won't buy it because it is simply too hard to figure out where to buy it. It is much easier to just buy the cookies that are at your every-day grocery store. Until the company can develop their channel, sales will likely be light, notwithstanding the fact that it is the most delicious cookie ever made.

The channel is that vital link to the customer base. It is the entity that knows who the customers are, has access to them in order to sell the product, and has the systems and commercial requirements to execute the transaction. This could be a direct salesforce or a distributor that calls on business customers. It could be a retailer where consumers shop. Or it might be a business partner with an overlapping customer base but non-competing, complementary products. Each target market will have its own unique needs and thus the channel must be appropriate to the task. **A successful productization effort comprehends the right channels and makes arrangements to have them in place and ready to sell the produc**t.

An effective channel strategy can be just as much of a competitive edge as any of the attributes of the product itself. Consider the example of a start up that was founded to provide real-time backup of data on an individual's cell phone, and rapid re-provisioning into a replacement phone if the original were to be lost. Users would never have to worry about losing pictures, phone numbers, settings, or music. This start up appeared to have two primary competitors with a similar offering, who were both at least one year ahead. The company was slowly picking up customers, but without a brand name or expensive advertising campaign, it was quite hard to grow rapidly. But then this start up did a very smart thing: they found and partnered with an insurance company that covered the replacement of lost mobile phone hardware. At time of purchase of a phone and cellular service plan, customers would be asked if they wanted to insure the hardware against theft or loss. If the answer was yes, the customer would be transferred to the insurance company's call center. The start up struck a deal with the insurance company to also add the data backup services as an additional choice to the customers. The insurance company would collect a royalty on the fees from each accepting customer. With this agreement in place, the start-up now had ready access to a very relevant set of customers and the means to solicit and service them. This type of critical customer access would never have been possible without the partnership.

There are some specific ways to analyze and evaluate a sales channel.

- *Matched to Segment/Technology*: A channel first and foremost has to have the "feet on the street" with ready access to the customer. In traditional models, this often means a salesforce that reaches out to create relationships with key decision makers, or a channel entity with which customers are already interacting for other commercial reasons (the mobile carrier above being an example of that; a distributor would be another example). The first role the channel fulfills is to separate the wheat from the chaff by knowing exactly who to communicate with and the most effective way to do it. If the internet is the channel, the challenges are the same: knowing how to stand out to relevant surfers among the millions of other web properties out there. Luckily there are tools such as Google's advertising scheme to help with that. But in both traditional and internet models the goal is to figure out who the right customers are and minimize scattershot methods of attracting them. A channel that is matched to the customer base and technology is critical for this. Problems arise when the organization tries to leverage its existing channels for existing customers into a new market segment or technology. Critical knowledge of the customers and their requirements, as well as key relationships, will likely be lacking. No channel is universal, so the organization always needs to scrutinize whether the channel strategy fits the product and market segment.

- *Motivated to Sell Product*: Simply throwing the product into the right channel will not necessarily lead to success. The individuals involved have to be sufficiently motivated to achieve the desired results. A salesforce shared among multiple product lines always means that your product has to contend for mindshare. The salespeople will be making choices everyday about how they spend their limited time. They will focus on what provides them the most personal gain. If the sales compensation system covers only a "chosen few" products because they are strategic to the company, you will have problems if your product is not on the list. If the product line is new and seems somewhat speculative, the sales team may not want to spend a lot of time on something that might fail. Also they are often slaves to the products currently generating revenue, so new products often get short shrift. The solution is to talk with the sales team manager and try to understand the motivators necessary to sell your product, and the points of resistance that might exist. Get a commitment out of them for a specific amount of time their teams will spend on your product relative to others. You can also work to put in place incentive programs specific to your product, such as rewards (paid for by the business unit) for hitting certain sales quotas. Whatever the method, the end goal is to **ensure that you understand the factors that motivate your channel to sell, and set up the conditions that gets your product the focus it deserves.**

- *Capable of Selling the Product*: So far, so good; the sales team has both the access and the motivation to sell the product to the right customers. The only remaining element is to ensure they are capable of doing so. It starts with the right skill set. If the sale is a technical one, then the salespeople should be technical or at least have enough pre-sales engineers on the team. If it requires strong domain knowledge of the market and technology, then salesforce hiring should take place with this experience in mind. Of course, the salespeople also need intimate knowledge of the product. A common function of the product management team is to train them. The sales training plan should be an integral part of the process of creating a complete product.

## Positioning

With the channel in place, the next challenge is to spark an initial interest in the product. This is Step 2 of the buying decision process discussed above – make them want to learn more about the product. This is done through **the *positioning* of the product, which is the art of presenting facts about the product in a way that grabs the customer's attention and leaves a memorable, positive impression**. A straightforward presentation of the facts (or features) likely won't do it. Why? Can't rational minds absorb these facts and reach a reasonable conclusion about the value of the product? In theory, yes. In reality, we should borrow some wisdom from Dilbert creator Scott Adams who stated that "we're all idiots". To some degree we should assume this about our customers. Not that they are unintelligent, but they can be counted on to be too busy to think through a barrage of facts and features thrown at them. You have to do the heavy lifting of something called the *Value Translation*: translating the attributes of the product into something that a customer believes makes his life easier. If done well, it can make a mediocre device seem good and a good device appear great. But if done poorly, even a great device can go unnoticed in the market. **Rarely are the benefits of a product so overwhelming and self-evident that they are obvious to the customer**. Nor will customers naturally perform this Value Translation for themselves. It is up to the Marketing team to do this right.

There is an identifiable framework for positioning, with five increasing levels of sophistication. This Positioning Hierarchy goes as follows:

Level 1: Communicate Features. Here, the features of the device are presented. This is the least sophisticated method of positioning because it really isn't positioning at all. Many product managers fall into this trap because they are too close to the product. During the entire Product Planning process, this is the level at which they operated. They spent a lot of time defining features for Engineering and discussing them within the organization. Once the Product Marketing phase begins, it can be hard to break from this mindset. Thus the marketing efforts focus mostly on features and function, without ever seeking to perform the Value Translation.

Level 2: Compare to Competition. The next level of positioning adds a comparison to the alternatives. This is usually a head-to-head feature and capability comparison against one or more competitors. This is slightly better than Level 1: at least it positions the product against some external reference point. But even so, this is a rudimentary approach; it merely says "we are better because we have these extra features." But customers don't always care about features, but rather the benefit derived from them.

Level 3: Translate Into Benefit. This tier takes the next step by seeing the situation from the customer's eyes. It comprehends what they care about, and translates the feature into a benefit relevant to the customer's priorities. This is the first level which could be considered "good" marketing. Understanding what the customer cares about and presenting the product in that context represents the essence of marketing. If the product was defined the right way, this should be easy because it will solve significant, real problems that the customer is having.

Level 4: Occupy a Unique Space. Al Ries and Jack Trout introduced the world to the concept of positioning in the 1970s. They stated that the pinnacle of this exercise is to reach a unique position in the customer's mind. When customers think of your product or company, a very simple and positive theme pops into their mind – whether it is "best technology" or "extremely reliable". There is no parity here – reality and perception combine to make the company or product stand out on some aspect. The benefit message is simplified and honed so tightly that it instantly sets you apart from the competition. This is your space in their mind, and nothing short of a herculean effort by your competition can supplant you.

Level 5: Influence the Buying Criteria. This level goes beyond simply solving a problem that the customer defines. It actually influences what the market uses as buying criteria. If you are at parity on the main buying criteria, then the best way to win is to change the rules. This is an exercise in educating the customer on a particular aspect of their usage environment or the product category that may not be currently high on their attention radar. By doing so, you may be able to make this particular aspect, which would obviously play to your product's strengths, become part of their buying criteria.

An example should help illustrate the application of this Positioning Hierarchy. There is a product called the "Sleep Number Bed". It became popular in the late 1990s due to heavy marketing. It is essentially a bed with a mattress that is a large airbag. It can be electronically inflated or deflated for varying degrees of firmness, based on the owner's preference (larger beds have two airbags so each sleeper can use a custom setting). Imagine if it had been marketed as such – the response would likely have been subdued. It would have been perceived as nothing more than an air mattress with a bed-like covering. In fact, inflatable beds had been on the market for years, and never achieved much success. It would have paled in comparison to the emerging bed offerings, each promising complete comfort achieved through large numbers of coils, cotton padding, and custom molding foam. The competition was defining the market's buying criteria to be not only the level of comfort but also the amount of technology applied to the problem.

Enter the Marketing team for the Sleep Number Bed. They realized they couldn't sell an inflatable bag against the advanced comfort technology that their competitors were pushing. So they invented the concept of the "sleep number". The sleep number is shown on a handheld display attached to the bed and reflects the firmness of the mattress (by how much air has been pumped into it). The advertisements state that each person will have their own unique number that represents the perfect and unique comfort point for their body and sleeping style. Advertisements show various celebrities extolling the comfort of the bed and stating their own particular "sleep number". This reinforces the message that "everyone has a unique sleep number". This positioning is therefore changing the buying criteria for a bed. Currently, the market assumes there is a universally "most comfortable" bed out there, and it is the new technologies that enable it. The sleep number concept tries to change this to a belief that there is no single most comfortable bed because each person is built differently and needs their own unique sleep number (level of firmness). Thus, the ideal bed is one that let's you customize it for your particular needs.

Let's see how the marketing of this product might play out when marketed at each of the five levels of the Positioning Hierarchy:

- Level 1 (Communicating Features): The pitch would go something like this: "This bed has an internal inflatable air bag, allowing you to customize the firmness to your desire. The bag is made of high tech Kevlar for 20 year puncture resistance, while at the same time conforming to every curve of your body." This approach is weak. It doesn't connect with a customer in any powerful way, and would seem inferior compared to competitors pushing coil counts and padding layers.
- Level 2 (Comparing to Competition): The messaging would sound like this: "In tests, this bed was shown to provide 25 more minutes of REM sleep per night than competing beds". The comparison to competition does elevate the impact of the message, but it still does so at the feature level. How many people would know exactly how 25 minutes of extra REM sleep would make them feel? Not many. Unfortunately, this places the burden for a Value Translation on the customer, who is probably not able to do it effectively.
- Level 3 (Communicating Benefits): The approach is as follows: " Users of the Sleep Number Bed experience 12% fewer colds than

non-users, and a 25% increase in perceived quality of life." Now the Marketing team is getting creative by making the Value Translation, creating a message the average person understands. They commissioned a poll of users to give their impression of their experience with the bed using two easily understandable parameters: frequency of sickness and quality of life. Of course everybody wants to optimize those, and the Sleep Number people are giving empirical evidence that it can happen. Does it matter who the interviewees were, whether the study was truly scientific, or how "quality of life" is actually measured? Not particularly. The most important thing is that product attributes are skillfully translated into a benefit that instantly resonates with the market.

- Level 4 (Occupy a Unique Space): The message is "What is your sleep number?" This signature tagline resonates with a unique and understandable embedded message. It says that each person has a distinct identity in the context of sleep comfort, and it can be reduced to a single number. The catchy tagline gives the Sleep Number Bed its own unique space in the perception map of the market. It owns the space know as "custom comfort", likely right alongside other vendors who each strive to own other spaces like "long reliability", "softest", and "European comfort".

- Level 5 (Influencing the Buying Criteria): The Sleep Number Bed has reached this highest level of the hierarchy because it seeks to change the notion that there is a universally "most comfortable" bed. Instead, it asserts that everyone has unique needs, so the buying criteria should instead be "most customizable comfort" rather than the amount of technology or universal comfort.

One of the most fundamental principles to observe in positioning is to keep it simple. Trout and Reis talk about an "overcommunicated society", which refers to the battle to be heard above the noise created by all players in a market. Customers develop a fatigue for the bold claims and promises of their vendors and often tune it all out. They also have little time or patience to sort through a complex message. An organization needs to keep its message short and simple, containing the bare essence of what makes the product valuable and unique. In their book

"Made to Stick", authors Chip and Dan Heath talk about "finding the core" of an idea. The full story of a product's value proposition is often complex. Helping the market to fully understand it would require the transmission of a lot of information. Unfortunately, you will rarely have the chance to do so. In an overcommunicated society, your window of access to a customer is brief. So **you have to boil down the mass of information to its most important and fundamental essence – the core of the idea**. This requires what the Heath brothers call "forced prioritization" – you *could* say a lot, but you have to pick only the most important part. They write:

> "Forced prioritization is really painful. Smart people recognize the value of all the material. They see nuance, multiple perspectives – and because they fully appreciate the complexities of a situation, they're often tempted to linger there. This tendency to gravitate toward complexity is perpetually at war with the need to prioritize"

Marketers tend to suffer from what they call the Curse of Knowledge: once you know something, it is difficult to remember what it was like not to know it. This makes it harder to explain to the uninitiated the value of the product. To combat this tendency, **relentlessly prioritize each nuance of the product story, and stick to the most important message in your positioning**. As Antoine de Saint-Exupery said: "A designer knows he has achieved perfection not when there is nothing left to add, but when there is nothing left to take away."

Good positioning is fundamental to turning a device sitting on a lab table into a living, breathing complete product that a customer desires. Good products can become great, and even mediocre products can compete with the right positioning. But without it, even the best device can seem lifeless. Go back to the Sleep Number Bed example. Imagine the situation without the positioning effort. Salesperson: "Want to buy an inflatable bed? It is really comfortable!" Customer: "Inflatable bed? You mean like the one I use in my tent when I go camping? No thanks." Great positioning transforms a product's true value (deriving from its attributes) into perceived value in the customer's mind. If done well it can even amplify it. Absent this, the customer will never appreciate the product enough to want to buy it. This represents a tangible inhibitor to the purchase decision.

## Product information

The positioning will spark the customer's initial interest. But to nurture that interest into a deeper engagement, **the right product information needs to be immediately available to quickly educate customers**. There are many common types of vehicles appropriate for various situations and forums:

- Press releases
- Sales collateral
- Websites
- Direct presentations
- Product seminars
- White papers
- Demos
- Performance test results

The use of product information items is a key piece of Steps 2 and 3 of the buying decision process. The nature of each of these will be addressed in detail in Chapter 19 "Product Information" and Chapter 20 "Press Releases". Here the focus is on their importance in creating a complete product.

If the Marketing team could visit each and every customer personally, they would have the opportunity to educate each of them on the product in depth. Obviously this is not possible in Steps 1 and 2 (if ever), and so the marketer must find ways to project the message and information through other means. Early in the process, a customer may be initially unaware of the product, or prefer to get their initial information anonymously. This is where press releases and web content are critical. When a salesperson becomes involved, product briefs and white papers can be critical in selling a complex product. The salesperson's skill set is often optimized for developing relationships and understanding customer decision dynamics rather than complicated product messages. Marketing collateral supplements their skills with succinct, effective product information that allows them to turn that initial customer interest into a deeper engagement.

Without it, Sales' may not be able to bring the right information to bear to move the customer beyond Step 2.

As the process moves to Steps 3 and 4, the customer may need to dig into the technical details of the product as a prerequisite to a purchase decision. This is when it is very important for the organization to have created comprehensive technical documentation (supplemented as necessary with activities like technical seminars). **A lack of such documentation can be a real inhibitor to the process; without it, most customers will never make a decision to buy the product** (discussed further in Chapter 19 "Product Information"). Of course, the information could be delivered through personal interaction between the customer and the organization's Applications Engineers, but it wouldn't scale across a broad customer base (and customer won't put much stock in technical information that is not written down). Hence, the written documentation is mandatory. Unfortunately most organizations fall into the trap of having to focus their scarce resources on development at the expense of documentation. Because a lack of documentation can be such an inhibitor to a sale, the organization must avoid a situation like this at all costs.

**Another significant obstacle to the buying process is the natural skepticism around claims made about the product**. Every vendor boasts that their product is the best. But eventually customers simply become numb to it. Fabricated claims and valid claims both look the same to the customer, who isn't necessarily able or willing to make the effort to figure out which is which. So the marketer's task is to assemble information that backs up the claims made. Preferably, the source is a (presumably impartial) third party. Let us look at some examples:

- *Claim: "We hold the #1 market share position"*. This is something companies like to say to prove their products are good and that they are a stable vendor. A third party market sizing report would help back this up.
- *Claim: "Our product offers the fastest performance in the market"*. There is no more common claim in most industries. A good approach would be to define a usage environment (which presumably reflects that of the customer) and an associated test methodology. Then hire a third party testing house to run the test and publish a document with the results. This gives the customer visibility into the test methodology (so they can evaluate

its validity) and proof that the test was run fairly; both help reduce the skepticism around the associated claims. Going a step further, a live demo of the product's performance can be a very powerful tool for combating skepticism.

- *Claim: "This is a real problem in the market (which our product solves)".* As discussed thoroughly in Chapter 7 "Market Problem" and elsewhere, the foundation of product planning is to determine the right Market Problems. In most cases you are learning about those problems directly from customers: in other cases you have to help the customer see the problem that exists. In the latter situation, third party analyst reports, polls, or quotes from articles and studies can be very valid data points to help establish these claims.

It is these important elements – product briefs, technical documentation, seminars, 3rd party reports, and demos – that all combine to deliver the right product information at the right time, in the right situation. Yet all too often the organization does not plan properly for these items. The most common cause is that all resources are consumed by the development effort or winning business and the product information pieces simply get de-prioritized. None of them are particularly difficult to create, certainly not when compared to the effort and creativity necessary to define and develop the product. So in order to create a complete product, these elements related to product information need to be planned for up front.

## Ecosystem

We now turn our attention to hidden inhibitors relating to factors that enable or enhance the usage of the product. If you are buying a trash bag, there is little else you need in order to use it to its maximum utility. But for more complex products, there may be some dependency on some complementary entities. Sometimes the dependency is absolute – to drive a car you need gas, or to use computer hardware you need an operating system. In other cases the complementary product is not absolutely necessary but does enhance the overall usage experience – that same computer seems more attractive if you know it has already been fully tested with the full set of applications you might someday be running on it. The set of these complementary items makes up what we call the ecosystem – a set of entities which enable or enhance the usage of the primary product.

Anticipating this ecosystem is the key to success here. If its important elements are understood, then effort can be applied to making sure they are addressed in a way that makes them non-issues for the customers. Going back to the computer example, the organization could seek to understand what applications will be run by their customers, put them in the lab and test them, then publish this 'tested' list to customers. These customers would no longer have to wonder if they will have problems running these applications on the computer they buy. This concern has now been removed, a powerful benefit for the product during the buying decision. But consider the opposite situation. If the organization does not concern itself with this ecosystem of applications, then the burden shifts to the customer to figure out if they will work with this particular computer. **This uncertainty could subtly inject a roadblock in the mental process of considering the purchase**. Studies have shown that even small amounts of uncertainty can irrationally stall a decision. Therefore it is not wise to leave it to customers to figure out which types of complementary products are needed, which vendors are the best, and whether they will work with the specific product. In some industries this may be the norm, but eventually one competitor sees the huge competitive advantage to be gained from simply putting all the pieces together for the customer. Customers no longer have these uncertainties around "how do I make this product work?" when dealing with this specific vendor. Removal of this concern can be a powerful advantage in the selling process. The truth is that customers don't want to do any work in order to use the product. They want to wake up one day, walk into the house or the office, open a box with your product inside, and have it be fully functional immediately without having to read the directions. They want it to "just work".

This is where so many marketers fall short in creating a successful product. **The root cause lies in confusing what your product "can" do versus what is "does" do right out of the box**. The two are separated by the effort to identify and acquire the complementary products, determine interoperability, and combine the two products in an operational environment. Sure, customers are capable of doing these things themselves. But a complete product that does it for them would be more attractive, both because it makes the customer's life easier by eliminating that work and because it removes from the purchase decision the uncertainty of whether it would work together at all. Doing this can provide a powerful advantage in the selling process.

The most striking example of successful ecosystem creation is the Apple iPod. Portable media players certainly existed before Apple entered the market. Digital music certainly existed as well. But Apple was able to make this combination a worldwide phenomenon. Why? It was because consumers experienced the same hidden inhibitors related to ecosystem mentioned above. There were several different music formats in use at the time – MP3, WMA, OOG, etc. Each didn't always work on a given player. Even when a particular format was supposed to work, sometimes it did not. There were also the legal issues involved, since the only type of digital music reliably allowed by law was that copied from your own compact discs – most online sources of music were questionable. There were many websites offering files, but consumers were never quite sure which were operating legally and most had limited choices. And the task of downloading and managing one's catalogue of music was never particularly easy. Apple came in and changed all this by putting the ecosystem in place *for* the customer. They set up the iTunes music service, and negotiated with record labels to legally sell music files over the Internet. The iPod used Apple's AAC file format, so it always worked. And they overlaid all of this with easy to use software to find, download, and manage all the music. Apple, primarily a hardware company, did not see their role as selling media player hardware while relying on the consumer to figure out the rest ("but the player is designed to work with any file format and website service!"). They lifted this burden from the consumer by putting all the pieces in place. It just worked. And that same consumer, free from the confusion and pain of their digital music world to date, responded by buying hundreds of millions of iPods and billions of songs. This was truly a textbook job building an ecosystem.

## Conclusion

Davidow's observations in this area were an earth-shaking epiphany in the field of marketing. With a view confined to the device itself, organizations were trapped into competing mostly on cost and features. If the device's attributes were better than the competition's, it won. But **by re-**

**moving the blinders and taking a broader view of your offering, you open up a whole new set of elements on which to compete**. If you can identify and eliminate the "hidden inhibitors" better than your competition, you become that much more competitive. You can win on elements that your competition might not even be aware of.  It only requires that you take this last step to create the complete product. It is a tragic mistake when Marketing wastes the enormous effort Engineering expended to create the device by failing to go that extra mile to maximize competitiveness by turning it into a complete product.

## Creating Complete Products: Real World Example

*The Marketing team was feeling very good at this point. The organization had agreed on a product definition, and Engineering was gearing up to staff the program. But their work was only just beginning. The General Manager was quick to remind them that the full process of turning Mason from a device into a product required more than just a locked definition. He knew from experience that there would be a host of "hidden inhibitors" that would create friction in the selling process. It was the job of the Marketing team to find and eliminate them.*

*The first step was to ensure an effective conduit to the target market segment. This meant getting the channel in order. Because the company had a long history of selling to the PC OEMs, a salesforce was already in place calling upon the groups making laptop computers. But the blade PC was a new market for TechCorp. There were no relationships in place with the groups within the major PC OEMs making blade PCs, nor with the group of startups also doing so. Part of the productization plan would be to officially task Sales to identify the right organizations and individuals. Sales would require some extra runway before the official sales cycle to do so. To arm the sales team with the right knowledge on Mason, a training plan would need to be created. The annual sales conference was coming up, so that would be the primary forum. A request to do a class at the conference was submitted to the organizer of the conference, and a training agenda was put together in order to guide content creation. Since the salesforce was shared with other product lines within the company, it was always a battle for their mindshare. The Director of Marketing took the initiative to meet with a few key sales managers to understand the goals they had set for their teams. It turns out that the current year's objectives had already been set; each salesperson was given a quota for three specific products that were tabbed as being strategic to TechCorp. Mason was not on that list, creating a clear obstacle to getting the sales team's mindshare. The Director of Marketing consequently asked his GM to work with the Vice President of Sales to somehow work Mason into the year's goals. Although he was not able to get it prioritized as high as the three products already on the list, an agreement was worked out whereby certain criteria of progress around Mason were codified. The Marketing team felt they could live with this, and a major potential inhibitor in the channel was now mitigated.*

254

*Marketing then focused on how to position the product in order to create that initial interest from the customer. Customers were not telepathic, so they wouldn't automatically understand what Mason offers them. The team wanted the positioning to succinctly communicate its value. One of the members of the team was new to Marketing, having recently come out of Engineering. He suggested that they focus on hard facts, highlighting the low power consumption while in Cable Sensing Mode, and the strength of the 256 bit encryption used to protect keys inside the TPM. But the more experienced members scoffed at him, kindly educating him that this focus on features would not resonate with customers. Yet he persisted, asserting that if they compared these attributes to what competitors were offering, the superiority of Mason should be undeniable. While they applauded his effort to move one step higher on the Positioning Hierarchy, they were still unmoved. What was needed was for the team to do the Value Translation for the customer: convert the features into benefits that are relevant to the customers' usage environment. They would start with a focus on the power attributes. While power consumption was interesting, what really mattered was the resulting battery life. So the team decided to position Mason as enabling longer battery life. This was good, as they were now operating at Level 3 of the hierarchy by focusing on benefits. But could they go higher and try to define and occupy some unique space in the customer's mind? Mason achieved longer battery life this through the intelligence the chip possessed to determine whether the cable was present. So instead of using the dull "Cable Sensing Mode", they named it "Intelligent Power", in stark contrast to competition's focus on low total power. This would help Mason stand apart from the alternatives within the customer's mind. This positioning would then be supported by marketing materials which helped explain why Intelligent Power was better and worthy of being a buying criterion.*

*Everyone agreed that this really helped take the positioning nearly to Level 5 on the hierarchy. Now, could the same be done for Mason's entire value proposition? Could power and security be wrapped up into a higher level message that was simple and memorable? Someone raised the point that laptop users, by definition, need easy mobility; they want to use the PC anytime, anywhere. Two elements that support this are long battery life and strong protection of data on the laptop, since it is particularly vulnerable to theft. Users also want the PC to "just work", because they are on the go and not necessarily close to a technician who could quickly fix problems. So the* mobility that users crave requires protection for their data, long battery life, and reliability. Mason supported all of these well, including the last one because the architecture had been field tested on two prior generations of product. Thus, this gave rise to the positioning statement: "True Mobility through security, long battery life, and stability." Now all of the key attributes of Mason for laptops rolled up into one simple message – True Mobility. The team felt by creating qualifiers for "mobility" that Mason best fulfilled, they could begin to own this space within the customer's mind.

Next was a discussion of any buying inhibitors that might exist as a result of a lack of information about the product. Of course, the more obvious product information pieces would be created: press release, website, and sales training aids. But it soon became clear that there would be two areas of concern which could require additional pieces. One was a possible confusion or skepticism that Intelligent Power was better than low total power. The supporting data was straightforward but not succinct, so the customer might not make the effort to validate the claim. The risk would then be that they would write it off as just another vendor making empty promises. In order to help customers understand this attribute of the product, the team decided to write a short white paper detailing how battery drain on a laptop PC was more likely to occur while the user was mobile, and thus not connected to a network cable. Thus, the majority of the time the PC is being used in a way that the network chip could be mostly powered down, thus conserving energy. The white paper was intended to give customers a way to absorb this message at their own pace, via a well organized and well written communication piece. Furthermore, in order to battle any skepticism about the actual performance of the product, a 3rd party performance test (in this case measuring battery performance of the PC with Mason vs. with a competing product) was planned. This would show an impartial 3rd party certifying that Mason did indeed enable a savings of 10 minutes of battery life using the Intelligent Power capability. Finally, the Applications Engineering team was asked to set up a demo showing a side by side real-time comparison of two PCs and the battery life impact of the Mason product. This could be used at trade shows and on customer visits to reinforce the message, as showing something is always better for retention than talking about it. All three of these pieces would serve to highlight and validate the positioning and benefits of Mason relative to power consumption. The latter two would help eliminate the hidden inhibitor that customer skepticism often created.

*The focus of the team now shifted to any ecosystem elements that needed to be in place in order to maximize or enable the utility of Mason's functionality. One thing that immediately came to mind was the software necessary to utilize the TPM capabilities. This technology had been created through an industry standard which specified a specific type of software must be run with the chip. This software was rather complicated, and so the organization had assumed that customers would source this through any one of several software companies which already offered it. But rarely do software and hardware work completely seamlessly out of the box. Forcing customers to do this integration and testing work themselves would be a big inhibitor to getting them to adopt the TPM technology. Since the organization was trying to drive TPM as a mainstream feature, this might hinder the strategy. So the decision was made to choose the two best TPM software packages, and do the integration and testing in-house. Now, Mason could be advertised to work with either "right out of the box", which would make it easier for customers to use the product. One more step was taken. A customer had given some feedback that most of the TPM software providers were smaller companies, and they were worried about basing their multi-billion dollar PC OEM business on a small corporate entity. In particular, liability indemnification and support were big concerns because the small company would likely not be able to adequately provide either. These concerns were so acute that it was essentially a show-stopper for using the TPM functionality. After much internal debate, the organization decided to directly license the TPM software, and simply bundle it with the chip. The PC OEM would then not need to have a commercial or support relationship with the small software companies. This alleviated the concern and removed several serious inhibitors to selling Mason.*

# Checklist

### Does the organization have access to target customers?
Successful organizations don't simply hope for access to customers – they create and enable a channel that offers the right exposure to the target market

## What to Look For:
- The right channel provides ready access to customers and is enabled to sell

### Will the product messaging be memorable?
Devices are characterized by attributes and comparisons, but complete products communicate their benefits in a way that is meaningful and memorable.

## What to Look For:
- Forced Prioritization was used to create succinct Level 4or 5 positioning

### Is all necessary product information planned for?
Successful organizations identify and plan for all necessary vehicles of product information that customers need to make a favorable buying decision

## What to Look For:
- Requirements for market and technical information are in the MRD and staffed

### Are all necessary ecosystem elements planned for?
Complete products encompass not just the device itself, but also all of the elements needed to enable or enhance use of the device.

## What to Look For:
- Every element to make the product work "out of the box" is planned for

*(Further discussion on this checklist available at www.systemnotcircumstance.com)*

# CHAPTER 18:

## Standard Marketing Presentation

*Modern political parties have perfected the art of message management. A large number of people are expected to deliver an effective and coordinated message across a variety of forums. Behind it all, a strong party organization manages to plan, unify, and control the message. Repetition and consistency are used to drive the message home. Product organizations need to apply the same discipline to their own message management. A well planned message needs to be codified as a single source slide set for multiple individuals to use in various selling situations. The goal is to ensure the consistency and repetition that is essential to marketing a great product. A core competence for great products requires that organizations have a distinct process and set of expectations on how this is done for each product.*

## Structure of the Marketing Pitch

Much time will be spent explaining the attributes of the complete product to customers. The whole endgame of the marketing effort is to communicate to customers what you offer, why it is valuable to them, and why it is better than their alternatives. This messaging will get transmitted in many ways by many people, and thus needs to be consistent across all communication paths. So it makes sense to codify your message in a single reference document called the Standard Marketing Presentation. It serves as the source document – a central repository for the story. As different selling situations arise, the unique set of information appropriate to the situation can be derived from the Standard Marketing Presentation. A product manager may use the superset of slides to give a detailed presentation to a group of midlevel individuals at one large customer. The General Manager may give a shorter high level presentation to the customer's executives. Or a salesperson may need two simple slides to email to a customer in order to generate enough interest to get a meeting. Each selling situation requires a slightly set of information and level of detail. So, problems can arise if each of these individuals has to cobble together the unique set of information appropriate for their unique presenting situation. Doing so is first and foremost inefficient. It also introduces the risk of the message being inconsistent or incorrect, especially if the positioning or status of the product is changing. Being able to quickly draw the material from a master set of slides, with little modification, is the best way to minimize all of these issues. **A Standard Marketing Presentation serves as the source document that feeds information to each messaging situation**, customized for the scenario but consistent with the overall story. It allows the Marketing team to scale and extend its effort by empowering a larger set of individuals with the right information to sell the product.

What follows is a template for a presentation for the marketing story. It is not intended to be entirely proscriptive, as every product marketing situation is unique. But it does cover four key elements of a presentation structure that has proven to be effective.

*Market Trends and Problems:* This is intended to give a view of the big picture. Too often marketers are like teenage boys – desperately wanting to cut to the chase. **They rush to talk about what the product *does* before taking anytime to establish the context for *why* the product**

**does what it does**. Customers become more open to the details when they can understand the big picture first. This starts with a discussion of trends in the market which are relevant to the product. Of course, the trends are chosen and presented in a way that reinforces the need for the product. Providing this type of content also positions you as a credible source of information and education on the market. Because you are providing them a valuable education service, they'll tend to be more open to you. So work to identify relevant trends and create a story around them. Yet this story must inevitably lead to a discussion of the specific problems that the customer is or will experience (as the trends play out). Recall the earlier discussion on how great products always solve real customer problems. Likewise, great presentations establish the problem first before any discussion of the solution. Doing so puts the customer in the right mindset to hear your messaging. Suddenly you are not just another vendor pushing yet another product to them; you are instead someone who understands their problems and can help solve them.

*Product Line Strategy*: Here you will describe the product line level strategy that is being pursued in response to the trends in the market. For the moment forget individual products – **overall, what are you trying to accomplish, and how are you competing?** Again, this is part of the big picture which will give your customers the right context to better understand and appreciate the individual products themselves. They want to know you have a vision for the product line that evolves and improves over time, rather than just a collection of point products. It positions you as a thought leader and a good long term partner. It is also a chance to use your strategy as a differentiator. Normally you compare your product head-to-head with that of the competition, hoping to convince the customer why you are better. Now you can take this battle to a higher plane. For instance, a manufacturing company who is the market share leader might tout their unique ability to leverage economies of scale. Thus, they are uniquely positioned to provide the lowest price and most stable supply over the long term. Although the company may not have the best price or performance at the moment, the case could be made that they have a fundamental long term advantage at the strategic level. Or, you could claim to have the largest R&D capability, and thus the most robust innovation engine and investment commitment to continue to drive new technologies. In effect, you are trying to expand the buying criteria; to the specific product attributes are added an evaluation of the company and its strategy. If you have the facts to back it up, take advantage of this technique to give your value proposition an added dimension.

*Existing Product Benefits:* With the context established, your audience is now ready to receive messaging about individual products. Start with those available today, including the one being sold in the current sales cycle. The primary job is to focus on the benefits of each, rather than simply relaying feature lists. Features are certainly meaningful to you, but don't always easily translate into something that resonates with the customer. **It is up to you to do that translation for them, using terms that are relevant to their problems**. This sounds easy, but is not always so in practice. You've spent the entire product planning phase talking about features, because that is the language which your internal teams speak. But do not carry this forward. A translation process *must* happen, and this is the phase where it should be happening. This step is always a good litmus test. If you are having trouble positioning your product to accomplish this, it may be that your features are not tied directly to a real customer problem. Of course this would be a sure sign to reconsider the definition. One final thought: try to target three benefits to show. There is something symmetrical to the human mind about three ideas that seems to optimize retention. You may have many relevant ideas about the product that could be communicated, but try to limit them to three.

*Future Product Roadmap:* This is where you begin to "sell the future". Of course you compete mostly on the product of today. But the buying criteria often include consideration of what the vendor will bring you down the road. There is a certain stickiness to a vendor relationship, and many customers prefer to maintain them over the long term. It may be because of personal relationships, commercial benefits, or high switching costs between products or technologies from different vendors. So, the preference is to buy today from a vendor who is competitive today but will also continue to offer very attractive products tomorrow. So a prime goal here is to "sell the roadmap". Don't be afraid to lean forward a little bit in terms of what you are promising for the future. You need not constrain yourself to products which are approved, or which you are fully certain you will develop. There is expected to be some movement on a roadmap. It is a statement of intent, but also a tool of inquiry. Tentative plans can be stated with certainty as a means of generating feedback from customers on those plans. This is far more preferable than meeting with customers and simply asking them "what do you want us to build?" Customers expect you to bring them the vision, not the other way around. They are not going to offer up their ideas unless you prime the pump first with your own vision and strategy. Confidently stating "this is where we are going" is an effective way to open them up so they provide candid feedback on whether it meets their business needs. **So, sell the vision and roadmap first, and then ask your questions**. The format for the roadmap is typically a slide with current and future product shown in an X- and Y-axis format. The Y-axis may mean nothing, or could denote different segments at which the products are targeted. The X-axis indicates time, and shows how your product line evolves over time. Your goal is to give the audience a view of the "big ticket" items that are being introduced in each upcoming product generation. Stick to the highlights, as details will only bog down the message and thus are better put in backup slides.

There is one final note worth mentioning on the structure of this presentation. Earlier it was stated that the Standard Marketing Presentation is intended to allow a custom set of content to be pulled quickly for each unique selling situation. This requires the presentation to be created in modular and hierarchical fashion. So, for instance, there should be a single slide that summarizes relevant market trends, supplemented with several other slides that explain these trends in more detail. Each of the sections would be created as such. For shorter presentations – such as to an executive or prospective customer – the high level slides can be easily extracted from the larger presentation with little or no modification needed. Longer presentations use more of the detail slides as needed.

## Presentation Style

The ability to create a great customer presentation is a bit of an art form. But there some basic principles that can help when followed. The first is to *organize* the presentation properly. **The structure of the presentation should be dictated by a logical flow of the ideas involved**. Before considering the content of individual slides, consider how you would like the story to unfold. If you had 30 seconds to tell it, what would be the main soundbytes you would lay out? The problem with most presentations is that they are built from the ground up. One or more slides are created for each individual topic that needs to be covered. Then the slides are thrown together into a jumbled mass of ideas. Instead, create from the top down. Establish your simple chain of logic, with natural progression from one idea to the next. This flow should then be codified in your agenda. As the presentation progresses, divider slides should show the transition from one major section to the next. A smooth flow, coupled with clear organization, is a powerful tool in increasing audience attention and retention. Each idea moves naturally into the next, and audience members will always know where they are in the overall presentation.

**Once the flow is set, only then should you begin to consider the *content* for individual slides**. Consider each slide as conveying a single important idea. In fact, it can be good practice to make the title of a particular slide explicitly state that single point. So if you have a slide that shows the large target market for a product, you might title it "The Market Opportunity is Immense for Product X" rather than "Target Market Size". The former sets up the audience member with an assertion which is then presumably supported by the data in the body of the slide. To some degree, the sequence of ideas that make up your flow simply become the titles of your slides. So not only does the overall presentation have a well thought out chain of logic, but it is clearly documented so the audience can easily understand it and follow along.

Another principle to remember is that the human mind only retains small chunks of information at one time. There is a tendency to put everything we know about a topic onto a slide, but ultimately an individual audience member will only retain a small part of it. You might as well **filter the information down to the part you need them to remember**. Most customers will have a level of impatience with vendors. They'll want you to get to the point quickly.

## Access to the Pitch

As we mentioned before, this marketing presentation serves a wide variety of people for various purposes. But that doesn't mean that it is open for anyone to access in its full format. This set of slides contains very sensitive information about products, strategies, and positioning. In the hands of a competitor it would be extremely dangerous. Thus, **access to the presentation needs to be controlled very tightly by Marketing**. Similar to the dilemma faced when deciding how much information to make public in a press release, access to the marketing presentation is a balancing act between the risks of a leak and the need to educate customers.

The main concern is a competitive leak via a customer. Often when you present, you'll be asked by someone in the audience for a copy of the slides. You should feel uncomfortable giving them a soft copy because you lose all control of where the information goes. The concern here is not with individuals in the customer's organization with whom you meet and some relationship exists. The problem is when these people email the slides internally, and those people pass it on again. At some point, someone you don't know has the slides. Those who eventually end up with them may or may not have loyalties or professional ethical standards which compel them to keep your information confidential. Or, you may be trying to break into a new customer that uses your competitor's product; their current loyalties and relationships could pose a risk to your information. In any such case, an uncontrolled soft copy is a leakage point you must consider. When presented with such a request, you may want to pare down the slides you send them to focus on safe information and minimize anything that is highly sensitive.

Exacerbating this is the fact that the Sales team will be continually requesting access to the presentation. Of course they'll want it to educate themselves so they are capable of selling the product; in fact, it is Marketing's job to facilitate this. But the problem comes when Sales gets lazy. Instead of putting in the time to train themselves to sell effectively, they might simply send the marketing presentation along to the customer hoping to generate some interest. Marketing cannot always rely on the Sales team to be discrete with sensitive information, or to filter out parts that are highly sensitive to leaks. This is not a knock on their integrity, common sense, or competence. It is merely a fact that has played out over time. So the Marketing team needs to approach this task smartly. Clearly, Sales needs some requisite set of information to proactively push to customers in order to do their job. Here we recommend creating a subset of the full marketing presentation which is appropriate for broader (but still confidential) distribution. Train the salesforce on the entire story, but only post the subset of slides for their use with customers. This should not be problematic – Sales isn't going to be able to present the full story in great depth anyway. The subset of slides should suffice for them to generate and/or assess customer interest, at which point more detailed information can be provided in controlled fashion.

It is also wise to create a set of guidelines for distribution. This includes clear criteria for Sales to vet customer opportunities, usually organized in the form of a set of questions they need to answer about the customer. Some criteria may cover the size of the opportunity (there is no sense in creating leak potential for a very small financial opportunity) or the applicability of the product (don't want to risk a leak when ultimately the product is not a good fit for the customer's needs). In the absence of guidelines, salespeople will often err on the side of making the customer happy, and customers inevitably want all the information. Marketing needs to define these engagement rules, and then enforce them with an iron grip; this means the ability to say "no" in the face of persistent salesperson who very much wants to engage a customer.

## Conclusion

The Standard Marketing Presentation serves as the "golden master" copy of the entire product line story. As the owner of the content, it is Marketing's responsibility to put this in place, and it is in their best interest to do so. It will save them a significant amount of time, as they can quickly peel off subsets of the information customized for specific situations. In its absence however, members of the organization that find themselves in a selling situation will improvise as best they can. They'll either make their own slides based on their current understanding of the product, or use whatever slides on the product they may have on their hard drive. This is dangerous, as the content could be out of date or simply not in synch with the overall message. Marketing needs to orchestrate the organization in what is presented externally, no matter the situation. The Standard Marketing Presentation is an effective tool that helps keep everyone in synch.

# The Marketing Pitch: Real World Example

*With the sales cycle for Mason about to begin, the Standard Marketing Presentation needed to be created. The team was particularly interested in putting this together because of the painful experience with the last product where one was not done. Customers had the perception that the product story changed slightly each time that it was told. In particular, Sales and Senior Management were not exactly in synch with Marketing on the exact positioning and details. The marketing effort ended up being somewhat incoherent. While the product fared reasonably well in the market, there was a lingering feeling that it could have done better with a more focused message. So the team was sufficiently motivated to codify the message into a Standard Marketing Presentation. This presentation would embody the message around the product's core positioning: "True Mobility through security, long battery life, and stability".*

*Marketing's first goal was to paint a picture of what was happening in the market. Of course this view would be biased towards supporting Mason's attributes. In the security arena, it was important to establish three things. First, that theft of PCs is a pervasive problem. Second, that the corporate data on these stolen PCs is very valuable. Finally, that the amount of data on a PC grows rapidly every year. In support of the first point, a member of the team was able to find an FBI report with crime statistics related to laptop thefts. It showed the number of reported cases to be large and growing over time. This was a good one – not only was it real data, but the FBI would be an incredibly believable source. To reinforce the third point, a graph was borrowed from a presentation by a hard drive company which showed the size of hard drives increasing over time.*

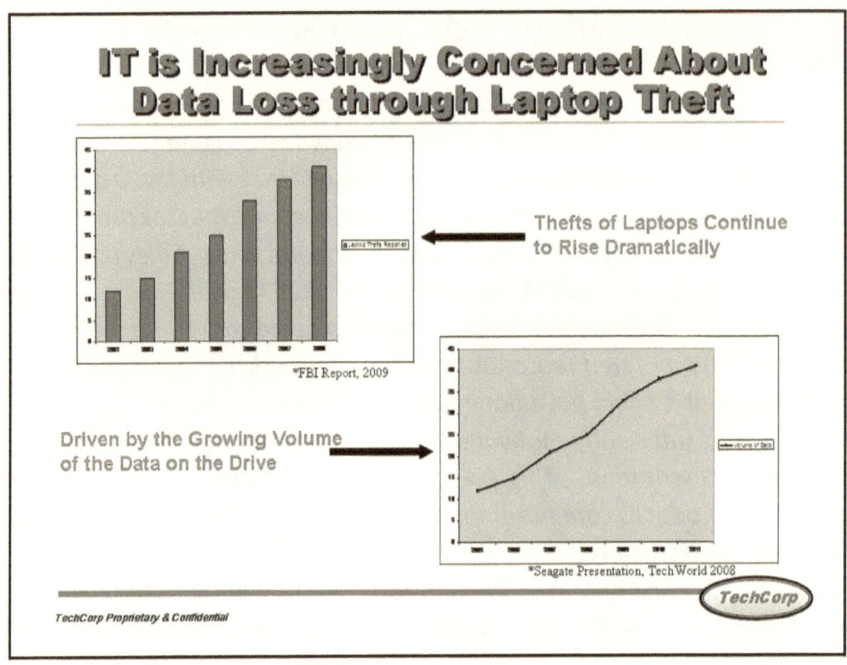

*Figure 18.1: Market Problem Slide*

Hard data, as shown in Figure 18.1, is very effective at shaping a customer's view of the market. Providing this type of information positions TechCorp as a credible source of market data. It certainly helps establish and focus the Market Problem so that the need for Mason and its security attributes becomes even more evident. A similar story was also created for trends in the market relative to power and battery life usage in mobile devices. Both of these stories served as market-based support for helping customers understand what is necessary to provide "True Mobility".

This characterization of the market set the stage for a description of Tech-Corp's strategy in this area. The Marketing team's approach was to demonstrate a corporate core competence in the area of data and content security. The goal would to be convince customers that since TechCorp has the intellectual property and knowledge to design systems trusted for highly sensitive applications (like content protection or financial transactions), then they must also be highly competent to secure PC data. So the strategy shown in Figure 18.2 was to apply expertise from these other industries to enable robust security and quick time to market in the PC space. With some of the other company level advantages discussed in the competitive analysis, they had made a pretty good case that TechCorp was a good long term partner.

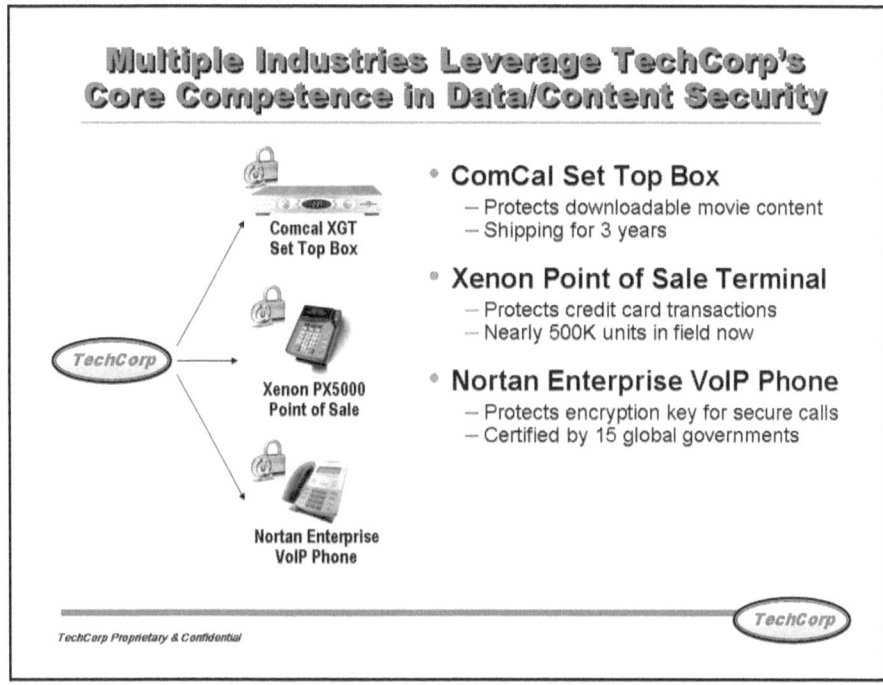

*Figure 18.2: Company Level Strategy Slide*

From a strategy standpoint, TPM was being positioned as the superior technology to protect corporate data, relative to Competitor A's approach based on bulk data encryption. To do this, the Marketing team created a few slides showing that physical theft was a much more relevant threat to corporate data than was network sniffing, against which bulk encryption protected. The overall goal of this part of the presentation was to show that TechCorp had a better <u>strategy</u> to address the market's security needs, and was well suited to <u>execute</u> on that strategy by leveraging core corporate competencies.

With TechCorp's strategic superiority presumably now established, the presentation could turn to presenting the products themselves. A slide was created for each of the organization's existing products. The goal was to convey the benefits of each product, with focus on how it solved customers' problems. The slide for Mason would of course focus on the core message around "True Mobility" as shown in Figure 18.3.

*Figure 18.3: Mason Core Message Slide*

This slide was intended to introduce the product and its benefits to the customer; backup slides were created for audiences that wanted more detail. But this was the slide that could be used universally by Marketing, Sales, and Management showing the main product positioning and benefits.

Next came the task of "selling the future" through the roadmap. The team had some very exciting technologies in mind for next generation products. They wanted to get the customers excited as well, but also solicit some feedback to make sure they were on the right track. They chose to show a different roadmap for each of the target segments. For mobile PCs, it was as shown in Figure 18.4:

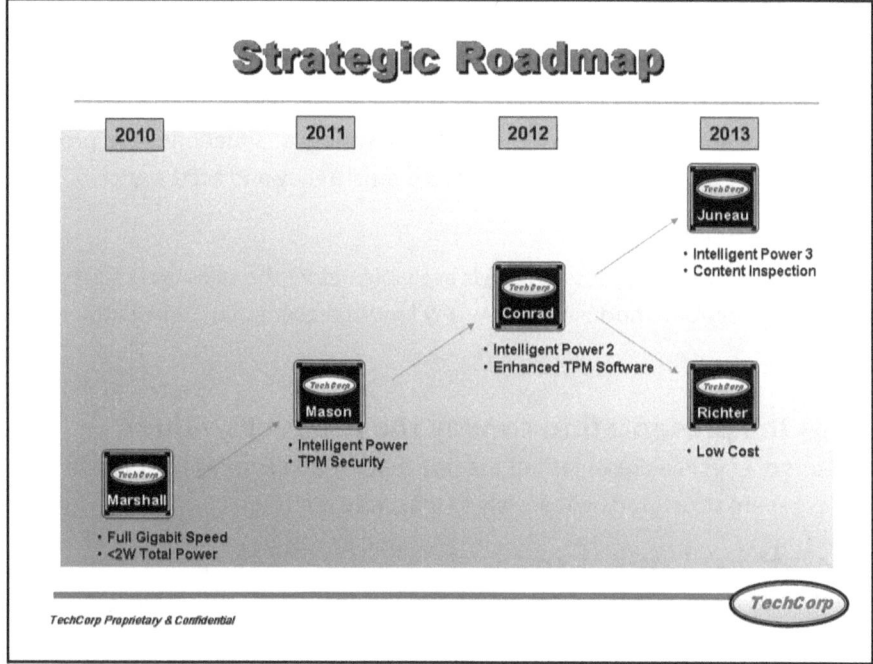

*Figure 18.4: Roadmap Slide*

*Without having to list all of the details, the high-level improvements of each product generation are shown. With only a quick read, the audience would easily understand how TechCorp would innovate in this space over the next several years. This was the type of slide which could be presented by all parties selling the product, with more detail provided as necessary in supplemental slides. This roadmap slide could quickly convey that TechCorp was the right partner for enabling True Mobility for the long term, thus reinforcing the motivation to become a customer now.*

*(Slides in this example are available at www.systemnotcircumstance.com)*

# Checklist

### Has a Standard Marketing Presentation been created?
Products are sold by multiple individuals in a variety of situations. The product story should be centrally codified to ensure consistency and accuracy

## What to Look For:
- A presentation (w/access policy) is available before the sales cycle starts
- It is scalable and modular to allow any length presentation to be extracted


### Does the presentation convey the product's value?
Creators of effective presentations assume that the audience will be passive, thus messages are structured deliberately to maximize retention.

## What to Look For:
- There is a core, fundamental theme supported by three sub-messages.
- Ideas flow logically like a story, rather than a jumbled of messages


*(Further discussion on this checklist available at www.systemnotcircumstance.com)*

# CHAPTER 19:

## Product Information

*"If a tree falls in the woods, does it make a sound?" That's the old adage suggesting that if one isn't directly aware of some entity or event, it may as well not have happened. Literally we know this to be just a parable, but metaphorically it is an analogy for your domain: if customers are unable to get the information they need about your product, does it matter how great it is? Product information pieces are the vehicle for the organization to project its message to a broad array of customers. Successful product dynasties make their product literature and technical documentation a critical component of influencing the market to desire, purchase, and use the product. They have repeatable methods for identifying which collateral or documentation is necessary for success, then reserving the necessary resources to execute it promptly.*

## The Importance of Product Information

We discussed in Chapter 17 "Creating Complete Products" how critical product information is to creating a complete product. Sales collateral is the conduit for conveying the value of your offering. Technical documentation makes it easy for the technical user or implementer to know how the device behaves. This is the information the customer needs in order to make a purchase decision in favor of your product. **Customers don't want to go on a fact finding mission – the right information needs to be immediately available**. Even great devices can fail in the market because of the hidden inhibitors that a lack of product information can expose:

- The customer may give up on the buying process simply because it was too hard to find out what he needed to know.
- The customer may not perceive the value because the salesperson or channel entity did not have sales collateral to supplement their (limited) personal knowledge in the selling process.
- The customer may perceive the product as not being "ready for prime time" because technical documentation is not ready. This is a common indicator that the product is more slideware than real.
- The customer may believe that technical support will be weak because technical documentation is not ready. If the organization can't dedicate the resources to support customers before the buying decision, customers will assume it only gets worse once the product is purchased.

Even if the feature set and price meet customers' needs better than the alternatives, any of these reasons could still cause customers to walk away. On the other hand, great product information makes it easy for customers to learn about the product and gives the perception that technical support will be good. This can be leveraged as a tangible competitive advantage.

## Sales Collateral

Early in the buying decision process discussed in Chapter 17 "Creating Complete Products", customers are marginally aware of the product, but don't yet know much about it. Their interest level may vary, as will the amount of time they are willing to spend learning about the product.

**The key to success is to have available the right amount of information in the right medium to support the customer's information gathering**. If a customer is walking by the organization's booth at the trade show, they may be unwilling to talk with a human but willing to take a one page product summary to read later. Or that customer may prefer to simply peruse the organization's website for more information. A salesperson having an initial 30 minute discovery meeting with a potential new customer may want to provide such a product summary. A marketer may wish to provide a detailed document describing a market trend or complex technology in order to expand upon the presentation she gave to the customer. All of these situations require information about the product's benefits and attributes in a written format. Through this sales collateral, Marketing can expand their reach and empower a broader set of individuals to successfully participate in the selling process. Because of the written format, it can also improve retention of the information because it can be crisply organized and the customer can read and re-read it at his own pace. Finally, well done sales collateral gives the impression of the product being "real". In a world dense with product offerings and the accompanying marketing 'noise', making a product seem more tangible is clearly helpful in standing out from the crowd.

The most universally useful sales collateral piece is the *Product Brief*, a one or two page document that briefly describes the product's features and benefits. It is very marketing-oriented, and for the most part offers only high-level messaging. A typical datasheet would include:
   o   Product name and ordering information
   o   SKUs that are available
   o   General feature set and positioning
   o   Benefits to the customer
   o   Sales contact information

A product brief gives a quick introduction to the product for those who know little about it. It gives enough information so that readers can decide if they want to learn more. **They are perfect for any situation in which the customer wants to do a bit of arms-length discovery before engaging directly with Sales or the channel about the product**. This document is typically made widely available – during sales visits, on the web, or handed out at trade shows – subject to whatever access policy marketing proscribes. An effective product brief will display the following qualities:

- *Succinct*: Shorter is better. The reader only wants to quickly determine the product's applicability to their need. It is not intended to answer all potential questions about the product.
- *Benefit Oriented*: As with all good marketing materials, the reader simply wants to know how the product helps them. You'll lose them quickly if you linger on technology and features in this written document. Save this for focused white papers or face-to-face discussions.
- *Visually Striking*: In this initial phase, you need to grab the reader's attention. The Marketing Communications team can usually handle this, and the company may have a standard template. Smaller companies are encouraged to hire a graphic artist to create something, rather than simply trying to home-grow something on a PC.
- *Vague*: The product brief will be widely available, so it should not reveal anything that would be devastating in the hands of your competitors (assume they will get it eventually). Seek to strike the balance between educating the customer and obscuring valuable details from competition. Remember, you don't have to say everything in this document.

A more detailed type of product literature is the w*hite paper*, which explores a product-related topic in depth. The value proposition of the product may only become clear once the customer understands the topic thoroughly. The white paper is the tool to help with this education process. Some examples might include:

- A description of some market trends, intended to highlight the unique value of the product as these trends come to fruition.
- An explanation of a complex technology related to the product, intended to supplement and reinforce explanations given verbally during presentations.
- A description of a Market Problem that the product solves, intended to reinforce the magnitude and scope of the problem and thus enhance the perception of the product's value.

Codifying these topics in writing allows for a well-organized presentation of the topic, supplemented with illustrative diagrams and graphics. Customers are able to read and absorb it at their own pace. They are a powerful tool in helping the customer truly appreciate the value proposition. The need for a white paper is relatively easy to spot: **if there is any part of the product story that proves difficult to explain fully in 2-3 slides, it is a likely candidate for a white paper.** The organization should make a concerted evaluation of the product story and situation to determine if a white paper could be of some help. The writing can be outsourced to a contract writer or an industry expert (whose own credibility may make the paper more impactful) to ease the burden.

The next category of sales collateral is the most common: *website content*. This is a default for most products and the value is commonly understood. But it can be the most challenging of all types of collateral because it is such a public medium. It makes it easy for customers to learn about the product, but makes it just as easy for competitors to glean information they can use against you. So it is a necessary evil that simply needs to be properly managed. Typically the MarCom team will build the website. It is up to the Marketing team to determine which information is appropriate to have openly available, and which should not be included or at least protected with some type of verification of who is accessing it. The best advice that can be given is **to determine the optimum balance between the benefits of broadcasting product information versus the damage from competition knowing it.** Marketing should never let MarCom run on their own, nor should they allow themselves to be pressured into releasing something that makes them uncomfortable. If there is no clear benefit to releasing a particular data point or piece of product information, then by no means should it be put on a website.

The final type of sales collateral to be discussed is the *product demo*. Unlike the other types, it is not an information piece but a physical demonstration of some aspect of the product's functionality. There are three typical reasons for doing a demo:

- To prove that the functionality is actually working, rather than simply slideware.
- To prove that claims of performance are actually true.

- To improve a customer's understanding of the value of certain functionality by showing rather than telling.

The first two address the natural skepticism that customers have regarding claims about a product, something created over time by a ceaseless line of vendors telling the customer anything needed to win. The third reason speaks to the natural human tendency to better appreciate things one sees than those that are simply described. There are some simple indicators to look for that would suggest a demo is appropriate:

- Claiming a level of performance that significantly surpasses anything available today, or is significantly superior to that from the competition. Every vendor claims to have the best performance, so making this point successfully will require more than pretty graphs.
- Claiming functionality that is new to the customer. It is harder to appreciate the value of something unfamiliar without a visual.
- Offering the first generation of a new technology. Developing new technology or product capabilities is hard, and often fraught with execution risks. But there is no more powerful proof than showing the product running.

If the organization's marketing efforts involve claims in the vein of any of the above, then a product demo can be immensely helpful. Once you decide to do one, it is critical to approach it in a disciplined manner. Simply describing the demo to an Applications Engineer and then waiting for it to appear is not a recipe for success. It is meant to impart a very specific message through a carefully crafted audience experience. This must be defined in detail by Marketing in a written document, including very specific dates of completion. Then, an Applications Engineer (who is probably already busy) must be assigned and given the priority to make the demo happen.

Sales collateral pieces are extremely important tools for conveying the product message to customers. They need to receive the proper priority within Marketing and Engineering. Marketers and senior leaders in the organization can ask three simple questions as a litmus test on what types of sales collateral are appropriate:

1. Is there an arms-length discovery process by the customer? If yes, a product brief is needed.
2. Are there complex technologies or relevant technology trends which customers need to understand? If yes, a white paper is needed.
3. Are there claims being made about the product's performance, functionality, or readiness about which the customer may have initial skepticism? If yes, a product demo is needed.

These three questions are intended to reveal *Collateral Indicators* – i.e. characteristics of a situation which indicate that certain types of sales collateral are necessary.

## Technical Documentation

Most products will require some form of documentation of technical characteristics. The information might describe how the product works (such as in a datasheet) or how to implement it (such as in a design guide). Or, the content may help an individual understand how to use the product (user manual) or correct a problem (help files). A lack of good documentation is a problem for two primary reasons:

- It can be a major hidden inhibitor to a sale if the customer wants to study the technical characteristics of the product during the investigation phase, only to find out that they can't because the product is not well documented. Thus, **they can't get the information they must have in order to make a decision**. Furthermore they will assume that if you can't dedicate the resources to create good documentation before the buying decision, then surely the post-purchase customer service will be weak.
- It can create a significant strain on technical resources to support the customer. Documentation is a tool to limit time-consuming direct interaction with a customer. Maximizing the technical details written down and questions answered in the documentation is what eliminates time-consuming support phone calls. As the product line begins to scale over a large number of customers, this is absolutely critical. **Without the documentation, every customer engagement will be an excessive drain on resources**, and many of them will be frustrating enough

for the customer that they may terminate the current or future engagements.

The Applications Engineering team will typically own the documentation. They are responsible for working with Engineering to get the necessary product data that forms the basis for the content. But this is not an exercise for the technical side of the house only. Marketing plays a key role in ensuring that the right documentation is available at the right time. Their responsibility begins in the Product Definition phase by creating a list of all documents that customers will need. They are guided by their own experience of what customers need, supplemented by further input solicited from Engineering and Field Applications Engineers. **The most important thing that Marketing can do to ensure the documentation gets done is to document the requirement in the MRD,** and get a commitment from Engineering and Applications Engineering on a completion date. This document-request-commit process helps avoid a common problem with documentation, which is that no one thinks about it until the customer is asking for it. Without the visibility of a process like this, documentation won't be planned for or staffed properly, and consequently will constantly be de-prioritized in favor of customer support issues and development work.

Marketing is also responsible for reviewing the content of the documentation. They are first checking for consistency with the overall product plan, including:

- Product features and their positioning
- SKUing and segmentation strategy
- Product names or numbers

These may be technical documents, but the presentation of the information must be consistent with the marketing plan. For instance, the segmentation strategy might use spanning via the creation of a low end SKU that removes some features. But to save time, the Applications Engineer might try to create one document that covers both high and low end SKUs. Clearly this would weaken the differentiation (and the two artificially created price points). Left to create documentation in a vacuum, the technical side of the house might not recognize this. Another problem is that the documentation is not easy to understand. Product companies are notorious for this: content that is technically correct but not useful for any non-technical reader. Marketing must review the documentation from a customer's point of view to make sure it is readable and effective. For both of these reasons, it is clear that Marketing should be very involved in the creation of technical documentation.

## Conclusion

Product information is commonly regarded as one of the most mundane aspects of product marketing. It tends to be neglected as a result, despite that fact that its absence can completely obviate a product's benefits. The antidote is system: the organization needs to simply make it a required part of the process at the same level of importance as less neglected elements such as the financial analysis. As it settles in as part of the organization's DNA, it will become an accepted, planned, and resourced part of the marketing process.

System, Not Circumstance

# Product Information: Real World Example

*The team proceeded to create a plan for the Product Information. The first element considered was the technical documentation that customers would need in order to use Mason. There would of course be the standard datasheet, which detailed how the device worked. The engineers had compiled the information during the design process. The Applications Engineers would then put it together into a usable format. The Marketing team then would do their review to make sure that it was both readable and consistent with the product strategy. Sure enough, there were some disconnects found. Marketing had planned to have a separate SKU for the blade desktop space because it had a very unique feature (serial interface) for that market for which a significant premium could be charged. Yet in order to save work for themselves, the Applications Engineers had tried to create one datasheet for all SKUs (instead of having to update two or more docs with future changes, they would only have to do it once). This meant that the serial interface showed on all SKUs. This would lead to inevitable questions from the blade desktop customers as to why they are paying a premium for a feature that appears to be available on some of the lower priced SKUs. To address this, Marketing requested that a separate datasheet be created for the blade desktop SKU.*

*One problem that Marketing had heard from customers was that the help files were poorly written and not very useful. This was not something on which the organization had previously put a lot of focus. But the GM had been pushing hard on the concept of "complete products", and this appeared to be something that made the product harder to use. The team decided that they would hire an outside firm to help create both a quick start guide and a very intuitive help interface. Though costly, it was deemed worthwhile because the product would be perceived as easier to use.*

*The Applications Engineering team was asked to commit to a schedule for the datasheet and the few other requested technical documents. This was actually the first time they had been asked to make a commitment, so their initial answer was that "staffing was tight, so they would fit it in as some of the urgent customer issues were resolved". But the GM pushed back, demanding a commit. So specific dates were produced, only to be judged by Marketing to be about two months past the start of the sales cycle. The GM asked what was needed to pull in the dates. The manager of the applications team responded*

282

that if they got their promised headcount approved within a week, they could hire in time to staff the documentation appropriately.

Next, the sales collateral needed to be planned. The team went through an exercise of looking for Collateral Indicators. They asked the three relevant questions, and visualized the selling situation to predict where collateral might help. Trade shows would be an important part of the plan, and customers visiting the booth would need some information on the product to take with them. This was a prime example of arms-length discovery, so a product brief would be appropriate for helping them understand the offering at a high level. For the most part, this would consist of the product positioning, some text describing the market's needs, and ordering information. Because of the open nature of trade shows, the team did not want to give away anything too sensitive.

Upon reflection, the team also concluded that there were some key trends and technologies that they needed the customer to understand. Hence, a few white papers would also be helpful. The addition of TPM functionality to the chip was risky because it was a new technology that the market as a whole didn't quite understand. This type of situation was ripe for a white paper which could explain the need for TPM, how it is enabled and used, and the benefits to corporate IT departments. This white paper could also help describe and establish the Market Problem related to laptop theft and the subsequent exposure of corporate data. This point was of course introduced in the Standard Marketing Presentation but could be presented in more depth in the white paper. Another useful white paper would be one describing how a battery's power is consumed in a typical usage model. Clearly this would be fashioned such that it supported the notion that most of the battery gets used while the user is mobile, and thus the network cable is not plugged in. This would help establish the value of the Intelligent Power capability. An outside writer was be engaged to write these, with content support from the Marketing team.

Finally, the need for a few demos was very clear with Mason because there were several fundamental claims being made about it. First, the TPM technology was very new to TechCorp, so there would be natural skepticism about how ready it was. A demo could go a long way in showing customers that it was real and working. It could be used at trade shows or taken onsite to a customer. Also, there was a claim about battery life performance (saving 10 minutes) being made which was quite impressive if true. This was also the type of situation where customers needed to be shown rather than told.

*A demo with two PCs, one with Intelligent Power turned on and the other with it off, would be the concept. An ammeter (this measured current being drawn from the battery) would be hooked up to display the difference in current draw while the PC was not connected to a network cable. Some graphics showing the battery level after 5, 10, 60, and 120 minutes would further reinforce the point. Both of these demos would need to be put together by the Applications Engineering team. With their newly approved headcount increase, they were now able and willing to commit to delivering these by the required date.*

# Checklist

## Is the product's value being communicated appropriately?

Sales collateral pieces help facilitate a customer buying decision by providing information about the product and making it seem "real".

## What to Look For:

- Marketing has conducted a "Collateral Indicator" exercise
- Product briefs and web info are readily available to prospective customers
- White papers and demos are planned to explain complex product attributes

## Are the technical capabilities documented properly?

Ready availability of technical information is a big part of making a product easy to use or implement, which can be a key criterion in the buying decision

## What to Look For:

- Marketing has gathered requirements from field engineers and customers
- Datasheets, design guides, and help files are comprehensive and clear
- Content is consistent with market positioning and strategy

*(Further discussion on this checklist available at www.systemnotcircumstance.com)*

# CHAPTER 20:

## Press Releases

*Public speaking in front of a large audience can be an anxiety-producing activity for most. The speaker is typically nervous about sounding incoherent or having incorrect information. The solution is to prepare a very clear message, check the facts, and practice like crazy. A press release for a product is a lot like this. It is an incredibly public statement by the company that is fraught with risks. It may give away too much competitive information, it could be incorrect and create legal issues or customer confusion, or it could be badly written and reflect poorly on the product or company. Because of the risky and public nature of these documents, much effort must be applied to doing them well. Great companies manage this process with a consistent methodology to ensure that press releases are justified relative to the risk, well and efficiently written, and interesting enough to be newsworthy.*

## Types of Press Releases

A press release is a vehicle for a company to communicate information that it feels is beneficial to be made public. It is usually 1-3 pages in length, and describes the topic of interest and why the reader should care. There are many types of events for which an organization may want to produce a release. Here are some of the most common:

- *New Product Launch:* This is by far the most common, and will get the most attention in this chapter. The goal is to alert the market of the existence or availability of the product, in hopes of stimulating customer interest.

- *Sales Milestone:* At times, a product or product line may achieve some notable level of sales volume. This reflects well on the success of the product and the value it brings. This type of release sends the message that "if this many other customers think the product is worth buying, so should you."

- *Industry Initiative Support:* An organization may decide to incorporate into the product some measure of support for an evolving industry standard or technology initiative. Since standards are only useful if enough companies participate, the intent of such an announcement is to show support and influence others to join.

- *Acquisition:* If one company purchases another, it is usually made public. The announcement alerts customers, analysts, and the press about the nature of the acquisition and the strategic synergies that the combination creates.

- *New Design Win:* An organization may choose to announce that an important customer has decided to purchase their product. This is of course done with the permission of that customer, who likely has deemed that it provides good publicity for them as well. The intent is to provide a proof point of the value of the product.

- *Joint Alliance:* Two companies may decide to jointly pursue a set of market goals. A key focus is the synergies between the two companies that would not be available with the companies working separately. The goal of this type of release is to inform customers of the value of the combination of the two companies.

In the interest of brevity, this chapter will focus mainly on releases related to new product introductions. But, most of the comments apply universally.

## The Format of a Press Release

Although there are no universal rules for the structure of a press release, most follow a typical format (individuals companies may have their own stylistic preferences).

- *Title and Subtitle:* These are the "headlines" of your release, similar to that of a newspaper story. They are the first thing a reader sees, and thus very important. Any editor or PR professional will tell you that most readers make their decision to read or not read the piece based on how interesting these lines are. Even a well-written release about an immensely exciting product will go unread if the header and sub-header are done poorly. **It is critical that they grab the attention of the reader** by using active language which immediately communicates the need to read the rest of the release. The header is the title of the release, usually 8-15 words in large, boldfaced font at the top. It should make a statement about what the product is uniquely accomplishing. For example: "Company X Announces the Industry's First...", "Company Drives the Mainstream Adoption of...", or "Company X Enables the World's Lowest Price..." It is this type of active language that will grab the reader's attention. Be sure to keep the message simple. Trying to cram two or three individual ideas into the title will only create confusion; pick the single most important idea and focus on it. Secondary points can be made in the sub header, which is a 15-20 word sentence just below the header in smaller font. Here is where the product name or number is usually introduced, and also where additional points or supporting information for the header can be placed.
- *Opening Announcement:* This first paragraph summarizes exactly what is being announced. In journalistic terminology, this is the "What" of the "Who, What, When, Why" theme. The information is

mostly factual – name of the product, what it does, who uses it, and so on. The threshold of interest for the reader to proceed further is even higher here. The title information used soundbytes to pique interest – **here you must sustain interest with greater detail**. A relevant audience is given the key themes of the product in a way that makes them want to read further to where more supporting detail is supplied.

- *Market Information:* Here you begin to paint a picture of the trends, problems, and/or needs in the market that necessitate the need for the product. This is the "Why?" The idea is the same as in the product definition process, where you always define the problem first. **Convince the audience of your view of the market and the need for your product becomes somewhat self evident**. Tying into a larger message gives the product more relevance and increases retention. Market statistics from unbiased third parties are especially helpful, as they add credibility to the story in the eyes of jaded readers.

- *Solution Statement:* The market's needs or problems should have been established in the prior paragraph. In this section, a description is given of how the product solves the problem or satisfies the need.

- *Quotes:* Statements of support from a customer, partner, or industry expert are a standard part of any release. Most quotes are intended to send the message that an intelligent person with appropriate credentials and domain expertise has looked at the product and feels it has a strong value proposition. It may also be intended to convey that the product is real, which is always a concern for fast-moving industries where vaporware is common. Alternatively, the quote might reinforce the assertions about market trends or problems.

- *Product Information:* This section provides some of the mundane detail about the product: the various SKUs available, benefits, feature list, pricing, and availability. In general, it is a straightforward description of what the product does, and how it may apply to different target market segments. **The emphasis should be on the benefits.**

## The Writing Process

Creating a press release is never a fun process. Writing is a hard activity for most people, made even worse by the fact the document is so public and thus will receive a lot of scrutiny. But the most difficult factor comes from the fact that it is a multi-party process, where Marketing drives the content but Management, PR, Legal, and Sales all play important roles. And the bigger the organization, the harder it gets. Larger companies (especially public ones) are bigger litigation targets, and so Legal tends to put more limits on what can be said. There are also more layers of management and therefore more opinions to be incorporated, thus complicating convergence on a message and the prose. The result? A convoluted process that takes too long and produces a sub-par product. Here is how it usually happens: PR sits with the appropriate product manager, gathers the key messages, and writes an initial draft. Of course, that PR person does not live and breathe the product and so the first draft is not likely to fully draw out the keys themes and subtleties. This means much iteration between the two until a suitable draft is produced. Then it is bumped up to the Director of Marketing , who (surprise!) has a slightly different take on how the product would be positioned. Comments are added, requiring substantial rework to accommodate them. Once this phase is completed, it goes up to the GM, who (surprise!) also has a different vision of the product, thus creating more rework. Each interation adds new themes that must fit in alongside the original messages. PR then jumps back in to massage the release using their expertise regarding the phraseology that will resonate in the editorial world. This requires a bit more negotiation between Marketing and PR. This "final" draft then goes to the attorneys, who proceed to strike out a few claims and phrases which might cause legal issues. That forces another round of rework, and then another review cycle. At this point the process is eight weeks old. Although each step by itself is reasonably simple, each individual likely has plenty of other work and travel that intervene to add latencies to every step.

**The most difficult part of this process is the wordsmithing** (deciding on the specific phrasing). Writing is a highly subjective endeavor. With multiple individuals involved, converging on the wording that satisfies everyone is difficult. But an already complicated process is made even harder when wordsmithing begins *before* the organization has converged on the key messages to be delivered in the release. The above example illustrates how different individuals at various levels of management may have their own vision of what is being communicated. Failing to get convergence (up and down the chain) before wordsmithing starts means you must work both at once. This can turn into quite a nightmare. Debate over the wording tends to obscure and crowd out the more important discussion over the fundamental points to be made. The result is often a release that lacks succinct and crisp messaging.

The solution is actually rather simple. **Before any writing of text begins, the organization has to come to complete agreement on the goals, themes, and messages in the release**. Free of the burden of wordsmithing, this becomes a simpler, more focused task. This is accomplished by creating a *Release Worksheet* as a first step. It spells out a few key points:

- *Timing*: when should the release happen? (more on this below)
- *Goals*: what will this release accomplish? (more in this below)
- *Overall Theme*: what 2-3 key messages should the reader receive?
- *Message Outline*: what key points will be made in each section?

The Release Worksheet serves as a vehicle to drive convergence on the strategy and message for the release. Marketing should start it, getting agreement first within the team. It should then be shared with PR and the management chain up through the GM to obtain their consensus. Only once this is achieved should anyone begin to write actual text. You will find that the drafts coming back receive approval much more quickly, and the end result is more interesting and effective.

## Goals of the Press Release

Press releases are accepted as an effective way to educate the market. But, it is a worthwhile exercise to consider for a moment why one would use such a public method of doing so. Clearly the type of information that goes into a release is useful to competition. It tells them where your attention is focused, allowing them to react strategically. It also reveals positioning and functionality, enabling them to react tactically. Rather than allowing this, why not simply rely on the salesforce to spread the word directly to customers, a much more discrete method? The risk of giving your competitor useful information may outweigh the benefits. The organization will have to evaluate each situation based on the circum-stances. To have an intelligent discussion on this there must be an under-standing of what the release is supposed to accomplish. Doing a release can't become a sort of Pavlovian response to the release of a new product, where everyone assumes one will be done but no one ever questions why. **The organization should have a clear set of goals for a press release before deciding to do one**. Some of the more common goals for a press release are:

- *To educate a diffuse market*. A salesforce or channel can often adequately cover a concentrated customer base. But covering a highly diffuse market can be much more difficult. The "broadcast" nature of a release may be necessary in order to get the message about the product out. A release for this purpose should use ben-efit oriented language that will capture the attention of the rel-evant audience by speaking directly to problems with which they are grappling.

- *To generate press coverage*. Articles about the product become yet another channel to project the message, amplifying the effect. So using the release to gain the attention of editors of relevant trade magazines is certainly a worthwhile goal. If this is in fact the goal, then the release must employ language that grabs the attention of information-overloaded editors. It must be clear what is new and different about the product, and a little sensationalism in the phrasing won't hurt a bit.

- *To educate financial analysts*. The intent is to demonstrate that the company has a successful new product which can fuel new growth. Within this there may be one of several specific messages:
    - We have or are taking significant market share
    - This market is growing rapidly
    - We have a defensible position
    - We have a large, solid customer base

You want the investors to believe that you are building a real and prof-itable business as a result of the investment made to date. If this is a goal of the release, then it should emphasize the large and growing nature of the product's TAM, and the specific strengths the company will employ to capture it.

- *To create confidence in the product's readiness.* In many industries it is common practice to "lean forward" – to communicate that a product will be available much earlier than is actually possible. Many customers have become wise to this and require additional proof of a product's readiness. Like a demonstration, a press release can help here because it carries such an obligation that the information be accurate.
- *To create momentum for a technology or industry standard.* New technologies or industry standards often need momentum in order to be successful. The market simply wants one scheme to win out so they know what to buy. So a press release indicating what the company will be supporting can be an effective tool in pushing the market in the desired direction. Releases with this as a goal should focus on statements of deep, long-term commitment to the particular technology initiative.

Each of these goals is a worthy one. But in the end, they must be weighed against the usefulness of the information to a competitor. Make no mistake – your competitors are quietly and hungrily waiting for you to do a release that tells them all about your product. They will be dissecting every sentence, looking for something to improve their strategy or use against you. So no one should assume that a release will always be done for every new product. Instead, the Marketing team should identify the goals they have for the release and how it helps the go-to-market strategy. **If the benefits are significant, by all means do a release. If not, question whether one needs to be done at all**. It may be smarter to simply operate under the radar of the competition and rely on more discrete means of accomplishing the same goals. If you do decide to put out a release, this logic can still be applied although in less binary fashion. You need not tell the world *everything* about the product. In fact, efforts should be made to state the minimum that will accomplish the particular goals of the release. This is one reason why it is so important to have a clear picture of what you are trying to accomplish. If a prime goal of the release is to demonstrate a new growth vector to analysts, there is no need to add much specific information about the product's features. The analysts won't care about that level of detail, and it will only serve to aid competition. Every word should be scrutinized for its necessity and for its utility in supporting the agreed upon goals.

## Quotes

The use of quotes can be effective in helping deliver the product's message. There are three main types of quotes:

- *From a company executive:* These are a standard part of most product oriented press releases. The executive will extol the virtues of the product or strategy. They are often structured into two sentences, the first typically a sweeping statement about a market trend or larger company strategy. The second usually addresses how this particular product addresses it. The size of the quoter's title is often perceived as a proxy for how important the product is to the company.

- *From an industry expert:* This type of quote is often from an industry analyst because of the presumed insight they bring from studying the market so closely. But it could also include high ranking individuals in 3rd party organizations associated with the industry, such as a government official. These statements add a credibility factor due to the presumed impartial nature of the provider. The quote should convey a view of the market that suggests the need for the product. It would comment on the market problem, the size or growth rate of a market segment, or the superiority of a particular technology or type of solution. Presumably it will directly support the statement made by the company executive. The industry expert could go even farther and specifically endorse the product, but this is not necessary.

- *From a customer:* The most important and effective type of quote comes from those who would actually buy the product. As they say, "a crowd attracts a crowd", so if the quoter has evaluated the product and found it worthy then it may influence the reader to do the same. As before, the bigger the title, the greater the perceived endorsement. However, there will always be resistance to providing such a quote, increasing as the title gets larger. The customer may not want to tip their competitors as to which solutions they are using, or may not want to favor one vendor too much in order to foster parity and competition. Relationships at the executive level are the most effective means to obtain good quotes from customers, but a last minute price concession (which probably would be made anyway to close the deal) could be traded to a commitment for a quote. Finally, creative wording could be employed to reduce the customer's resistance. For example, the following press release from Microsoft: *"Microsoft is a strong believer in the advantages Bluetooth can bring to the PC market, enhancing user experience and creating new opportunities for mobility around the desktop work environment," said Sharon Brassert, Development Program Manager of Microsoft's PC Hardware Division. "As a market leader in the mouse and keyboard markets, we believe the BCM2040 offers the kind of features, cost, power and reliability necessary to stimulate the broader adoption of Bluetooth within the industry."* Nowhere in the release does Microsoft ever say that the product is superior to alternatives. It merely states that it "could catalyze the market". Yet on a quick read, the reader is left with the overall impression that Microsoft believes this product is a good one. Creative wording allowed both parties to maintain their interests.

## Other Aspects

There are a few other aspects of the press release that should be considered, each driven by the company's norms. It behooves Marketing to be in synch with these. It can make the release writing process much faster, as early drafts will be more stylistically aligned with the expectations of senior management.

- *Level of boastfulness*: Some companies like to make big, bold claims in order to create maximum impact. Others may choose to be more conservative for either of two reasons. First, they may want to maintain long-term credibility with editors and financial analysts, who eventually begin to apply a filter on statements from companies that consistently exaggerate. The individuals in PR and Investor Relations can lose credibility with these communities if Marketing makes claims that turn out to be less than accurate. Second, there can be legal consequences (such as shareholder lawsuits) to any unsubstantiated claims. A little hype is expected, but statements about market share should be backed up with 3rd party reports. Those about being "first", "lowest", "fastest", and "only" need to be based on demonstrable, objective criteria.

- *Timing of the release*: PR will want to time the release for maximum press coverage. Conventional wisdom says to announce during an industry trade show. More editors are likely to be writing about an industry in this time period, and it allows for face-to-face interviews with them. There is merit to this, but it should be weighed against the downside that the message will have to compete with that from every other company making an announcement. It also limits the ability to be in a position to be the first to announce a certain type of product. If you do, you can claim "World's first...", while a competitor who announces even five minutes after you cannot. Being able to say this increases the impact of your announcement; and, as they say, no one remembers who finishes second.

- *Threshold to do a release*. Every company will have its own view on how important an event warrants a press release. Some may want to generate a steady stream of announcements in order to keep the company in the industry's collective consciousness. Others may want to maximize the impact of any one release, and therefore only do them for important events. The choice is entirely stylistic, but carries some of the same risks as above of causing editors to begin develop of 'fatigue' for the company's statements.

## Conclusion

What at first seems to be a straightforward marketing tool is revealed to be a rather complex animal. 'To release or not to release' is a question which deserves some hard thought. This process is always one of knowing the goals and benefits of a particular release and balancing them against the negative consequences of telling the competition anything useful. Then if the decision to move ahead is made, it marks the beginning of a difficult writing process. Multiple visions, opinions, and messages must be integrated into a single document that is both effective in the market and acceptable to all stakeholders in the organization – two goals inherently at odds. The most important thing the organization can do to make this process effective is to agree on all key themes and messages before any wordsmithing begins.

## Press Releases: Real World Example

*A press release would presumably be needed for the product launch, and so PR was anxious to get started on it. But the Director of Marketing wanted to be convinced that this was really in their best interest. The PC OEM market was concentrated on less than ten large customers. Because the salesforce could touch each of them, a release was not necessarily required to raise awareness among customers. But there were two other audiences that the team wanted to reach. The first was comprised of IT managers who would buy the PC (the OEM's customers). Marketing hoped that they could educate this group as to the solution that Mason represented for their very real problems around battery life and data security. If a release could raise their awareness of Mason, it could create a pull-through of demand for PCs equipped with it. The second group was the software developers who would write software that leverages the TPM to protect data. Creating an ecosystem of compatible software was critical to creating a complete product. The release would educate them on the fact that TPM was being driven into the mainstream through integration and low cost, and so was a technology they should begin to support. With these reasons the Director of Marketing agreed that doing a release was the right thing to do, even at the price of alerting competitors to the strategy. An additional decision was made to not address the blade desktop market in this release. It was a small, emerging market, and inclusion in this release would distract from the main messages for the core laptop market.*

*A release worksheet was then put together to give form to important goals and messages:*

- *Timing: Anytime between May 1st and July 30th. The product would be nearly locked and confidence in imminent production would be high.*
- *Goals:*
  - o *Reinforce to customers the benefits of Mason*
  - o *Educate IT managers about how Mason can help their problems with battery life and data security; influence them to request Mason-based PCs from the PC OEMs*
  - o *Inform software developers that TPM would quickly become a mainstream technology because the cost point is dropping from*

$4 to a negligible premium; influence them to begin modifying their software to take advantage of TPM

- Overall Theme:
  - o Long battery life, data protection, and a stable technology are all very necessary to enable a user to be truly mobile
  - o Mason saves 10 minutes battery life through Intelligent Power
  - o Mason protects against physical theft by securing the data with TPM1.2 hardware at negligible premium
  - o Mason is a third generation product that is very stable and reliable
- Message Outline:
  - o Title:
    - Mason enables True Mobility for laptop users
  - o Sub-title:
    - 10 minutes extra battery life and integrated TPM based security provide a better mobile experience
  - o Opening Announcement:
    - TC151 is the product name
    - It is targeted at laptop PCs
    - Today's mobile user needs three things: long battery life, data protection against physical theft, and stable technology
    - Mason delivers a world class solution for all three
  - o Market Information:
    - Battery life is one of the most important attributes to a laptop PC user
    - Users demand a PC that consumes the minimum power necessary at any given time for the task at hand
    - Laptop users are keenly concerned about the risk of exposing sensitive corporate data due to physical theft
    - The amount of data on any given PC is growing significantly year-on-year
    - Today's best available data protection is software encryption, which is vulnerable to a hacker who can find the encryption key stored on the PC's hard drive
    - Users and IT managers are demanding stronger protection of the data on the laptop PC

- o *Solution Statement:*
  - *Laptops are unconnected over 50% of the time, but most networks chips burn power as if they are always connected*
  - *Mason's Intelligent Power can sense when PC is unplugged and drop into a lower power mode until the cable is plugged back in, saving 10 minutes battery life according to the BatteryMark test*
  - *Mason is integrating TPM1.2, a standards-based hardware security technology; key cannot be hacked*
  - *TPM is more secure than software encryption*
  - *By integrating TPM it is available for negligible price premium rather than $4 of today's discrete solution, driving TPM into the mainstream*
- o *Quotes:*
  - *GM:*
    - *Users are demanding the battery life, security, and stability to enable True Mobility.*
    - *Our corporate competencies in low power design and secure solutions uniquely enable us to deliver True Mobility*
  - *PC OEM Customer*
    - *Many customers talk to us about the need for out laptops to continually provide better security and battery life*
    - *Mason will help us do that*
  - *Analyst*
    - *We have seen a dramatic increase in theft of laptops and corporate data*
    - *Mason is an ideal solution to help*

*This Release Worksheet was circulated among PR and MarCom for comment, then up the chain to the GM. When all comments were incorporated, PR proceeded to write the actual text of the release. Because convergence on the key messages had already been achieved, the first draft was ready rather quickly for review.*

# Checklist

## Do the benefits of this release outweigh the risks?

Not every new product needs a press release – the organization should be convinced that the resultant attention will provide real benefit.

### What to Look For:

- Marketing and PR have identified the goals and the benefits are clear
- The release reveals only what is necessary to accomplish the goals

## Is the release being written efficiently?

Press releases must deliver multiple complex messages in a finite space. The right process can make the effort faster and the end result more effective.

### What to Look For:

- A Release Worksheet has been completed by Marketing and PR
- Messages and themes are agreed upon by all before text writing begins

## Is the release newsworthy?

The release will only grab the attention of customers and editors if it quickly conveys that the product is somehow new and novel.

### What to Look For:

- The title and subtitle convey an attention-grabbing core message
- The release clearly conveys why the product is novel and noteworthy

*(Further discussion on this checklist available at www.systemnotcircumstance.com)*

# CHAPTER 21:

## The Product Launch

*First impressions are critical, and nowhere is that more important than with a product launch. This point of introduction in the market is a unique opportunity to generate interest in the product. So much has been accomplished by the Marketing and Engineering teams to date – wasting it with a poor product launch is not an option. Successful companies know how to manage this process in predictable fashion each time. Every functional group knows what is expected of them, and takes very seriously their obligation to deliver on time.*

## The Launch Deliverables

The product launch is the process by which the product is publicly revealed. It will involve multiple functional groups across the organization managing a defined set of deliverables. It is a complicated process, one that always feels a bit like herding cats. Each element has its own level of unpredictability, so arranging all of them to coincide with the launch date is difficult. This is compounded by the fact that the launch is entirely dependent on the development schedule, which can be highly variable. But if managed properly with appropriate program management techniques it can be brought under control. The following are the most common deliverables necessary for a launch:

- *Product Name*: To date, the product has probably been referred to by an internal code name. Now it is time to create something for public consumption. In some industries, this may simply be a product number. In others, particularly in consumer industries, it may be some type of proper name (i.e. Canon SureShot). There are some basic principles which would apply to both situations. First, there is often brand equity associated with a naming convention for a product line. It is always in your best interest to build and preserve this through consistency across product generations. Brand equity is a factor that provides customers a measure of familiarity and therefore comfort with a product. At some point, the product line may be segmented to address distinct market segments. So **build in a mechanism from day one that anticipates and allows this so you can maintain the naming scheme but customize it appropriately**. You don't want to get into a situation where limited options on naming cause you to have to change the product name, and therefore lose some brand equity, just to support your segmentation or upsell strategy.
- *Market Message*: Probably the most critical element of the launch is the specific set of messages that are to be delivered to the market. **It is critical that it be consistent across all of the various mediums of communication, as repetition and consistency are powerful tools to help retention**. Created by Marketing, it will be used throughout the launch: in product briefs, white papers, packaging text, advertisements, and sales presentations. Most

importantly, it must be simple, effective, and memorable. And obviously it should be fully consistent with the product, the strategy, the overall positioning, and the press release. Typically it is in the format of a core umbrella message supported by three benefit-oriented bullet points. Again, forced prioritization is key here.

- *Market Development Plan*: The communication vehicles for your market message should be laid out in a *Market Development Plan*. This lists all of the activities that will be undertaken to create awareness of and interest in the product. It could include:
  1. Trade show activity
  2. Advertising
  3. Press events
  4. Channel program

Typically, MarCom will lead the charge on putting this together, with heavy involvement from Marketing.

- *Marketing Collateral*: Per the discussion in Chapter 19 "Product Information", it is important that all necessary pieces be identified up front. Marketing, PR, and MarCom should meet to determine which pieces will be needed to support the launch goals as well as the Market Development Plan. The development of the pieces identified can then be program managed in the context of the overall launch.
- *Press Release*: Discussed in Chapter 20 "Press Releases", this is the piece that is the trigger event for the launch. It is the first look the public will get at the product and its positioning. Accompanying the release is a *Press Briefing*, a presentation which will be given to a select group of journalists to give them insight into the product and its significance. The goal is, of course, to entice them to write favorable articles about the product in order to generate more awareness in the market. This will be discussed more in Chapter 22 "Talking with the Press".
- *Supply Chain Plan*: This is an often overlooked part of a product launch: the plan to make sure Operations is producing enough product to satisfy a steep demand curve while attempting to minimize excess inventory. It is hard enough to do this in full

production, but the complexities of a launch make it a real challenge for a number of reasons:

o   The demand is uncertain because the product is new. There is a significant risk of over or undershooting actual demand. Operations teams are universally known to operate such that they minimize inventory and scrap, so expect them to push to limit early production.

o   Production and quality issues are common in the very early phase of production. At any moment the factory could go lines-down, or poor yield could significantly limit production.

o   The lock down of the design could get pushed out due to problems in the design phase. So, the product cannot be pushed into the production line until this happens. This is particularly problematic when manufacturing has a long lead time. The pressure to start material early to improve time to market sharply conflicts with Operations' natural tendency to try to minimize scrap and reduce cost. A painful but all too common scenario is for Operations to be lined up to support a whiplash ramp, only to find a bug in the product and have to push out the ramp several months, something that typically causes a big inventory problem.

All of these factors conspire to make it very difficult to ramp a product. But **failure to execute here can instantly kill the momentum of a hot new product**. How tragic that huge demand for a great product that is well launched could be instantly extinguished when Operations can't supply enough product. To avoid this, Marketing and Engineering need to work closely with Operations during the launch planning. Marketing needs to make the case that lost opportunity hurts more than the cost of inventory. They should push for a healthy buffer, even in the face of inevitable resistance from Finance and Operations. Another technique is smart staging of material. If WIP ("work in progress", or component material which is assembled into the product) can be staged right before irreversible and expensive manufacturing steps, you can reduce cost while eliminating from the critical path the time needed to gather the WIP material.

## Supporting Roles

It should be clear by now that the launch process involves important participation from several functional groups within the company. But it is Marketing that plays the central role. Each of the other groups either requires something from them or provides something to them (or both). Figure 21.1 summarizes the role and needs of each group in this launch process, relative to the Marketing team:

| Groups | What they Provide to MKT for Launch | What they Need from MKT to Support Launch |
|---|---|---|
| **Sales** | • Pricing guidance<br>• Guidance on how well positioning will resonate with customer<br>• Customer agreement to provide quote for release | • Good sales collateral and technical documentation<br>• Readily available product supply line |
| **Sr. MGT** | • Approval of press release<br>• Approval of launch plan<br>• Quote for the press release<br>• Serve as spokesperson for press events | • Comprehensive launch plan, including all deliverables |
| **Customer Service** | • Set up of product information in ordering system | • Part numbers<br>• Description of product |
| **OPS** | • Production capacity to meet customer demand<br>• High quality, stable supply line | • Forecast of production needs<br>• Product launch schedule |
| **PR** | • Guidance on press release and briefings<br>• Arrangement of press briefings | • Completed PR Worksheet<br>• Launch goals and schedule<br>• Press briefing presentation |

| | | |
|---|---|---|
| **MarCom** | • Coordination of advertising campaign<br>• Delivery of necessary marketing and sales collateral | • Product messaging<br>• Launch goals<br>• Launch schedule<br>• Content for sales collateral |
| **ENG** | • Production ready product<br>• Support for technical documentation | • Product definition<br>• Target schedule |
| **Apps ENG** | • Creation of technical documentation<br>• Pre-sales and customer support | • Requirements for technical documents<br>• Review of technical documentation |

KEY: Apps ENG – Applications Engineering; ENG – Engineering; MKT – Marketing; MarCom – Marketing Communications; PR – Public Relations; Sr MGT – Senior Management

*Figure 21: Summary of the roles and needs of each group in the launch process*

## Conclusion

Organizing this process to the point where all the functional groups are in lockstep is no easy task. Depending on the organization, Marketing, MarCom, or PR will take charge and drive the process. But in all cases Marketing must play a strong role in the process. They are the group that determines all of the key messaging and is intimately involved in all other aspects of the product, including the engineering development side. They also own the product forecasting and supply chain aspects. Thus, they clearly hold most of the knowledge needed in this process. But, no matter who takes the lead, the organization needs to be serious about disciplined program management of the product launch. This means that processes and expectations should be put in place so that everybody knows their role, and Management should request to be updated regularly about progress.

# Product Launch: Real World Example

*With the product defined and development well underway, the team began to focus on planning for the launch. The Marketing, PR, and MarCom teams would all be involved, and so a core team was formed with participants from each. They met weekly in order to coordinate and plan for the product introduction into the market.*

*The first decision to make was the timing of the launch. This tended to dictate how much could be planned. The product would be nearing the end of the development cycle by April, and in a relatively robust state. TechCorp's corporate norm was to not make speculative statements about products, and so the requisite level of confidence would be achievable by then. There was a major trade show in the middle of May, and so the team decided that this was the target. It also gave them a little cushion in case the product schedule slipped a bit.*

*They then chose a product name. The currently available product was the TC150. The immediate suggestion was for Mason to be called the TC160, and each subsequent product would increment the number by ten. But of course they would run out of 1x0 numbers within 4 generations, and switching to a 2x0 designation would waste some of the numbering scheme's brand equity. Also, the product line was starting to segment – Mason would in fact span across the laptop and blade segment. Further out in time, the roadmap showed that the product line for laptops would further segment into a high and low end offering. So a decision was reached to use TC15x for the laptop segment and TC16x for the blade segment. TC151 and TC161 would be used for Mason in each segment respectively. TC14x would be reserved for future low end laptop products. Each segment would have its own unique number set, allowing customers to develop some familiarity with each (i.e. a form of brand equity).*

*Next, the marketing message needed to be established. The positioning that had been agreed upon during the productization exercise was to em-phasize "True Mobility through security, long battery life, and stability". Since MarCom likes to have the market message be in the form of three bullets, the team converged on the following:*

1. *Intelligent power usage increases battery life*
2. *TPM security protects data from theft*
3. *3rd generation technology ensures stability*

*This market message would be used as a consistent theme across multiple communication vehicles.*

*The Market Development Plan was tackled next. The trade show at which the launch would take place would be an important event to meet face-to-face with the press and prospective customers. The plan was to conduct a round of press briefings the day before the launch. The release would then go out the next morning, and TechCorp would sponsor a presentation at the show. A booth would also host a demo of the product, as well as have available the product brief and white papers. Further market development activities would be planned throughout the year. There were other trade shows held in the European and Asian markets, so one was chosen in each market for TechCorp to have a booth and provide demos and collateral. Because most of the main customers did not seem to be influenced by advertising in trade magazines, none was requested for Mason. To round out the market development activities, the team decided to focus some attention on information technology (IT) end users. A series of webcasts would be organized to educate IT managers on the benefits of TPM security for protection of their data. This was intended to generate a "pull" for the technology; in the best case, these IT managers would start adding TPM to the Requests for Quote (RFQs) they put out to the PC OEMs.*

*At this point, the budget for the launch and all of the required activities and deliverables now totaled $110,000. This would be Public Relations and General Manager for consideration, but it appeared to fit within the allotted marketing budget for the year.*

*Finally, the Marketing team needed to collaborate with Operations on the Supply Chain Plan. This would prove very difficult because the forecast was going to be rather difficult to create. Although overall volumes in the PC market were stable, it was not quite clear which specific customers would need to be supplied right out of the gate. Winning or losing even one late in the game would cause a dramatic swing in volumes. Since the lead times for manufacturing the chip were rather long, and the schedule required by customers was tight (relative to the development schedule), the Marketing team needed to guess which customers would use Mason right out of the gate. They decided to guess on the high side, because in their world winning a design only to put the customer "lines-down" due to a lack of product was a cardinal sin. The Finance and Operations, of course pushed back, advocating a more conservative ramp plan until the real customer list (and therefore volumes) could be determined more firmly. The decision was ultimately bumped up to the GM and the VP of Operations. The Marketing team put together an analysis showing the costs vs. benefit of a large buffer. It made clear that a four month supply of material sized to meet Mason's "best case" volume scenario could be fully consumed in only seven months at a "worst case" run rate. So the price of ensuring no product supply issues was only the inventory costs for three months, which turned out to be less than 3% of the total COGS. Marketing's view won out.*

# Checklist

### Is the launch being program-managed?
A launch is a complicated affair with many moving parts that must all converge on the launch date. Activities must be managed with discipline.

## What to Look For:
- A complete launch plan (with milestones) exists several months in advance
- A cross-functional group meets regularly to coordinate launch activities

### Is the Market Message used effectively?
A launch is intended to capture customers' attention, enticing them to learn more. Crisp messaging soundbytes are essential in this type of interaction

## What to Look For:
- Repetition of the product's core message is used across all mediums
- The core message is supported by three succinct bullet points

*(Further discussion on this checklist available at www.systemnotcircumstance.com)*

# CHAPTER 22:

## Talking to the Press

*The product launch and press release are designed to generate interest from many parties, among them the press. But be careful what you wish for – talking to the press is a tricky business. Like an actor rehearsing his lines, you have to prepare yourself to deliver a simple, newsworthy message. Anything less and you can be sure the reporter or editor will forget about your product five minutes after speaking with you. Successful companies know how to interact with the press in order to generate articles. They employ a known set of best practices to manage the press briefing to maximum benefit. This means delivering a carefully crafted message, and revealing exactly what you intend, no more, no less. The product is portrayed in the best light, and the journalist walks away believing it is worthy of his writing an article.*

## The Press Briefing

A press briefing is a presentation given to members of the press, either individually or in a group format. It is usually conducted just before the press release goes out. **It is intended to educate the editors on the product and stimulate their interest in writing an article about it**. This is the organization's chance to convince them of the newsworthiness of the product. Because of the sheer number of products being announced, it is difficult for editors and journalists to know which to write about. Press briefings are an effective tool for getting them focused on your product. Instead of hoping that editors notice the release and contact you to get more information for an article, you are proactively approaching them. This takes away a few common obstacles to getting press coverage:

- All journalists are looking for a "scoop", where they are the first to break a story. If the announcement has already happened, the impact of their article is diminished, as will be their motivation to do one.
- They simply may not be aware of your announcement. Actively engaging them is more likely to bring it to their attention.
- They may not understand or appreciate it, and so the detail in the presentation and the chance to ask questions will help.

The process starts with the PR team contacting a core set of editors who cover the relevant industry. Good PR professionals should have established relationships with many of the relevant publications and editors. They will schedule a round of conference calls or face to face meetings (particularly when announcing near a trade show) for members of the press to meet with the company's spokesperson, typically an executive or someone from Marketing.

The organization's representative would start by giving a short presentation on the product being announced. The most important principle to follow here is to **boil everything you know about the product into a single overarching message supported by a few succinct bullet points; repeat this multiple times during the presentation**. Journalists don't know your market, your jargon, or your technology nearly as well as you do. But they are quite good at understanding the needs of their audience. They are not tolerant of complexity, so stick to a short, simple message that they can turn into an interesting article. Remember to use the forced prioritization mentioned in Chapter 17 – there is a lot you *could* say but only present the most important messages and discard the rest for now.

Keep this theme in mind as we examine the typical format for a press briefing presentation. It begins with an Executive Summary. This is the "elevator speech" on what is being announced – your ability to boil it down into a few simple messages is tested immediately. The content can be derived straight from the title, subtitle, and opening announcement sections of your press releases. Your audience needs to clearly understand what is uniquely new in this product that hasn't been available so far (this is likely based on your competitive advantage, which you presumably do have). Then you absolutely need to answer the unspoken "so what?" question. In other words, why is this significant and why will people care?

The second slide would cover the dynamic in the market that makes this product valuable to the intended customer base. The content can of course be taken straight from the Market Information section of your press release. Most importantly, here is where you establish the Market Problem(s) on which your product is based. You should have clearly documented this during the Product Planning process, so the information should be readily available. Be sure to identify how existing products are failing to meet the market's needs. If you can characterize the problem or trends clearly enough, the need for the product being announced should be self-evident.

The next section covers the product itself. You are filling the "vacuum" that you created in the previous section. As with all marketing messaging, **focus on benefits and avoid too much detail**. You may have a lot to say because the product has a lot of good attributes, but absolutely stick to your core messages. Force yourself to avoid overcommunication by de-emphasizing any aspects which are outside these central themes. Finish off with a deeper look at how other available products are not meeting the market's needs, and are thus inferior to the product being announced.

Next, you should take the content up a level and describe the strategy at the product line level. Give the audience a better understanding of what your company is trying to do in the market. Is this a first product, or the latest in a long-term investment by the company? How does it mesh with other initiatives or product lines within the company, or with those of complementary companies in this space?

Finally, you finish off with a summary slide that repeats the key messages. This repetition is what will cause the audience to retain them.

## The Interview

The communication is not all one way. The journalist will undoubtedly ask questions throughout and afterwards. This is the interview portion of the briefing. It is a great opportunity to help the journalist understand your message, and provide information in a style and format that helps the writing of the article. But because interviews are live and in real time, there is also a very real risk of doing something to hurt your cause. **If you appear disorganized or lack clarity around your message, it will negatively impact their interest in the product and confidence in your company**. But editors very much appreciate a good interviewee, someone who is knowledgeable about the product and can deliver a memorable and succinct message. There are certain people who have natural aptitude for the interview. But the vast majority have to develop these skills. If you are going to be the company spokesperson, you absolutely need to get training. There is a well-understood body of knowledge and principles that can help you become a good spokesperson. Then, be sure to put in the necessary preparation time. Create and practice your message until it is crisp. Also get to know the people who will be interviewing you; solicit advice from your PR team on the style and tendencies of editors that they know. Try to understand the level of detail and types of soundbytes that they like. Mimic their style as best you can. Also be prepared for their interviewing style – whether aggressive, provocative, or laid back – so you can compensate accordingly. A standard technique to help in this regard is to prepare a practice "Question and Answer" sheet (be sure to include even the difficult or controversial ones). Practice answering these beforehand so you appear more polished in the interview.

During the interview, there are three common techniques you can use to improve your effectiveness:

- *Speak in headlines.* Most humans give way too much information. Editors want you to quickly get to the bottom line. They live in a world of soundbytes, so you must too. The burden of translation of information to soundbyte cannot be on them. When most of us explain something, we take a deductive approach. We present all the relevant facts as we lead up to our conclusion; we in effect deduce the conclusion through the use of undeniable facts. But the opposite is more effective – **lead with your conclusion**, establish it momentarily as semi-fact, let the audience's mind get oriented to it, **then back it up with supporting facts**.

* *Repetition*. Your job is to create one to three key messages that best characterize the product, and then repeat them often throughout the interview. **Repetition creates retention**. This is because the first time someone hears a message, it gets mentally categorized with all other information. The second time, the listener recognizes it and unconsciously considers whether it could be important; it starts to stick in the listener's memory. The third time they hear it, it becomes very clear that this is an important concept; a normally functioning brain will store it appropriately. By definition of the format of the press briefing described above, you should have at least three chances to mention a key message: in the executive summary, in the body of the briefing, and in the summary.

* *Bridging*: there are going to be times where you are asked a question that you really don't want to have to answer. It may be that it is a controversial topic, and you either don't know a good answer to give or are worried that the answer will end up in print. In other cases, you may feel the question takes you away from your key messages, and you want to keep steering the interview back on point. In either case, you use a *bridging* technique, whereby you **give a token response to the question asked, but then quickly lead back to what you really want to say**. There are three specific types of bridging, so let us look at an example of each:

  o *Deflection Bridging: "I don't know about that, but what I do know is…"*

  o *Big Picture Bridging: "I understand what you are asking, but let's look at this from the 50,000 foot level…"*

  o *Better Days Bridging: "Yes, that was an issue, but the good news is what's going on now…"*

Now that we have covered what you should do, it is helpful to know what you should not do during an interview. For those that have ever been a witness in a trial, this guidance is remarkably similar. The goals are to clearly communicate to an audience that is far less knowledgeable than you on the topic and to avoid doing anything to offend anyone.

- Don't use technical jargon. If they don't understand it, you muddle your message.
- Don't be provoked. The journalist may be trying to get you to say something in anger.
- Don't lie or fake an answer. You will get caught, and the impact to your reputation and the company's will be painful.
- Don't be vague. This makes it look like you don't know or are hiding something, and only invites more questions on the topic.
- Don't say "no comment". Use your bridging technique if you can.
- Don't answer anything "off the record". There are no real rules governing how this information should or should not be used.
- Don't answer a difficult question that hasn't been raised. You may be feeling tense about the topic, but if the journalist doesn't raise it, let it pass.
- Don't answer multiple questions at once. The journalist may simply be trying to confuse you into saying something silly.
- Don't comment on topics for which you are not the right spokesperson. These likely include financial or sales projections, legal matter, personnel matters, or unannounced products.
- Don't answer hypothetical questions or artificial choices. They carry too much risk and none of the upside. Challenge their premise and bridge out.
- Don't say anything negative about competitors. It only makes you look petty.
- Don't agree with a statement by inadvertently shaking your head. This is an unconscious habit for some, but gives off the wrong non-verbal message.
- Don't let an unsupported statement go unchallenged. The journalist may be fishing for information or trying to misquote you.

## Conclusion

The key to success here is to simply make this the interview an easy and pleasant experience for the reporters. Work with a small set of key messages. Give short answers and frequently summarize for emphasis and clarity. Basically you are trying to make it easy for them to do their job by delivering a clear message in an easily digestible format. Although speaking skills and organized thinking are critical, thorough preparation is just as important. Put in the time to create and rehearse your delivery – this is the prime determinant of how effective your interactions with the press will be.

## Talking to the Press: Real World Example

*With the launch date set, PR was now able to set up the press briefings. The lead PR person sat down with the Marketing team and mapped out the type of publications to be targeted. The general consensus was to focus on periodicals read either by IT managers or design engineers. The desired effect was for IT professionals to request the product from PC OEMs, or for the PC OEM's own design engineers to read the article and want to design Mason in. A list of 15 editors was created and PR proceeded to schedule the interviews.*

*Work then began on a standard set of slides that would be presented in these briefings. The first slide was, of course, the Executive Summary as shown in Figure 22.1:*

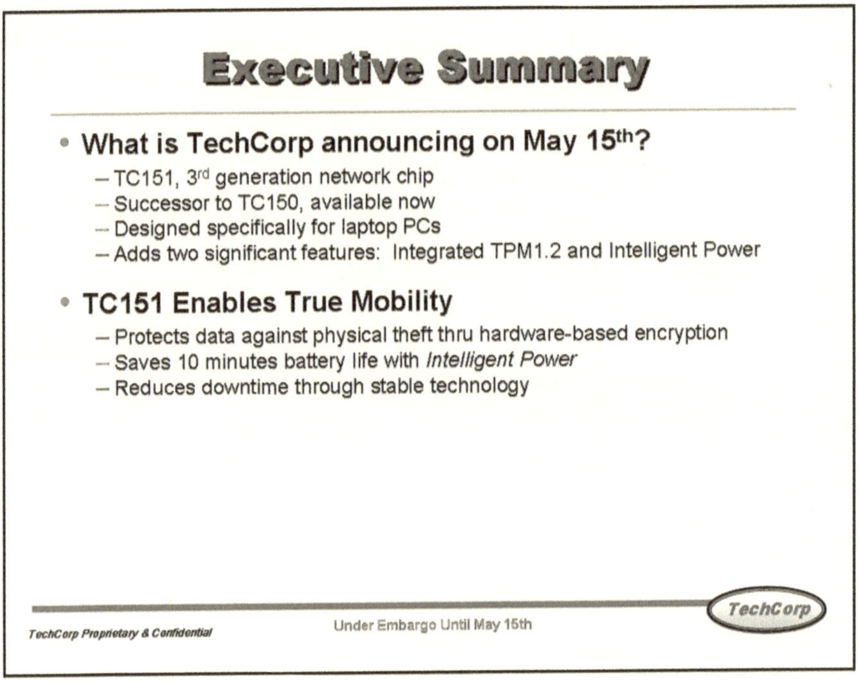

## Executive Summary

- **What is TechCorp announcing on May 15th?**
  - TC151, 3rd generation network chip
  - Successor to TC150, available now
  - Designed specifically for laptop PCs
  - Adds two significant features: Integrated TPM1.2 and Intelligent Power

- **TC151 Enables True Mobility**
  - Protects data against physical theft thru hardware-based encryption
  - Saves 10 minutes battery life with *Intelligent Power*
  - Reduces downtime through stable technology

*TechCorp Proprietary & Confidential*          Under Embargo Until May 15th          *TechCorp*

Figure 22.1

*Now, the presentation needed to describe the dynamic in the market that makes Mason so important. Clearly the theme of True Mobility (as shown in Figure 22.2) was the best vehicle for this, because it perfectly described the needs of the laptop buyer:*

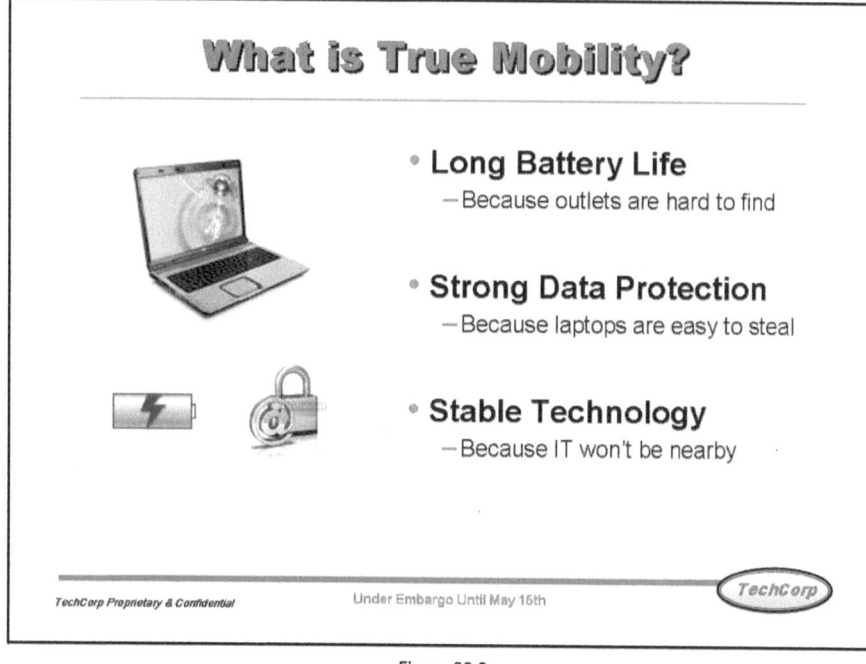

*Figure 22.2*

The heavy use of soundbytes was intended to give the editors easy messages to grab onto in the writing of their articles. In only 25 words of explanation, the slide was able to convey the important needs of users trying to achieve real mobility in their PC usage.

In support of each of these points, a slide would be added to describe the problem the user faces today and what Mason does uniquely to solve it. On the subject of battery life extension, the slide would create a narrative explaining how most networking chips waste an inordinate amount of power under normal usage patterns, as shown in Figure 22.3:

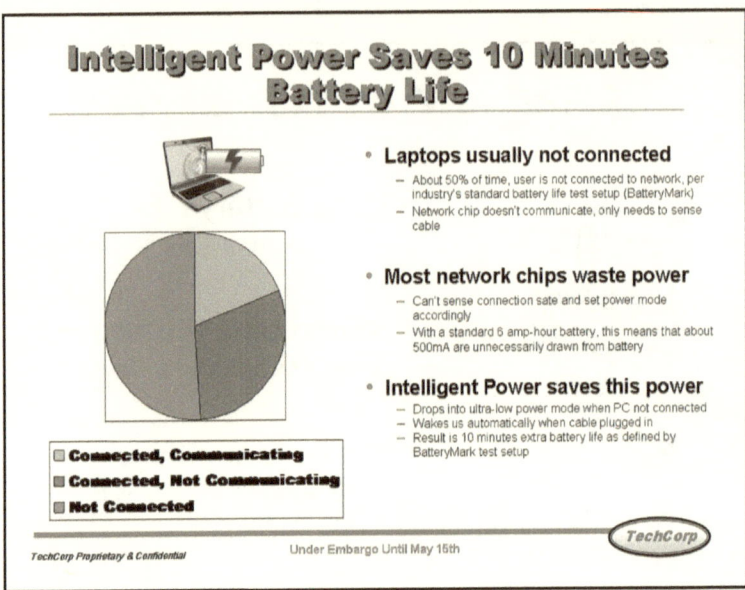

*Figure 22.3*

Similar slides each covering the security and stability aspects of the product were also added. The presentation was then followed up with a summary repeating and rein-forcing the key themes of this product (shown in Figure 22.4):

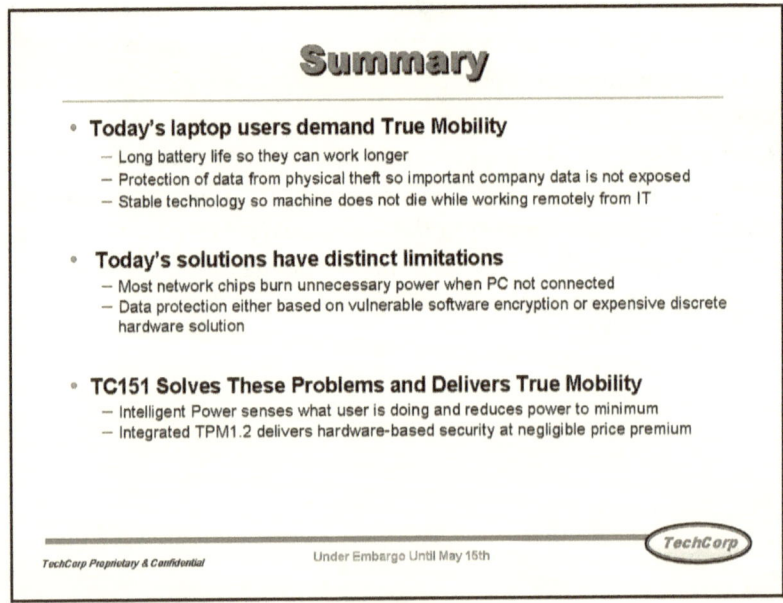

*Figure 22.4*

*(Slides in this example are available at www.systemnotcircumstance.com)*

# Checklist

## Has a newsworthy press briefing been created?

A newsworthy briefing with a crisp message can significantly increase the number of articles generated and thus the attention on the product.

## What to Look For:

- Slides ready for review three weeks before press tour
- Messaging clearly answers the question "why should I care about this?"

## Does the spokesperson have the necessary skills?

There are a core set of important techniques that are essential to being a good spokesperson. Innate talent helps, but most of the skills can be learned.

## What to Look For:

- A training course has been made available to the spokesperson
- Spokesperson speaks in headlines, uses repetition and bridging techniques

*(Further discussion on this checklist available at www.systemnotcircumstance.com)*

# CHAPTER 23:

## Sales Strategy

*Now that the product is defined and the marketing plan is in place, it is finally time to go win business. Your success will largely be a factor of the value and differentiation inherent in the product. But if selling to a larger customer, there is another factor at play: your ability to discern and influence the customer's unique decision making process, which is likely spread across multiple individuals and organizations. You may have a great product, but if you don't know how to cause all key decision participants to converge on a decision to buy it, it may not matter. Great companies know that simple "closing" techniques from Sales 101 will not cut it. The situation requires a holistic engagement plan with Sales, Marketing, and Management all actively participating. It is this disciplined approach which consistently increases the probability of a win in each and every sales engagement.*

## The Nature of Strategic Sales

It has been said that the job of the sales team is to figure out how customers make decisions, while Marketing should drive the right information into that process. Both parties play a significant role. The emphasis on a "decision process" is important. It is never as simple as just showing up to give a great presentation, then waiting for the customer to send a purchase order. It is much more complex than that with a large customer. Selling to a small customer can be a relatively focused effort. There are typically one or two decision makers, so determining their buying criteria is straightforward and fast decisions can often be reached. In contrast, large customers may have many decision makers or influencers, each possibly with their own buying criteria. You may not have relationships with or access to all of them. Worse yet, you may not even be aware of certain individuals with significant influence or veto power over the process. Mastering this environment and moving the customer towards a decision in your favor is a complex venture. So while **small accounts may be won with tactics, large ones are only won through execution of a carefully planned strategy**.

Several groups have a role in this process. It starts with Sales, who are responsible to their management for the wins. As stated before, they perform the due diligence to figure out what is important to the customer and how they make decisions. Sales will then manage the entire process in order to drive to successful closure of the business. But this does not alleviate the Marketing team from responsibility for a win. On the contrary, the successful business unit will instill in their product managers a sense of personal responsibility for winning business. They are directly affected by the impact of a win or loss to the P&L, so they cannot simply sit back and wait for Sales to generate wins and revenue. Their participation is key, although the official split of responsibility is determined by the culture of the corporation. In some cases, Sales may want to exert tight control over their accounts, to the point of even excluding Marketing from customer interaction. At the other end of the spectrum, Sales may operate more as meeting-getters and note-takers, relying on Marketing to dictate and drive the process. Typically **the most successful model is a balanced one, where Sales brings strong knowledge of the customer to the table, Marketing brings strong product knowledge, and both sides collaborate equally on the engagement strategy**. To participate effectively, Marketing needs to understand the landscape at the key accounts, provide messages customized to them, make personal visits for meetings and presentations, and coordinate activities internally to meet the unique needs of each large account. Marketing should also manage the participation of Management in this sales process. The GM in particular needs to be available to meet with executives from the customer company in support of the sales engagement.

## The Sales Process

The sales process need not be a "black art". There are a basic set of fundamentals that can be followed to significantly increase the chance of success. In their book "Strategic Selling", Miller and Heiman did a wonderful job of helping bring form to this process.

The first step is rather straightforward: *Identify the Opportunity*. What is the specific piece of business that is being pursued? Although this may seem a bit mundane, there is an important subtlety here. In complex accounts, **each selling situation may be different**, with its own unique buying criteria, decision makers, and decision process. There is a tendency to get lazy, believing you can simply follow the same playbook that won the business last time. Don't assume this is the case. Clearly identify what is being pursued right now. But more importantly, use this as a reminder to fashion your strategy for the circumstances at hand. One more thing – you should quantify the opportunity so that everyone's efforts can be prioritized accordingly. This helps rally the troops on the big ones and avoids crying wolf on the smaller ones.

Your next step is to *chart the players and their roles*. This starts with the organizational chart, but this is only the first step. This document only tells you everyone's functional role. But it doesn't necessarily tell you how decisions get made. Of course assumptions can be made based on title, but this doesn't necessarily account for the impact of individuals' personalities, the organization's culture, and the unique circumstances of this particular buying decision. **Do not fall for the illusion that an organizational chart provides**. In this process of charting the players, look beyond titles and rely on first hand due diligence on how this particular buying decision will happen. Also do not fall into the trap of simply approaching the people with whom you have already developed a relationship. They may be irrelevant on this *specific* buying opportunity. Within the set of relevant individuals, Miller and Heiman were able to identify a specific set of roles:

- *Decision Maker*: This is the person who will make the ultimate decision. This person is often higher up in the organization, but not always. The guy at the top of the organizational chart might simply be rubber stamping a recommendation from someone below him. He may get the "final" word, but in reality is not making the decision. This makes things tricky because Sales often wants to engage the "top" guy first; little do they know there may be a powerful advisor hidden behind the "puppet king". This is up to your due diligence to determine. But even if you find the decision maker, don't then give into the temptation to immediately start selling to him. He will probably be taking recommendations from others in the organization, and it is often more fruitful to engage broadly so as to influence that recommendation rather than try to circumvent it.

- *User.* The person making the ultimate product decision is often not the one who actually will use it in his day-to-day job. So unless the customer's organization is completely autocratic or bureaucratic, these individuals will have significant input into the process. And they will likely have some strong opinions. An example would be the engineer who has to implement your database product into their PeopleSoft system. He will, of course care about features and performance and all of the other things you are marketing. But by talking to him you might discover a pet peeve he has about clear documentation and ready technical support. If your attention is focused solely on the decision makers, you might never have learned this. Nor would you know that this guy could kill you behind the scenes with a negative recommendation. This may not be out of spite (although it could be), but rather that you didn't take the time to seek him out, determine what he cares about, and address it, either through educating him or by tweaking the product plans. **Never overlook the users of your product because they can play a role as critical influencers in this decision process.**

- *Technical Screener.* This player is someone whose role is to evaluate your product against a specific set of objective criteria. This might be someone from Purchasing (only looking at price and supply chain terms), Quality Control (quality process or defect levels), or Legal (contract terms). They are not aware of or care about the product's overall value proposition. They come to the table with perspective of "Does this product meet the criteria I have been given?" They have veto power, buy they are not an influence path for winning the business. **In other words, they can say "No" but not "Yes"**. So the best you can do is to neutralize them. At all costs avoid them becoming a gatekeeper to the rest of the organization – try to find other points of first contact. The ideal strategy is to cement relationships and position with other influencers first, then engage the screeners. But when you do finally approach them, do so sincerely. Learn their acceptance criteria and take the job of satisfying them very seriously, because they can sink you quickly with their veto power.

Once the players and decision making process have been charted, it is now time to engage the customer with a comprehensive plan. There are a few basic steps in the process:

- *Develop a coach*. Navigating the customer's decision making process can be difficult from the outside looking in. It won't necessarily be obvious, even to a talented salesperson. You'll need someone on the inside to guide you. Miller and Heiman called this person a "coach" – someone within the customer's organization who is willing to give you informed advice on how to proceed. Presumably he is in a position to help you map the paths of influence, users' needs, and organizational hot buttons. He may also help you better understand the latest status on the decision process, and where you stand competitively. And why would this person be so kind as to do this? It has to be someone who sees benefit in you winning, or at least getting a fair shot at doing so. Maybe it makes his life easier because of the great support you provide to him. Possibly he simply believes in your company and/ or the product, and feels this is the best choice for his company. It could even be for selfish reasons, such as to perpetuate the lavish entertainment activities that your sales team provides him. In any case, he is motivated to help you. **It is critical for the organiza-**

**tion to have such a person in place for every engagement**. But this is a process that takes some investment. Just like there are certain things you shouldn't ask for on a first date, you also need to develop a coach over time. Rarely is someone willing to give you the right level of information right out of the gate. Also, be careful how you use this person. Don't ask them to sell for you internally, only to help create the map. If you ask them to put their own credibility on the line for you, you may either scare them off or burn them as a coach if they are perceived within their own organization as being biased.

- *Identify each player's "win"*. It is a fundamental fact of human nature that most people are motivated to do what benefits them the most personally at any given moment. So **if a particular player in this process sees personal benefit in you winning, they are much more likely to be your advocate**. That is why it is so important to put thought into what each player would consider a "win" for them. They may want to do what benefits their company the most, either out of loyalty or a belief that their own fortunes will follow. Features and price are often important in such situations. Another individual may have a strong family commitment, and his goal is to finish his work more quickly so he can go home sooner. Great documentation and strong technical support may appeal to him. Certain users may exist in a situation of high accountability, so they would be highly risk averse. Anything your product can do to reduce their personal risk would be perceived by them as a "win". At the same time, a young aggressive manager who wants to make a big splash may be open to a cutting edge technology that helps her change the game. Each individual responds to something different. While a product can't be all things to all people, it is still critical to ferret out these preferences in the sales process and cater to them as well as possible.

- *Develop an action plan*. Now that the map is drawn, it is time to chart the course across it. Prioritize the list of players in order of importance for being influenced, and determine the information and messaging that would appeal to them best. You will then assign to each one the most appropriate person on the Sales or Marketing team to own the relationship. A technical screener would likely be matched with someone similarly technical on your side. Business people should be approached by individuals within Marketing and Sales. The customer's executive should be matched with your own; this technique, which Heiman called *like-rank selling*, is effective because most people are more comfortable with those at a similar level in the corporate food chain. Presumably each member of your team participating in this process should be working to develop the relationship and initiate frequent interactions with their assigned counterpart.

At this point, you should be ready to execute on the plan. As you engage each player, always remember that "fire and forget" does not work. You don't meet with a player once and then check the box next to his name. In a complex sale, no one wins after just one presentation. Continue to follow up until you are sure each player is aligned in your favor. And always remember that this selling phase is somewhat of a test for you. You will likely come out of customer meetings with action items to gather and provide more information they need to make a decision. Follow through swiftly and reliably – if you can't do this during the sales process, the customer will safely assume you won't be particularly responsive after they've given you the business.

## Developing Relationships

**Developing relationships is by far the most important success factor in winning new business.** The resulting familiarity breeds trust. Marketing is all about making future promises, so the customer's trust in you is a cornerstone of your success. Familiarity also breeds openness, which means the customer is more willing to give you information on their plans and hopefully those of your competitor as well. And quite frankly, if the customer knows and likes you, they are simply more willing to advocate for you. When you can't win solely on features and price, strong relationships can close the remaining gap (but they can't overcome incompetence or bad products).

Let us for a moment examine the nature of a professional relationship. It is a bond that is formed after a requisite number of interactions in which you demonstrate credibility and reliability, whether through personality or delivering on commitments. Don't assume that after one meeting you now have a 'relationship' with a person and that you can now leverage the associated trust and benefits. These things take time. Often, they only happen after two or three interactions in which you prove yourself by delivering on your promises. These could be significant commitments, or just as easily could be a small item such as following up with a note containing a small bit of information you promised to dig up. Often, the magnitude does not matter, but rather that you kept your word. As mentioned before, these interactions are an evaluation on whether you do what you say. So to bolster your cause, proactively look for opportunities to prove yourself in this regard. Then, **only after several successful interactions and follow-throughs should you begin to assume a useful relationship exists**.

This customer puts you through this evaluation process because they know they may eventually need something from you. They want the "red phone" in case anything goes wrong. And they want to know that you keep your word, because then they can more easily bank on the promises your company is making during the selling process. These facts, coupled with the value that your product brings to them, are what make customers believe that you and your company can help them meet their goals. You now represent an entity that makes the customer successful in what they are trying to accomplish. Once this belief is established in their mind, then you truly have a relationship built. Assuming you continue to maintain the relationship by dedicating the necessary time for regular contact and new opportunities to deliver on your word, this can be an indispensable tool for winning new business.

## Conclusion

All of us know that influencing another person can be hard. But the process of influencing multiple people (who each have different personalities, perspectives, and goals) to act in concert to your benefit can be a monumental task. A good sales team that collaborates well with Marketing is often the only way to succeed. An effective sales system that guides the team to map the influence paths and then directs the right information to them is what great companies use to increase the probability of winning business for their great products.

# Sales Strategy: Real World Example

*As the sales cycle approached, Marketing and Sales got together to strat-egize on how to attack a particular major customer – Bell Computers. PC OEMs have large organizations with complex decision making processes. It was going to take more than just some simple sales techniques to close a ma-jor piece of business with a powerhouse company like Bell. The first task was to identify which individuals within the Bell organization would be involved in the decision process. The lead salesperson stated that she had previously won a large deal for another TechCorp product by leveraging Bell's Chief Tech-nology Officer (CTO). He had been influential in advocating internally for the product because he recognized the value it brought to Bell. But after some discussion, the team quickly realized that the CTO would not be as influential in this case. It was a different group within Bell that would be making the de-cision related to Mason, and they had an entirely different group of personali-ties and decision making tendencies involved. No, this one would need a new plan. After some further discussion, the following list was generated, mostly from the knowledge Sales had about how Bell makes decisions*

1. *Decision Maker:*
   a. *Catherine Harper, Senior Vice President of Laptop PCs. Cath-erine owns the business unit that designed the laptop PCs at Bell. Ultimately she would sign off on any final decision. It was believed that she would rely on her staff (mainly Donovan and Robby below) to make the choice and present her a recommendation. It would be very unlikely that she would overrule their choice outright. But, if she were engaged early and sold on the benefits of the product and the roadmap, she could develop a preference that could trickle down to her staff before the decision process get very far along. This could help influence those two early, and could also open up the door for extended face time for the selling process. Sales believed she would respond to a message that po-sitioned TechCorp as a partner who would help Bell differentiate now (with interesting features) and would be a good long term partner with a compelling roadmap and an executive manage-ment team who was committed to Bell's success (they wanted*

Catherine to believe she always had an executive "red phone" to call if there were ever a serious problem).

2. Influencers:
    a. *Donovan Taylor, VP of Marketing, Laptop PC; Donovan is responsible for creating a competitive product in the market. He is a power player around Bell, and his recommendation for component choices would carry much weight. He tended to be very hard to access; not particularly open to meetings and certainly not social engagements. He would not be won over through relationship. But he was keenly interested in how Bell could differentiate their products and continue to raise the bar of performance and functionality. He also understood security, which was a big help in trying to sell him a leading edge security technology. He would respond to a message about the value and benefit of features, and how he could push the technology envelope to differentiate his products. Getting access to him would be difficult, but if they did a good job with Catherine, the team hoped he could help open this door a bit.*
    b. *Robby Zhang, VP of Engineering. Robby's team would be responsible for implementing Mason into their PC system. He was wholly unlike Donovan, in that he relied a lot on trust and relationship in choosing vendors to work with. As an experienced guy, he was aware of market trends and the need for Bell to differentiate. So he cared about features, but his top concerns were that the solution met the requirements, was on time, easy for his team to implement, and worked well. So, Sales felt that he would respond to a message that gave him confidence in this for Mason. It would also pay to target some social engagements with Robby to continue to build the relationship.*
3. Users
    a. *Dan Nguyen, Platform Architect. Dan was the person who created the architecture of the system. Although not high in the organization, he was influential because of his domain knowledge. If he said there was a problem with Mason, the sales engagement could stop immediately. So it was important to get close to him to vet out any concerns he might have. Although he was*

*interested in high level features and functionality, the bulk of his concern would exist in how the product would interact with the system at a low level.*

    b. *Mike O'Brien, Software Manager. Mike managed the process of integrating the software of each vendor into the overall software module for the entire PC. Mike was a heads down type of guy that cared mostly about execution. He wanted to know that the vendor's software was complete and completed on time. He was very risk averse.*

4. *Screeners*

    a. *Vahid Rankor, Product Quality Manager. Vahid was well known within Bell as a guy who was very hard on the vendors. It was his job to ensure that Bell products met a high standard of quality, and much of this related to the quality of the component parts. Features and market related issues were not within his field of concern. He had a very detailed list of criteria that he measured chip vendors against; he knew his business well and was nearly impossible to fool.*

    b. *Beth Richardson, Procurement. True to form for all procurement people, she cared mostly about price. She could be expected to negotiate hard to get the best one she could out of TechCorp. But, Beth would also concerned with continuity of supply issues, and terms and conditions of the purchase agreement.*

*Marketing took this information and offered their own suggestions for the core message to be communicated to each individual:*

*Catherine Harper:*

1. *Message: TechCorp knows low power design better than anyone. Proof: show examples from across the company.*
2. *Message: Bell can create a major technology initiative around TPM security. Proof: show list of IT shops using software security who could be converted to hardware-based TPM solution.*
3. *Message: The TechCorp executive team is available at any time to address issues. Proof: set up face-to-face meeting with Catherine and TechCorp CEO.*

System, Not Circumstance

_Donovan Taylor:_
1.  _Message: Bell will win more battery life shootouts with Mason's Intelligent Power feature. Proof: show battery life demo and story._
2.  _Message: TPM provides better data security, something that would appeal to end users concerned about laptop theft, helping Bell differentiate. Proof: explain threats to software security; supplement with statistics about increasing laptop thefts and value of data._
3.  _Message: TechCorp will have the best technology long-term. Proof: show roadmap and story about corporate competencies around low power and secure solution design._

_Robby Zhang_
1.  _Message: Mason gives Bell fundamental advantage in hardware-based TPM security and 10 minutes extra battery life: Proof: show TPM and Intelligent Power story._
2.  _Mason will be easy to implement. Proof: show list of available technical documentation and make promises of on-site support._
3.  _Message: Mason will not add risk to Bell's own schedule. Proof: show Mason schedule versus Bell's schedule requirement._

_Dan Nguyen_
1.  _Message: Mason will help reduce total system power consumption. Proof: show him battery life demo and discuss power modes in depth._
2.  _Message: Mason will meet Bell's low level system requirements. Proof: The team will spend significant time with Dan to map Mason into his system architecture so that he is fully confident it will meet his needs._

_Mike O'Brien_
1.  _Message: Mason software is complete. Proof: meet with Mike to map out all Mason deliverables. Focus on the fact that a "complete product" with deep consideration of ecosystem is being delivered._
2.  _Message: Mason software will be on time. Proof: conduct a schedule and program management review with Mike._

_Vahid Rankor_
1.  _Message: TechCorp products meet a high quality standard. Proof: bring members of TechCorp's Operations team to meet with Vahid to demonstrate quality infrastructure and historic defect level metrics._

<u>Beth Richardson</u>
1. Message: TechCorp will provide strong continuity of supply for Bell. Proof: bring members of TechCorp's Operations team to meet with Beth to discuss capacity planning and techniques to assure continuity of supply.
2. Message: We will work with you on price. Proof: the team did not want to have a price discussion until the perception of value was driven with the decision makers and influencers. So the strategy would be to placate her but delay any specific price discussion.

Marketing and Sales then finished off the plan by mapping out how each player would be engaged:
- Catherine Harper: Would be matched up with the business unit's GM and Techcorp's VP of worldwide sales for a like-rank selling situation. A dinner would be set up within a month.
- Donovan Taylor: Would be focused on by the business unit's Director of Marketing and the sales person covering Bell. They would go to meet with him within two weeks.
- Robby Zhang: Same coverage as Donovan.
- Dan Nguyen and Mike O'Brien: The Mason product manager and the local salesperson would cover Dan and Mike. Because both were new contacts, some relationship activities would need to take place in addition to marketing and working through any issues they raise.
- Vahid Rankor and Beth Richardson: The Mason Product Manager and the salesperson would cover these two individuals as well. They would use an initial meeting (within two weeks) to pave the way for a follow up meeting with Operations.

# Checklist

### Has a strategic engagement plan been created?

Large accounts are not won through tactics – they require a comprehensive plan that covers both organizational and influence structure.

## What to Look For:

- Sales has mapped how the decision will get made on this opportunity
- Key individuals are targeted for approach with a custom message for each

### Do Sales and Marketing have key relationships in place?

Business is rarely won on the merits of the product alone – strong relationships provide the trust and communication necessary to win consistently.

## What to Look For:

- Marketing/Sales spend significant time cultivating customer relationships
- A coach is in place for every engagement with a large customer

*(Further discussion on this checklist available at www.systemnotcircumstance.com)*